DEPRESSION IS FUN!

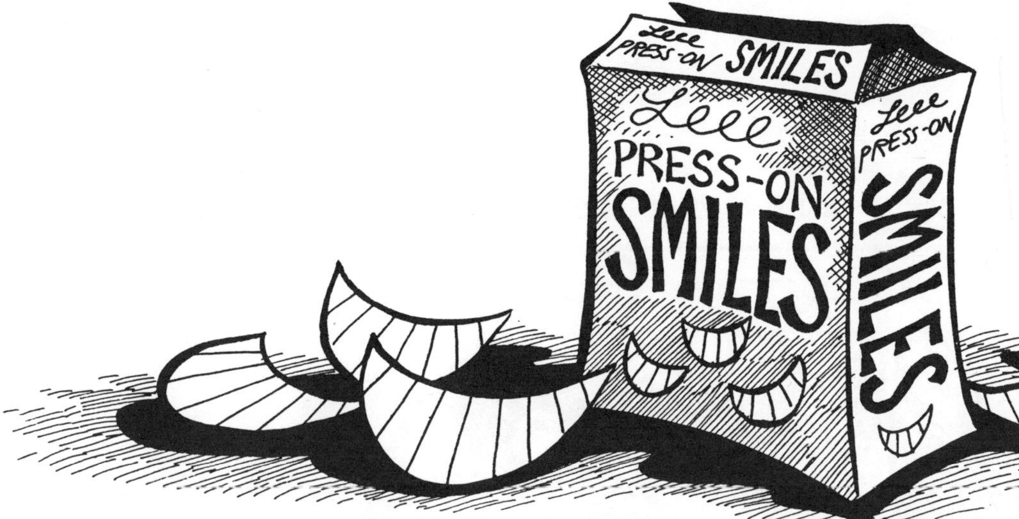
Leee PRESS-ON SMILES
Leee
PRESS-ON
SMILES
Leee PRESS-ON
SMILES

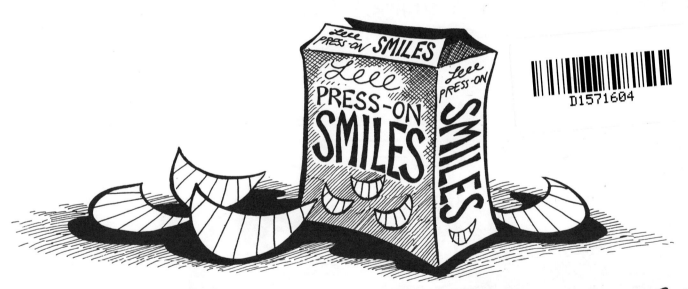

A "NINA'S ADVENTURES" CARTOON COLLECTION BY Nina Paley

T.H.C. PRESS • CAPITOLA, CA

SOME OF THE CARTOONS IN THIS BOOK PREVIOUSLY APPEARED IN NEWSPAPERS INCLUDING THE NO-JOKE NEWS, THE SANTA CRUZ COMIC NEWS AND THE FUNNY TIMES.
COVER AIRBRUSH BY RAY GARST, SANTA CRUZ

THE HINENI CONSCIOUSNESS PRESS
1840 41st AVENUE #102-286
CAPITOLA, CA 95010
PHONE: (408)662-9340

LIBRARY OF CONGRESS CATALOG CARD NUMBER: 92-072579

ISBN: 0-9628913-3-9

PRIVATE EDITION • T.H.C. PRESS
AUGUST 1992

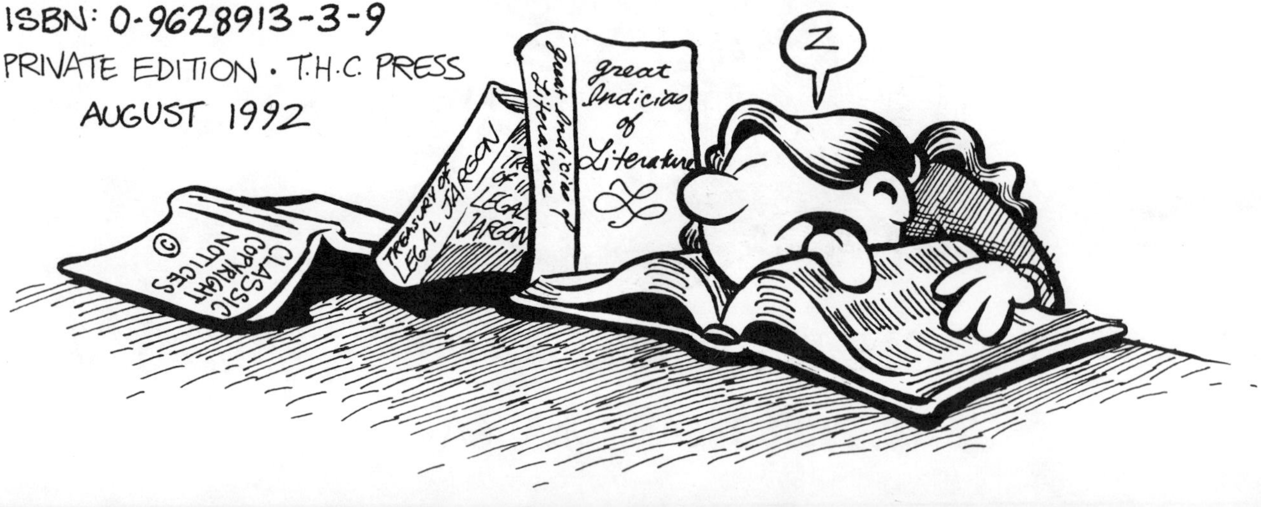
Z
great Indicias of Literature
Great Indicias of Literature
TREASURY OF LEGAL JARGON
LEGAL JARGON
CLASSIC COPYRIGHT NOTICES
©

THIS BOOK IS DEDICATED TO
MY PARENTS,

Jean & Hiram Paley

WITHOUT WHOM I WOULD NOT HAVE BEEN POSSIBLE,
AND WITH WHOM I WAS IMPOSSIBLE.

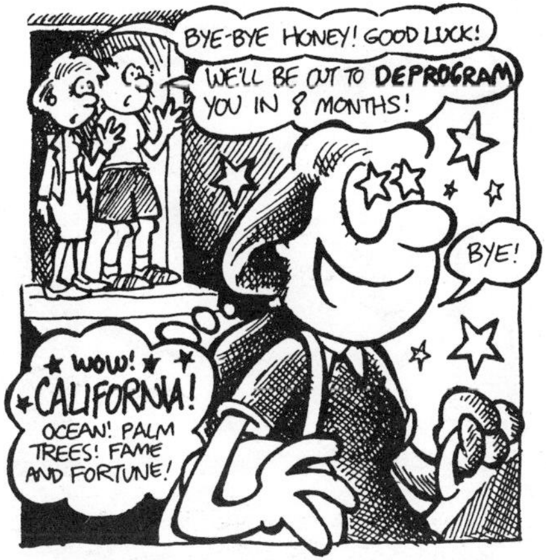
BYE-BYE HONEY! GOOD LUCK!
WE'LL BE OUT TO DEPROGRAM YOU IN 8 MONTHS!
BYE!
WOW! CALIFORNIA! OCEAN! PALM TREES! FAME AND FORTUNE!

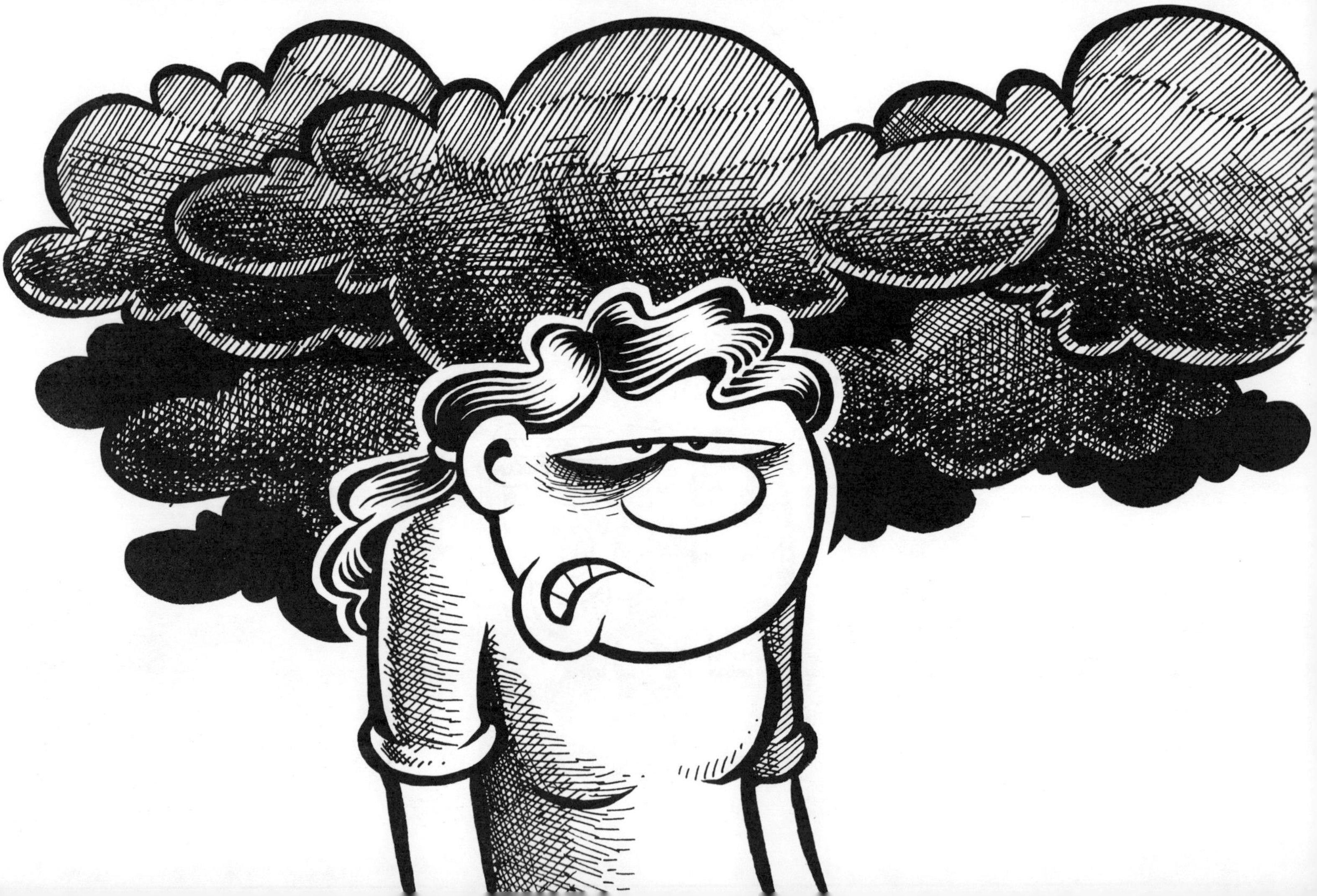

CHAPTER ONE:
DEPRESSION

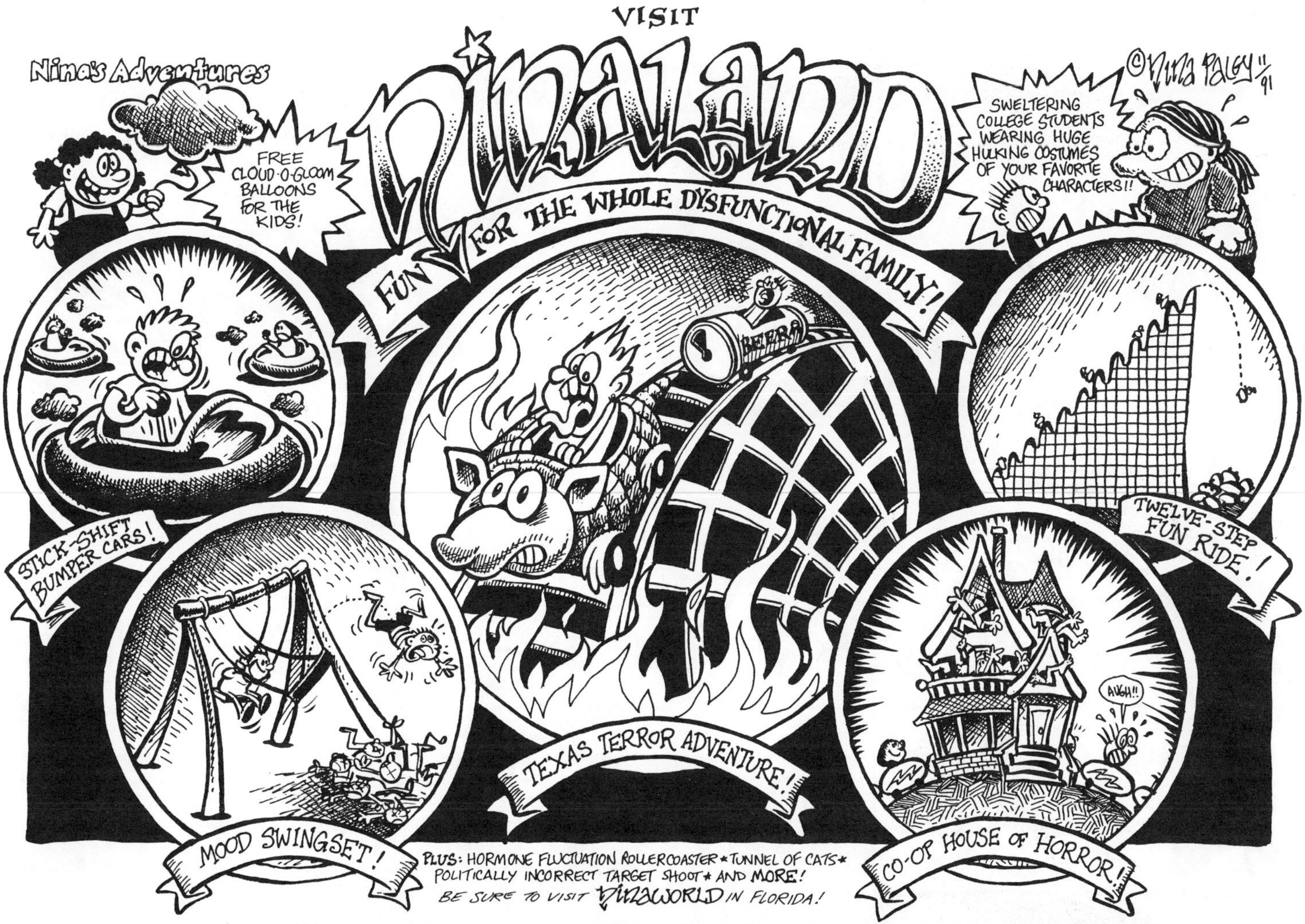

VISIT
Nina's Adventures
NINALAND
©Nina Paley 11/91
FREE CLOUD-O-GLOOM BALLOONS FOR THE KIDS!
SWELTERING COLLEGE STUDENTS WEARING HUGE HULKING COSTUMES OF YOUR FAVORITE CHARACTERS!!
FUN FOR THE WHOLE DYSFUNCTIONAL FAMILY!
BEER
STICK-SHIFT BUMPER CARS!
TWELVE-STEP FUN RIDE!
AUGH!!
MOOD SWINGSET!
TEXAS TERROR ADVENTURE!
CO-OP HOUSE OF HORROR!
PLUS: HORMONE FLUCTUATION ROLLERCOASTER ★ TUNNEL OF CATS ★ POLITICALLY INCORRECT TARGET SHOOT ★ AND MORE!
BE SURE TO VISIT NINAWORLD IN FLORIDA!

NINA'S ADVENTURES

"HOW TO ACT LIKE AN ARTIST"

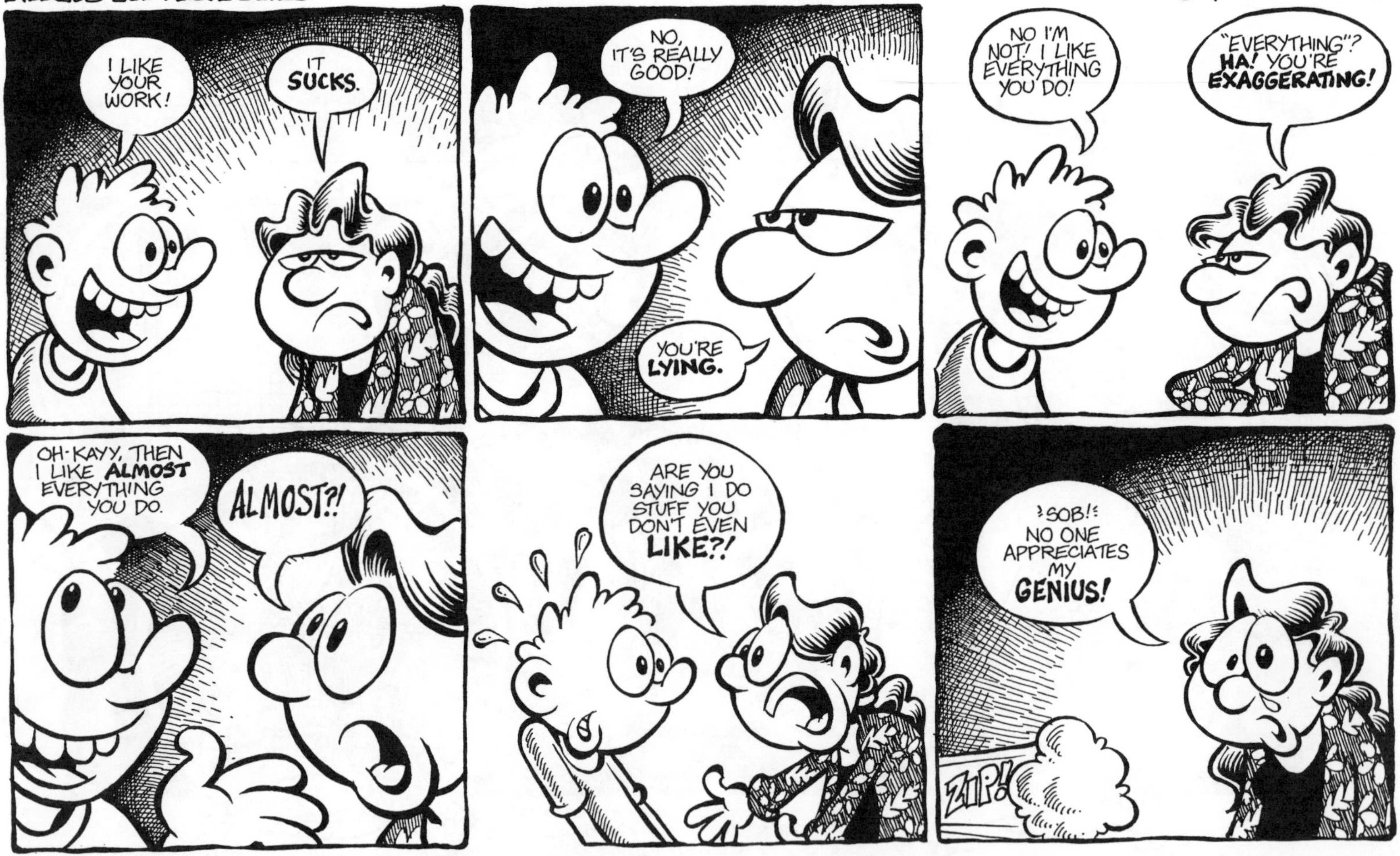
I LIKE YOUR WORK!
IT SUCKS.
NO, IT'S REALLY GOOD!
YOU'RE LYING.
NO I'M NOT! I LIKE EVERYTHING YOU DO!
"EVERYTHING"? HA! YOU'RE EXAGGERATING!
OH-KAYY, THEN I LIKE ALMOST EVERYTHING YOU DO.
ALMOST?!
ARE YOU SAYING I DO STUFF YOU DON'T EVEN LIKE?!
SOB!
NO ONE APPRECIATES MY GENIUS!
ZIP!

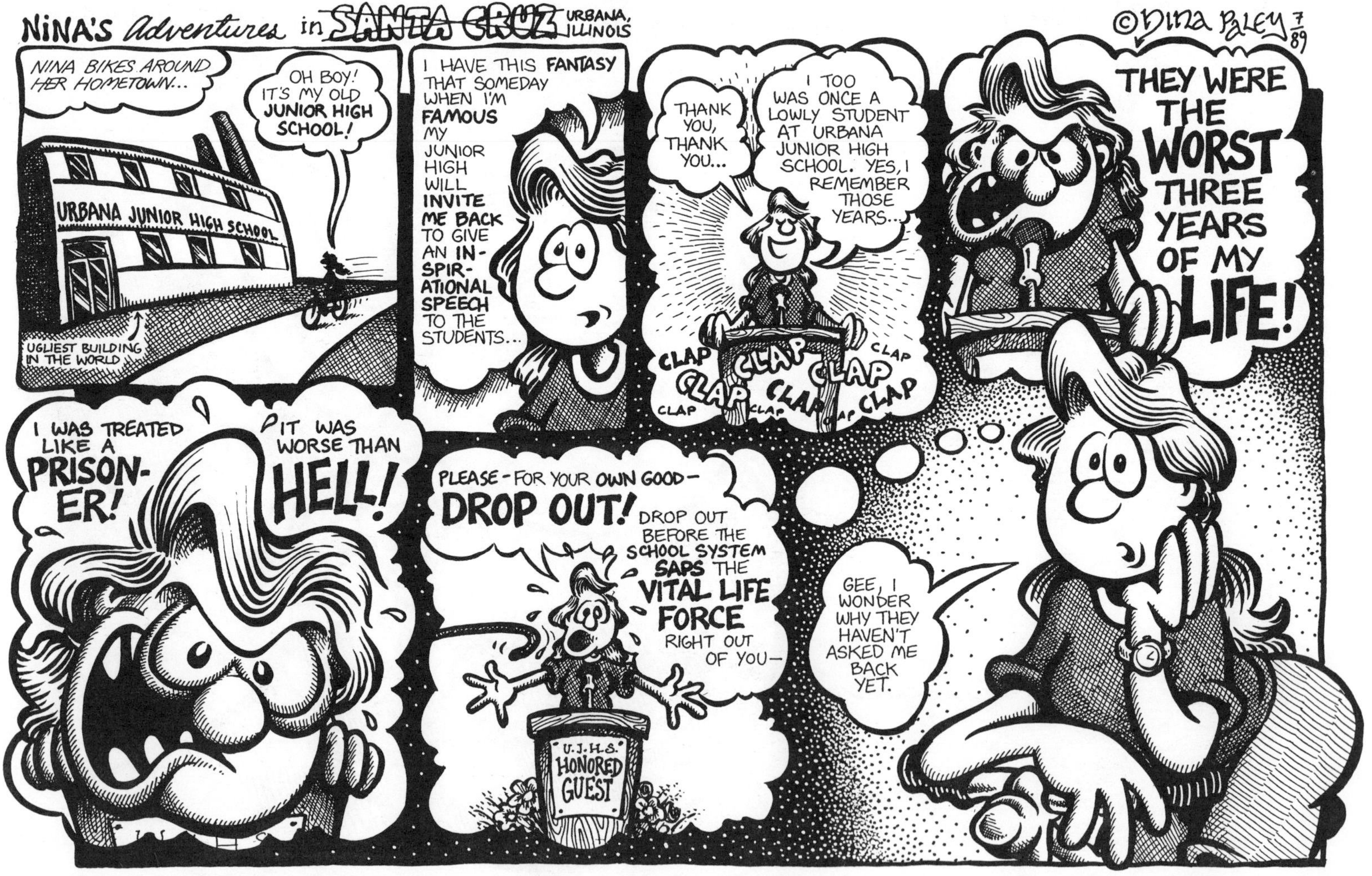

NINA'S Adventures in ~~SANTA CRUZ~~ URBANA, ILLINOIS
©Nina Paley 7/89
NINA BIKES AROUND HER HOMETOWN...
OH BOY! IT'S MY OLD JUNIOR HIGH SCHOOL!
URBANA JUNIOR HIGH SCHOOL
UGLIEST BUILDING IN THE WORLD
I HAVE THIS FANTASY THAT SOMEDAY WHEN I'M FAMOUS MY JUNIOR HIGH WILL INVITE ME BACK TO GIVE AN IN-SPIR-ATIONAL SPEECH TO THE STUDENTS...
THANK YOU, THANK YOU...
I TOO WAS ONCE A LOWLY STUDENT AT URBANA JUNIOR HIGH SCHOOL. YES, I REMEMBER THOSE YEARS...
CLAP CLAP CLAP CLAP CLAP CLAP CLAP CLAP CLAP CLAP CLAP
THEY WERE THE WORST THREE YEARS OF MY LIFE!
I WAS TREATED LIKE A PRISON-ER!
IT WAS WORSE THAN HELL!
PLEASE - FOR YOUR OWN GOOD - DROP OUT!
DROP OUT BEFORE THE SCHOOL SYSTEM SAPS THE VITAL LIFE FORCE RIGHT OUT OF YOU-
U.J.H.S. HONORED GUEST
GEE, I WONDER WHY THEY HAVEN'T ASKED ME BACK YET.

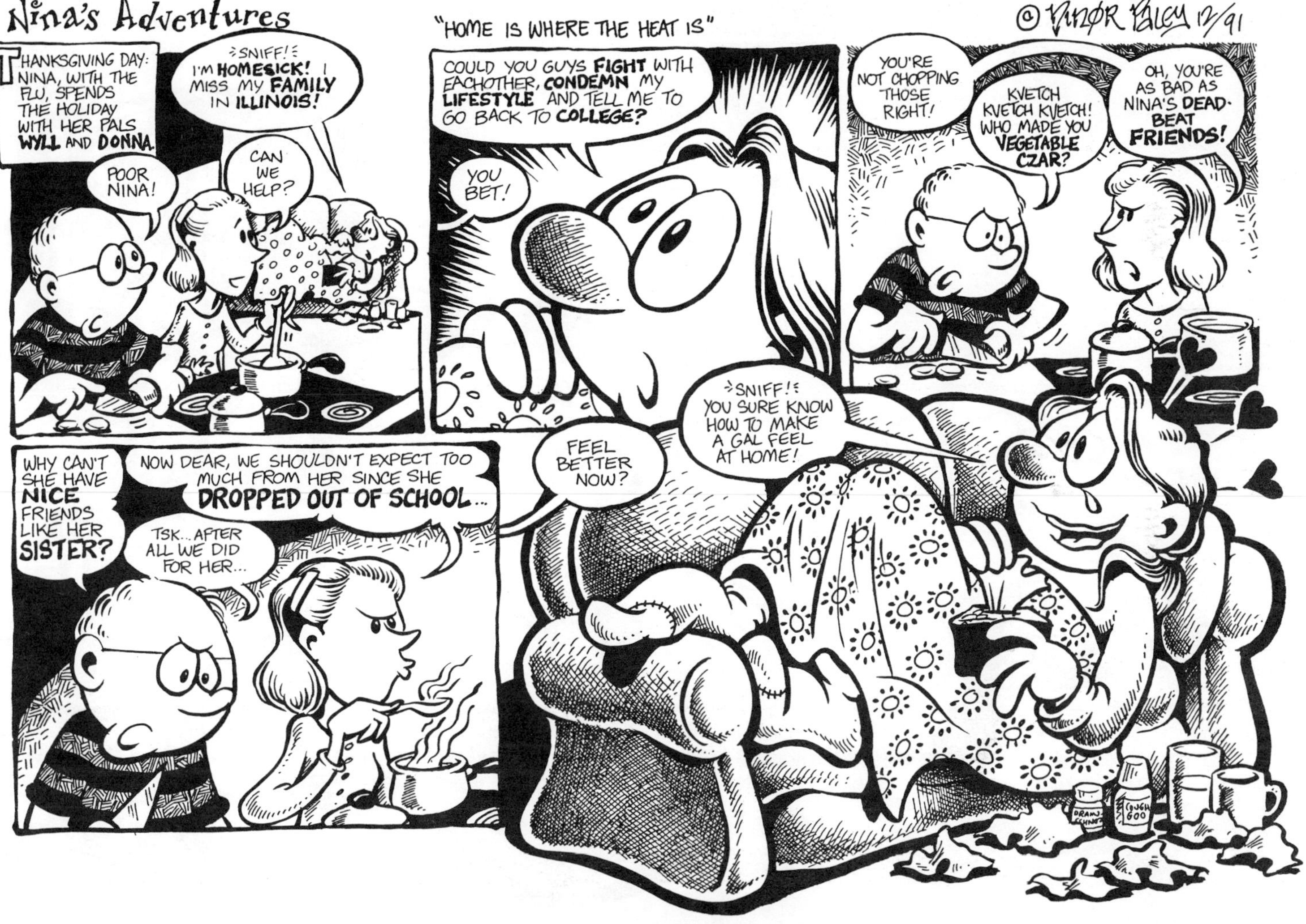

Nina's Adventures
"HOME IS WHERE THE HEAT IS"
© NINA PALEY 12/91
THANKSGIVING DAY: NINA, WITH THE FLU, SPENDS THE HOLIDAY WITH HER PALS WYLL AND DONNA.
SNIFF! I'M HOMESICK! I MISS MY FAMILY IN ILLINOIS!
POOR NINA!
CAN WE HELP?
COULD YOU GUYS FIGHT WITH EACHOTHER, CONDEMN MY LIFESTYLE AND TELL ME TO GO BACK TO COLLEGE?
YOU BET!
YOU'RE NOT CHOPPING THOSE RIGHT!
KVETCH KVETCH KVETCH! WHO MADE YOU VEGETABLE CZAR?
OH, YOU'RE AS BAD AS NINA'S DEAD-BEAT FRIENDS!
WHY CAN'T SHE HAVE NICE FRIENDS LIKE HER SISTER?
NOW DEAR, WE SHOULDN'T EXPECT TOO MUCH FROM HER SINCE SHE DROPPED OUT OF SCHOOL...
TSK... AFTER ALL WE DID FOR HER...
FEEL BETTER NOW?
SNIFF! YOU SURE KNOW HOW TO MAKE A GAL FEEL AT HOME!
COUGH GOO

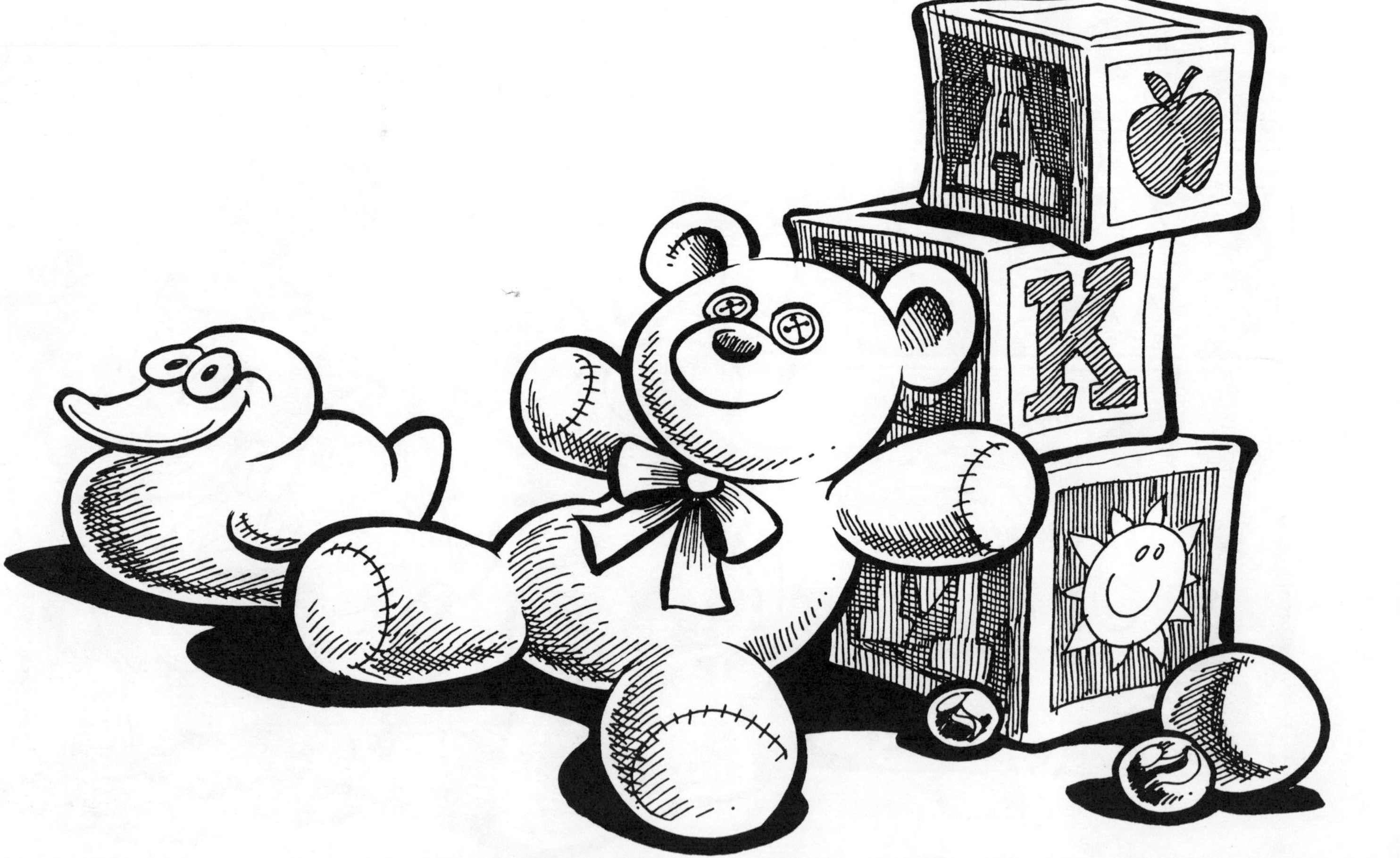
A
K

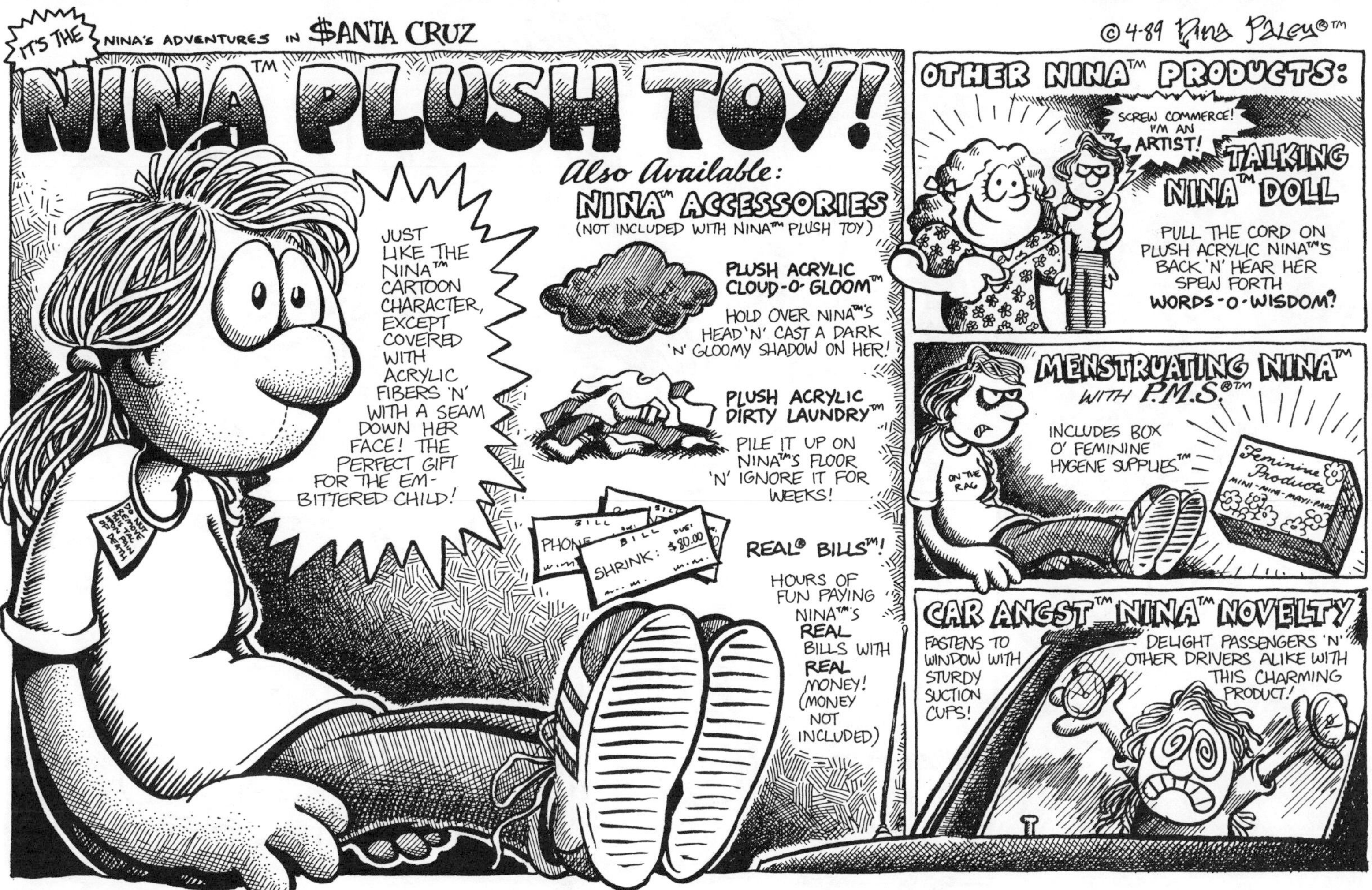
IT'S THE
NINA'S ADVENTURES IN $ANTA CRUZ
©4-89 Nina Paley®™
NINA™ PLUSH TOY!
JUST LIKE THE NINA™ CARTOON CHARACTER, EXCEPT COVERED WITH ACRYLIC FIBERS 'N' WITH A SEAM DOWN HER FACE! THE PERFECT GIFT FOR THE EM-BITTERED CHILD!
Also Available:
NINA™ ACCESSORIES
(NOT INCLUDED WITH NINA™ PLUSH TOY)
PLUSH ACRYLIC CLOUD-O-GLOOM™
HOLD OVER NINA™'S HEAD 'N' CAST A DARK 'N' GLOOMY SHADOW ON HER!
PLUSH ACRYLIC DIRTY LAUNDRY™
PILE IT UP ON NINA™'S FLOOR 'N' IGNORE IT FOR WEEKS!
PHONE
SHRINK: $80.00
REAL® BILLS™!
HOURS OF FUN PAYING NINA™'S REAL BILLS WITH REAL MONEY! (MONEY NOT INCLUDED)
OTHER NINA™ PRODUCTS:
SCREW COMMERCE! I'M AN ARTIST!
TALKING NINA™ DOLL
PULL THE CORD ON PLUSH ACRYLIC NINA™'S BACK 'N' HEAR HER SPEW FORTH WORDS-O-WISDOM®
MENSTRUATING NINA™ WITH P.M.S.®™
INCLUDES BOX O' FEMININE HYGENE SUPPLIES.™
ON THE RAG
Feminine Products
CAR ANGST™ NINA™ NOVELTY
FASTENS TO WINDOW WITH STURDY SUCTION CUPS!
DELIGHT PASSENGERS 'N' OTHER DRIVERS ALIKE WITH THIS CHARMING PRODUCT!

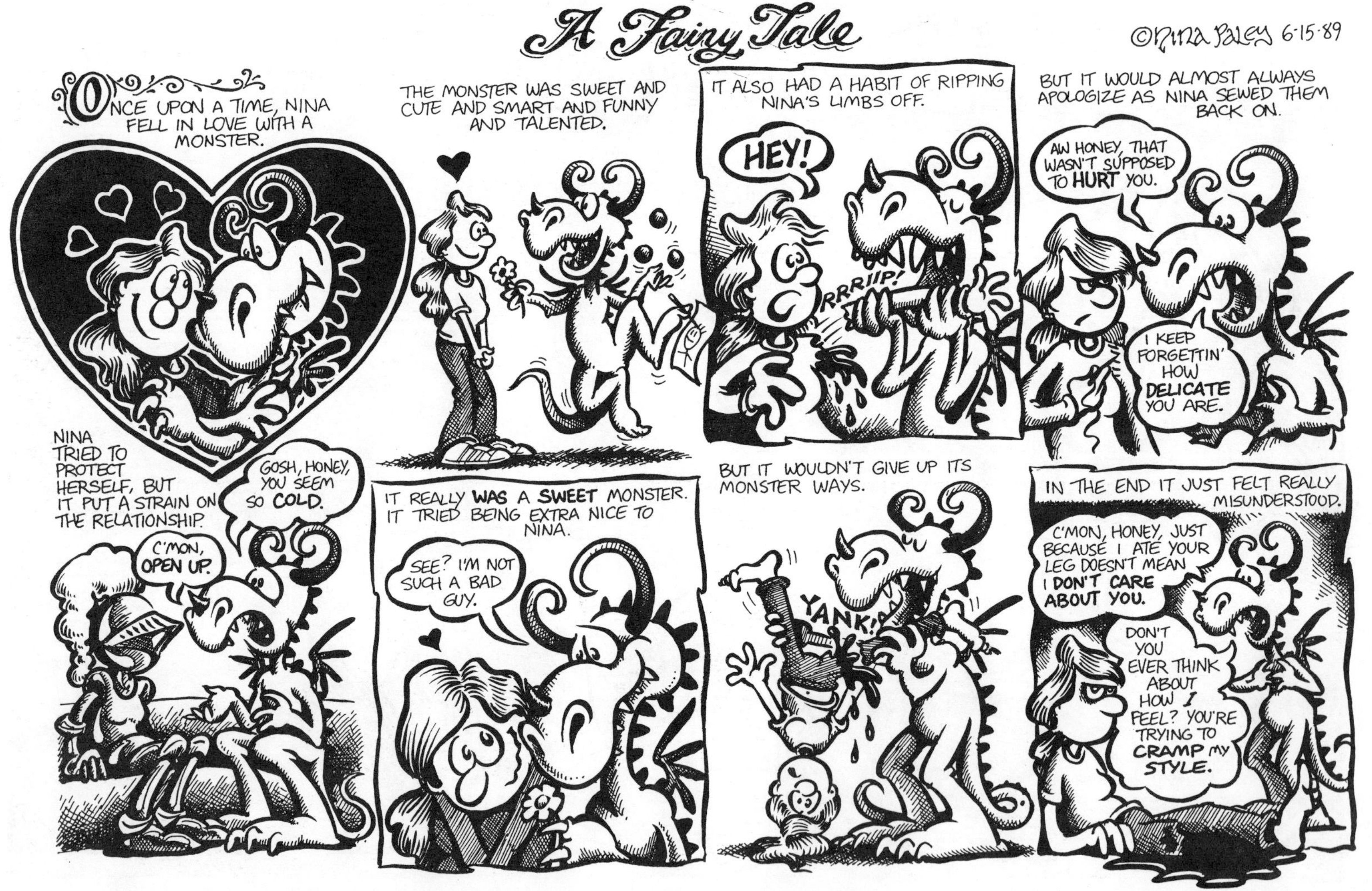
A Fairy Tale
©Nina Paley 6-15-89
Once upon a time, Nina fell in love with a monster.
The monster was sweet and cute and smart and funny and talented.
It also had a habit of ripping Nina's limbs off.
HEY!
RRRIIP!
But it would almost always apologize as Nina sewed them back on.
Aw honey, that wasn't supposed to HURT you.
I keep forgettin' how DELICATE you are.
Nina tried to protect herself, but it put a strain on the relationship.
Gosh, honey, you seem so COLD.
C'mon, OPEN UP.
It really WAS a SWEET monster. It tried being extra nice to Nina.
See? I'm not such a bad guy.
But it wouldn't give up its monster ways.
YANK!
In the end it just felt really misunderstood.
C'mon, honey, just because I ate your leg doesn't mean I DON'T CARE ABOUT YOU.
Don't you ever think about how I feel? You're trying to CRAMP my STYLE.

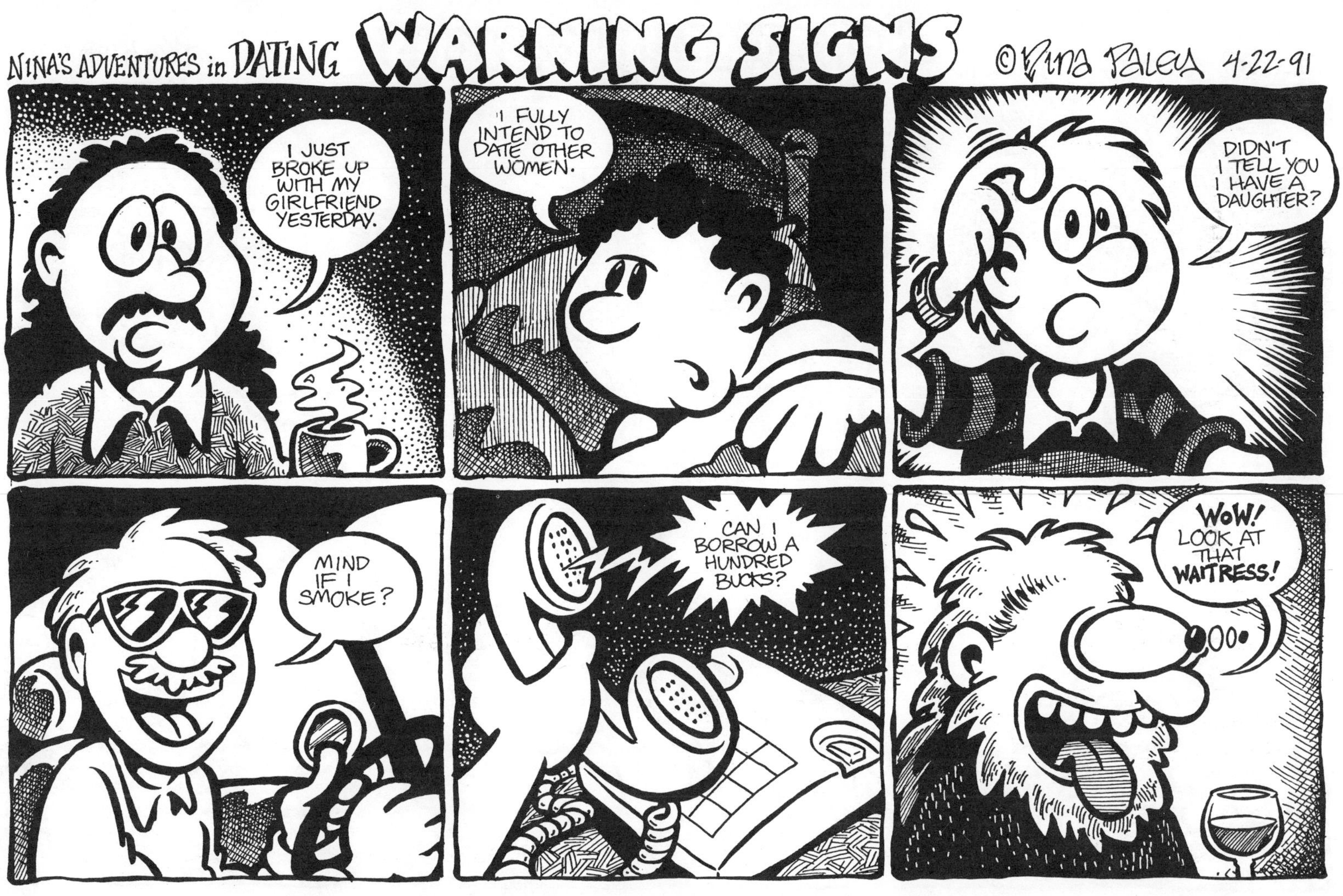
NINA'S ADVENTURES in DATING
WARNING SIGNS
© Nina Paley 4-22-91
I JUST BROKE UP WITH MY GIRLFRIEND YESTERDAY.
I FULLY INTEND TO DATE OTHER WOMEN.
DIDN'T I TELL YOU I HAVE A DAUGHTER?
MIND IF I SMOKE?
CAN I BORROW A HUNDRED BUCKS?
WOW! LOOK AT THAT WAITRESS!

Nina's further adventures in DATING

MORE WARNING SIGNS

© Nina Paley 2/24/92

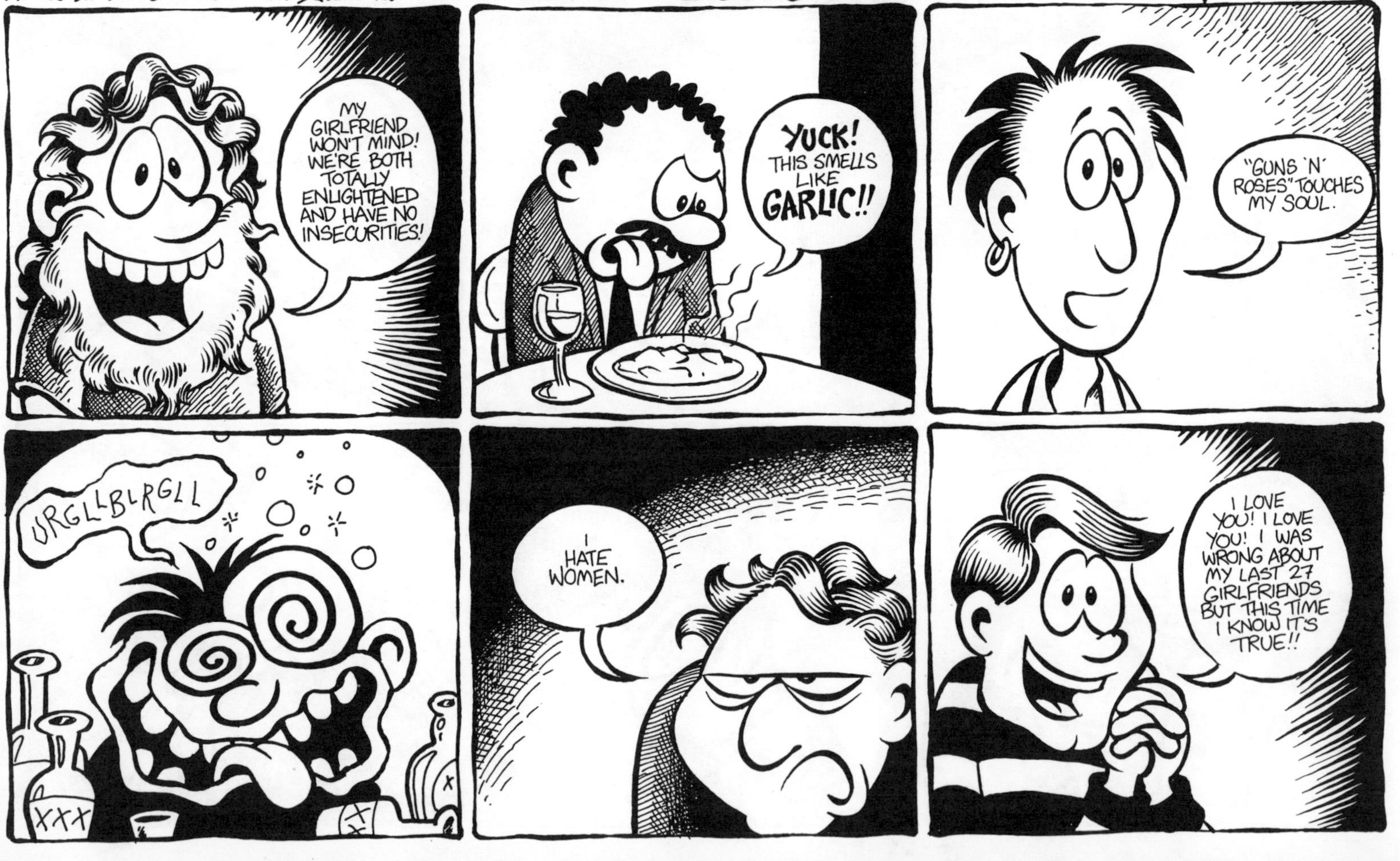
MY GIRLFRIEND WON'T MIND! WE'RE BOTH TOTALLY ENLIGHTENED AND HAVE NO INSECURITIES!
YUCK! THIS SMELLS LIKE GARLIC!!
"GUNS 'N' ROSES" TOUCHES MY SOUL.
URGLLBLRGLL
XXX
I HATE WOMEN.
I LOVE YOU! I LOVE YOU! I WAS WRONG ABOUT MY LAST 27 GIRLFRIENDS BUT THIS TIME I KNOW IT'S TRUE!!

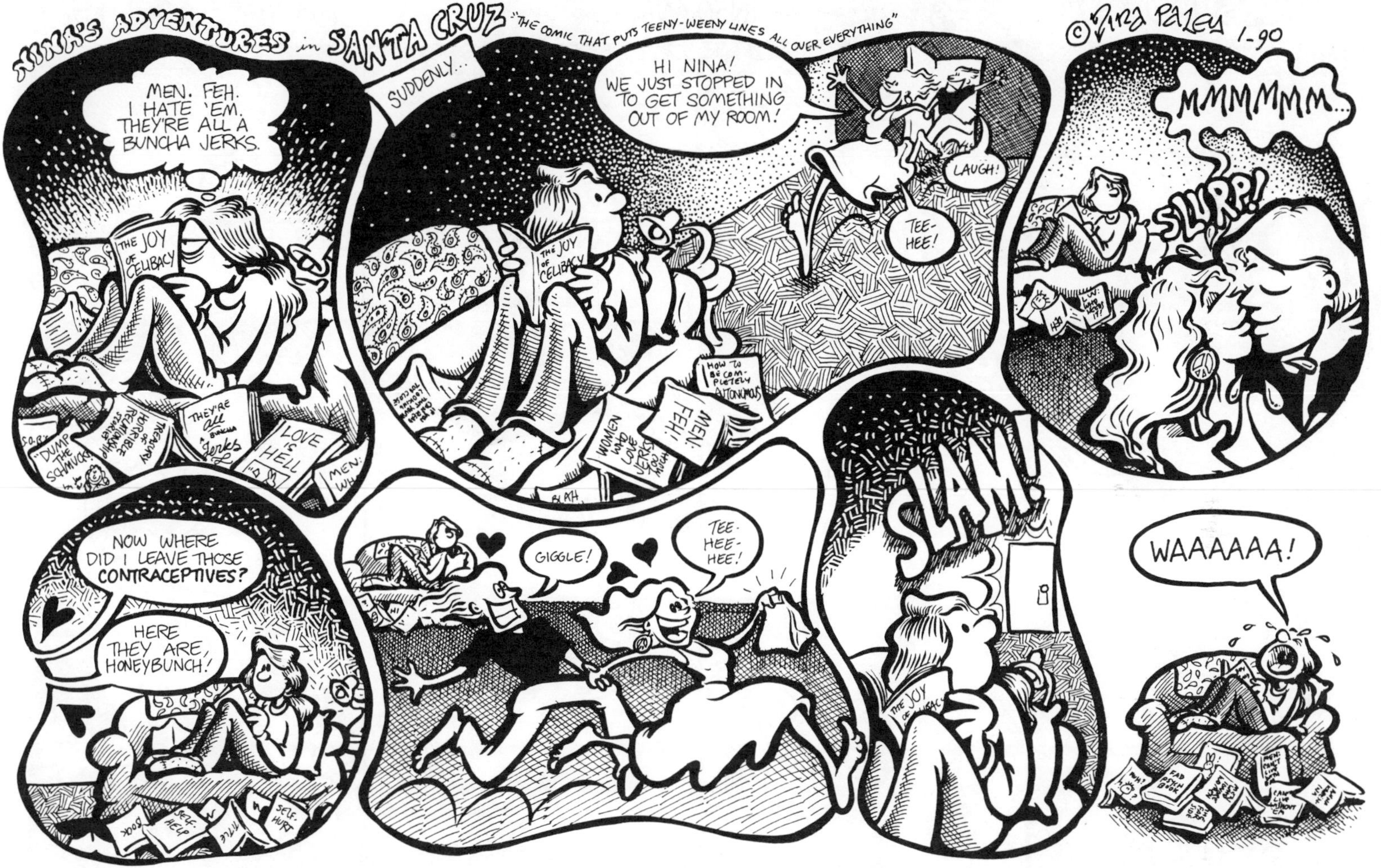
NINA'S ADVENTURES in SANTA CRUZ
"THE COMIC THAT PUTS TEENY-WEENY LINES ALL OVER EVERYTHING"
© Nina Paley 1-90
MEN. FEH. I HATE 'EM. THEY'RE ALL A BUNCHA JERKS.
THE JOY OF CELIBACY
TREASURY OF HORRIBLE RELATIONSHIP STORIES
THEY'RE ALL A BUNCHA JERKS
DUMP THE SCHMUCK
LOVE IS HELL
SUDDENLY...
HI NINA! WE JUST STOPPED IN TO GET SOMETHING OUT OF MY ROOM!
LAUGH!
TEE-HEE!
HOW TO BE COMPLETELY AUTONOMOUS
MEN: FEH!
WOMEN WHO LOVE JERKS TOO MUCH
BLAH
MMMMMM...
SLURP!
NOW WHERE DID I LEAVE THOSE CONTRACEPTIVES?
HERE THEY ARE, HONEYBUNCH!
SELF-HELP
SELF-HURT
BOOK
GIGGLE!
TEE-HEE-HEE!
SLAM!
WAAAAAA!

NINA'S ADVENTURES

"INSOMNIA"

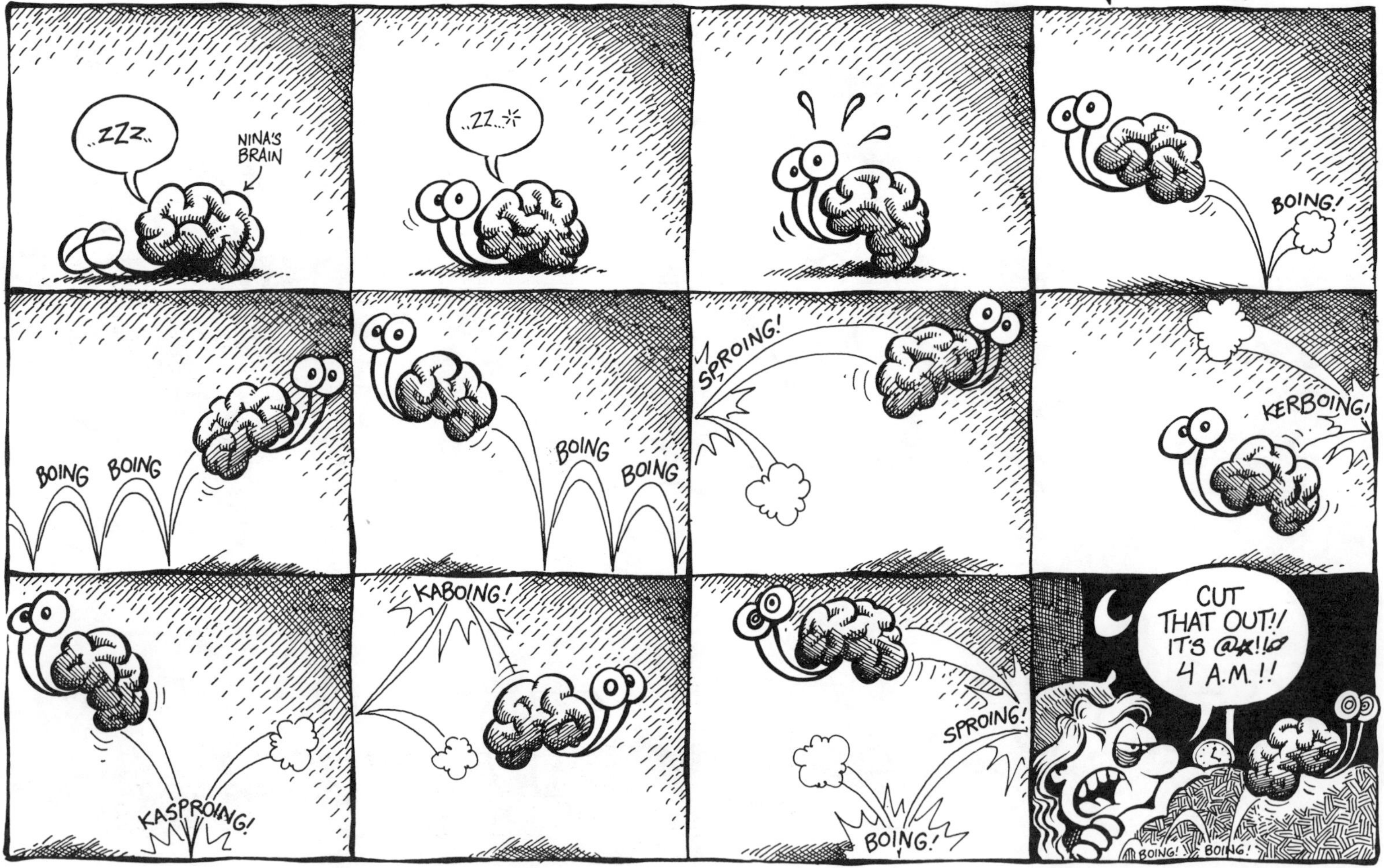
..ZZZ..
NINA'S BRAIN
..ZZ..
BOING!
BOING BOING
BOING BOING
SPROING!
KERBOING!
KASPROING!
KABOING!
SPROING!
BOING!
CUT THAT OUT!! IT'S @*!!& 4 A.M.!!
BOING! BOING!

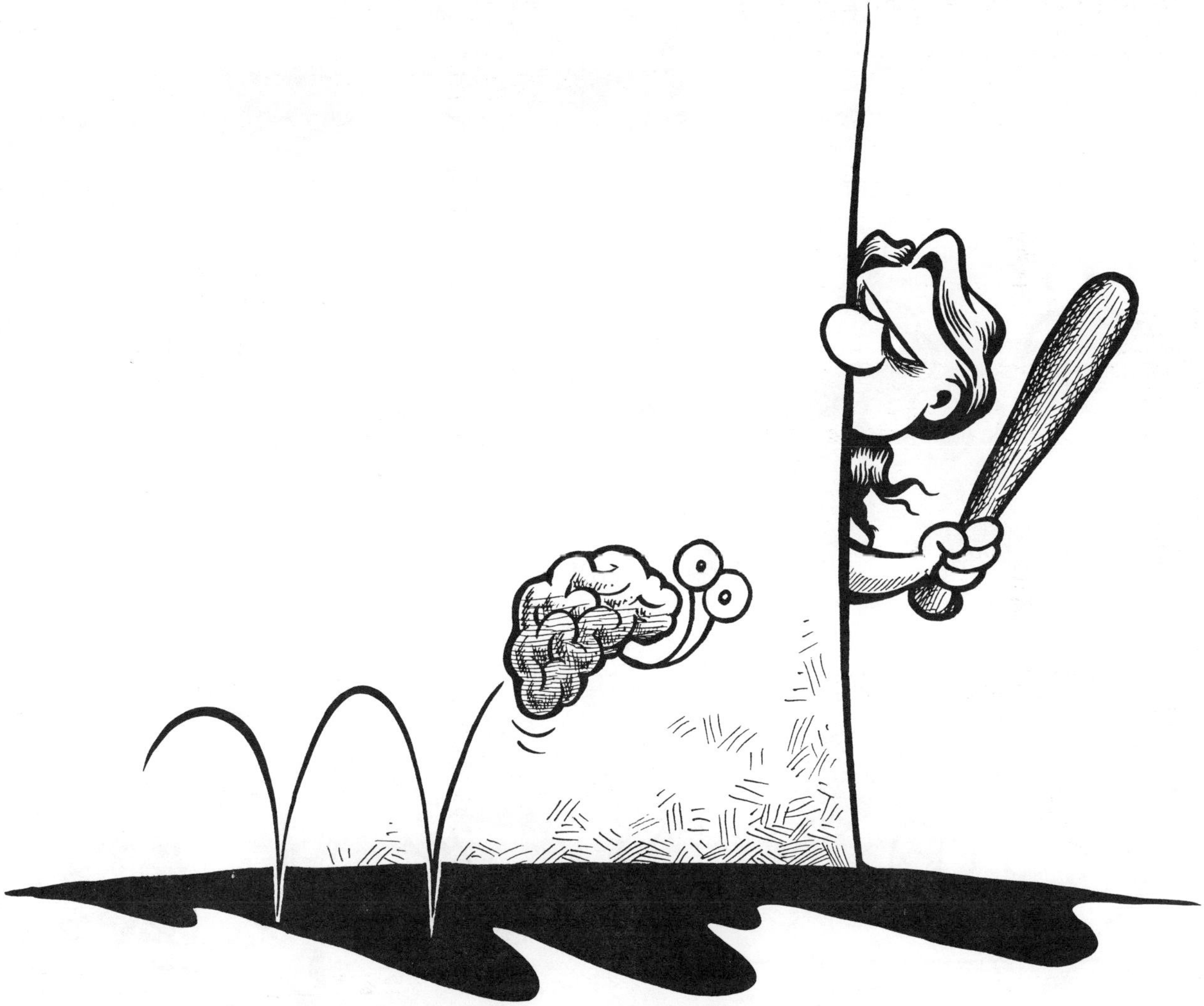

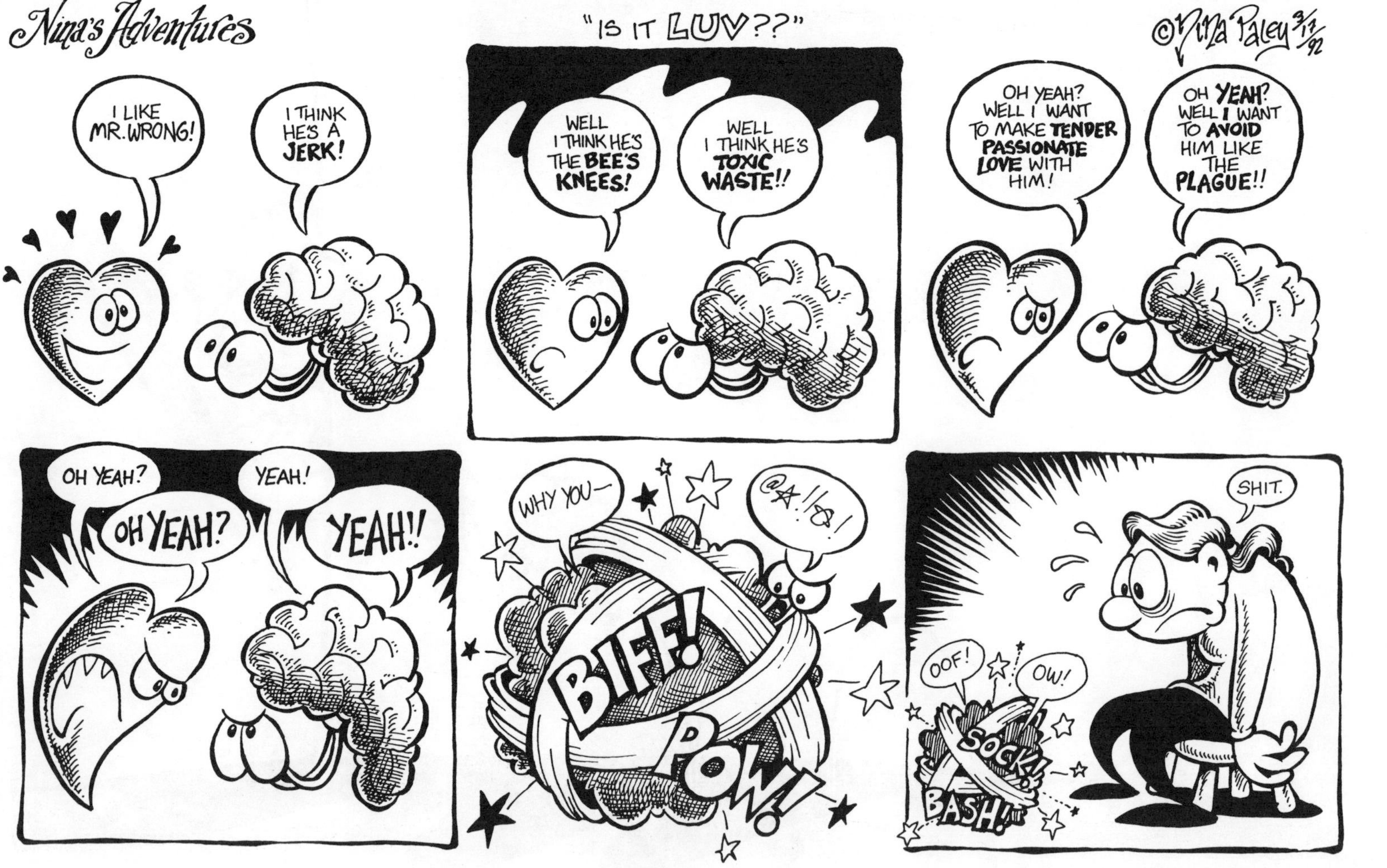
Nina's Adventures
"IS IT LUV??"
©Nina Paley 3/17/92
I LIKE MR. WRONG!
I THINK HE'S A JERK!
WELL I THINK HE'S THE BEE'S KNEES!
WELL I THINK HE'S TOXIC WASTE!!
OH YEAH? WELL I WANT TO MAKE TENDER PASSIONATE LOVE WITH HIM!
OH YEAH? WELL I WANT TO AVOID HIM LIKE THE PLAGUE!!
OH YEAH?
OH YEAH?
YEAH!
YEAH!!
WHY YOU—
BIFF!
POW!
SHIT.
OOF!
OW!
SOCK!
BASH!

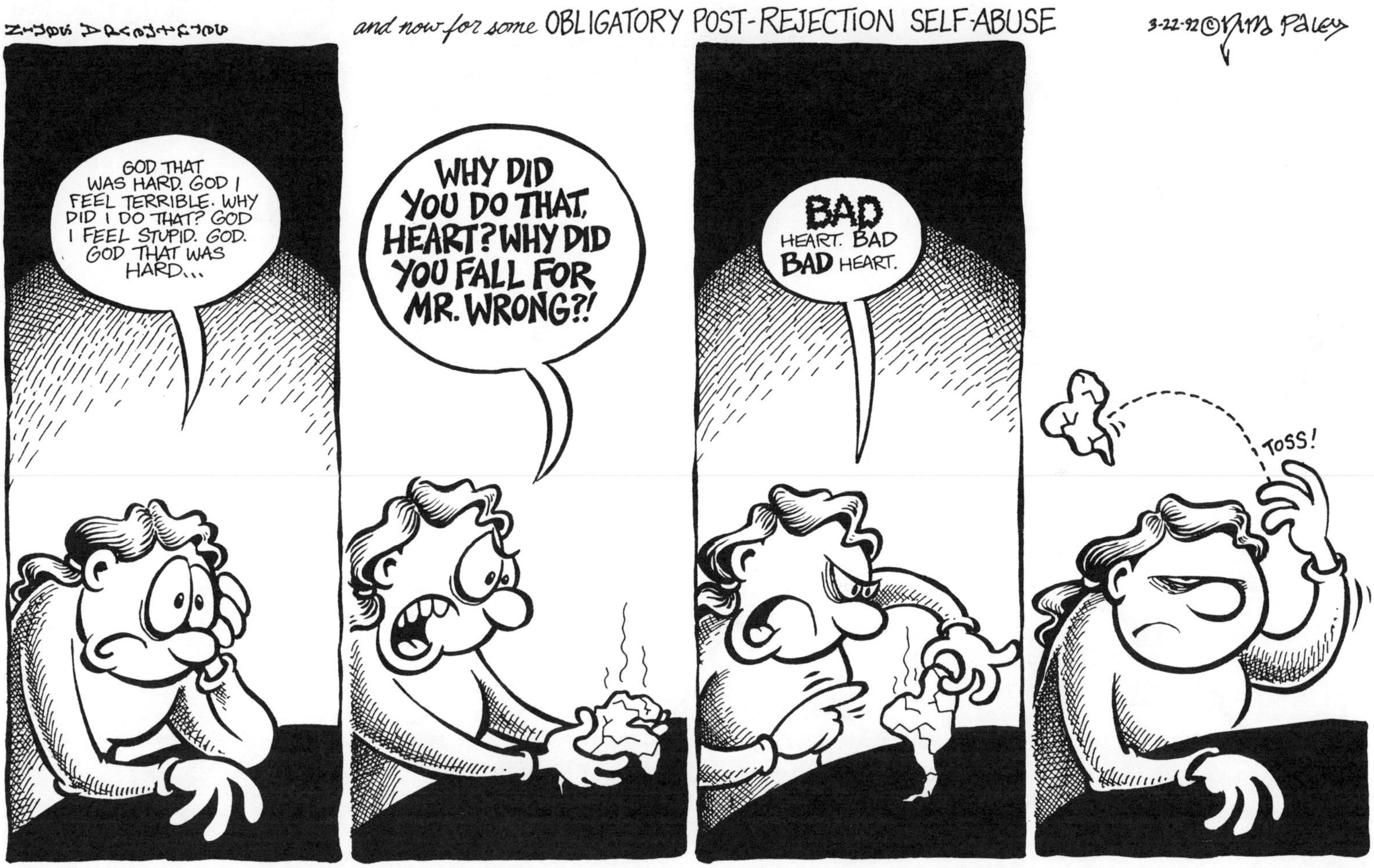
and now for some OBLIGATORY POST-REJECTION SELF-ABUSE
3-22-92 © Nina Paley
GOD THAT WAS HARD. GOD I FEEL TERRIBLE. WHY DID I DO THAT? GOD I FEEL STUPID. GOD. GOD THAT WAS HARD...
WHY DID YOU DO THAT, HEART? WHY DID YOU FALL FOR MR. WRONG?!
BAD HEART. BAD BAD HEART.
TOSS!

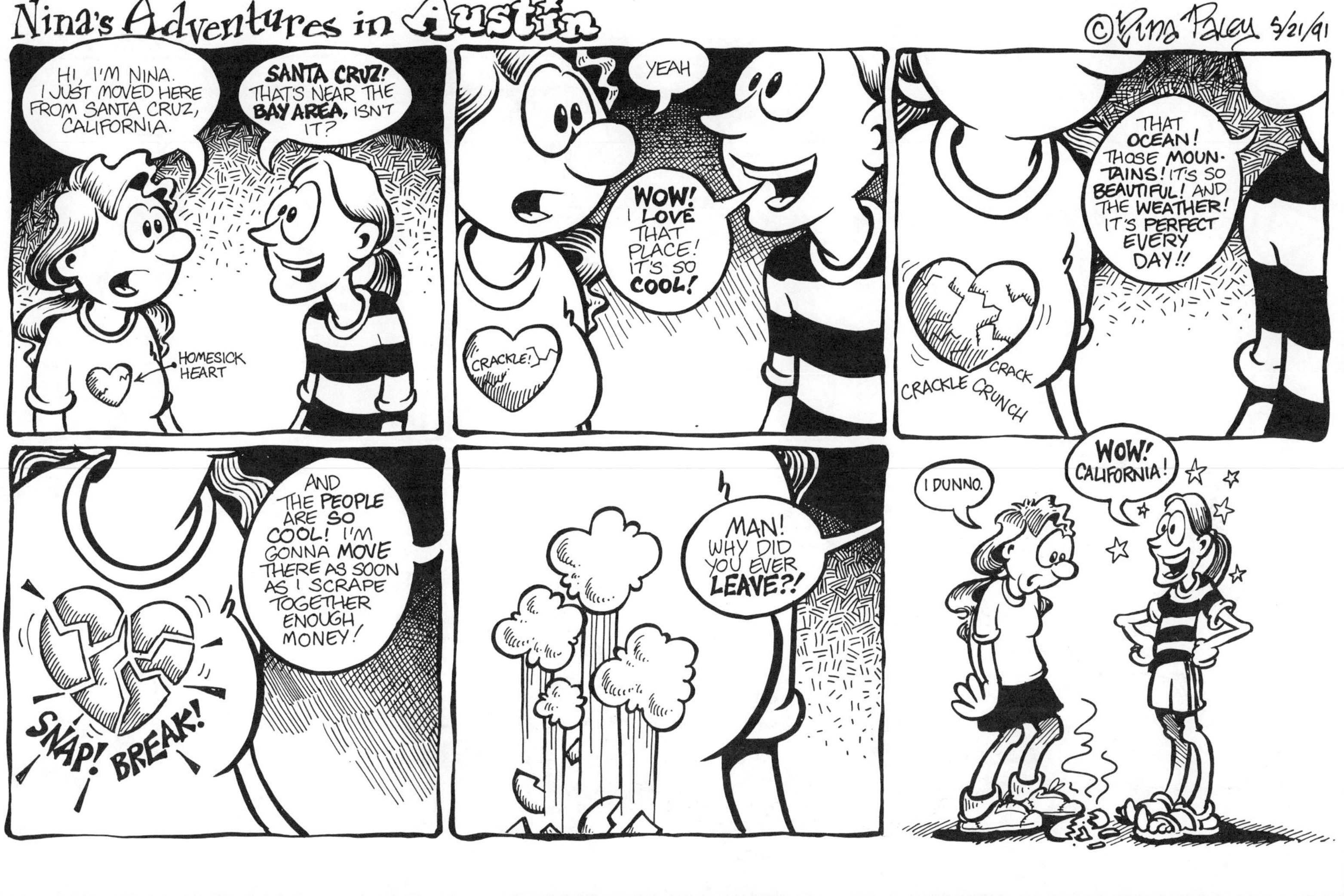

Nina's Adventures in Austin
©Nina Paley 5/21/91
HI, I'M NINA. I JUST MOVED HERE FROM SANTA CRUZ, CALIFORNIA.
SANTA CRUZ! THAT'S NEAR THE BAY AREA, ISN'T IT?
HOMESICK HEART
YEAH
WOW! I LOVE THAT PLACE! IT'S SO COOL!
CRACKLE!
THAT OCEAN! THOSE MOUNTAINS! IT'S SO BEAUTIFUL! AND THE WEATHER! IT'S PERFECT EVERY DAY!!
CRACKLE CRUNCH CRACK
AND THE PEOPLE ARE SO COOL! I'M GONNA MOVE THERE AS SOON AS I SCRAPE TOGETHER ENOUGH MONEY!
SNAP! BREAK!
MAN! WHY DID YOU EVER LEAVE?!
I DUNNO.
WOW! CALIFORNIA!

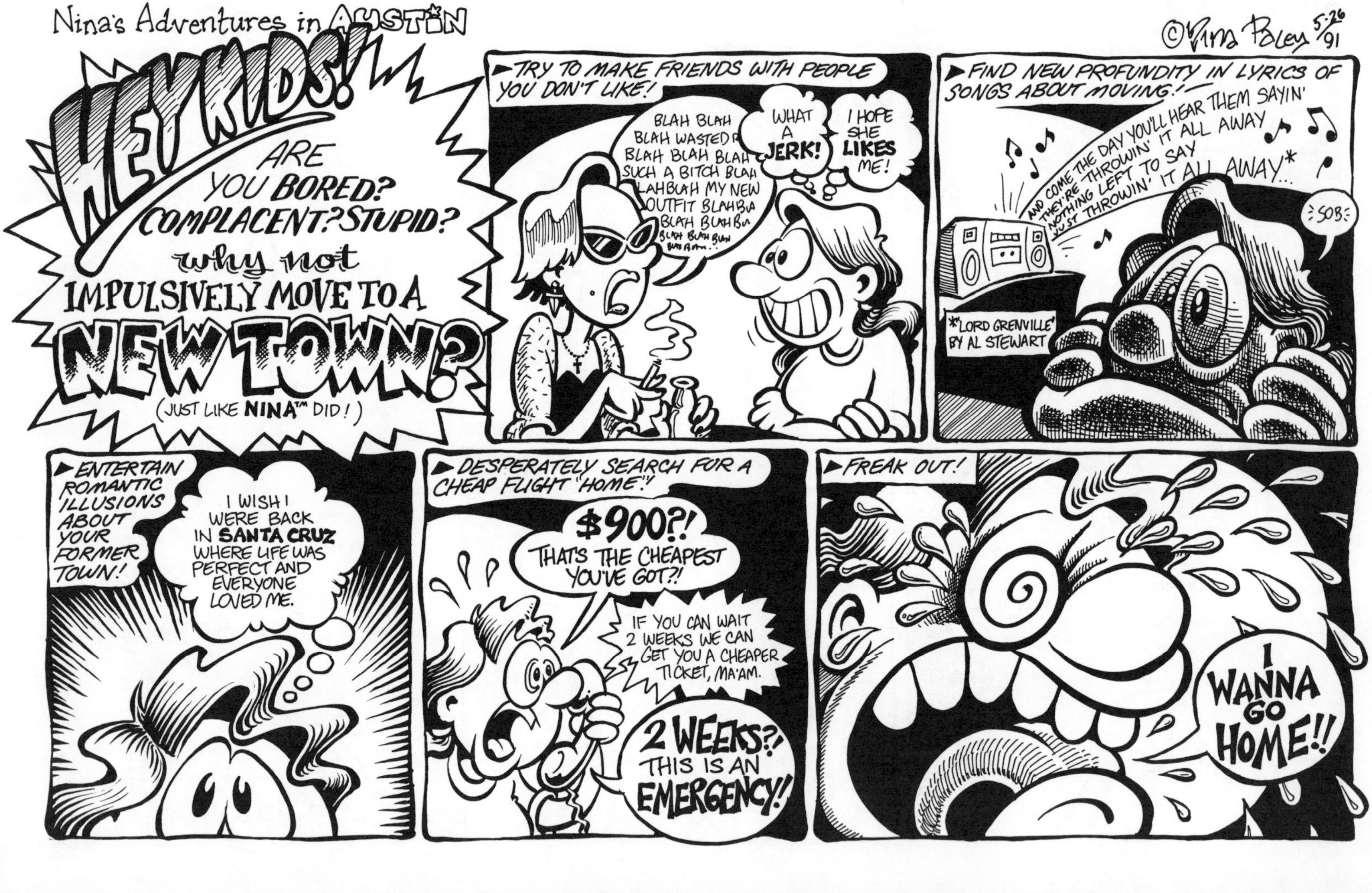

Nina's Adventures in AUSTIN
©Nina Paley 5.26 91
HEY KIDS!!
ARE YOU BORED? COMPLACENT? STUPID?
why not IMPULSIVELY MOVE TO A NEW TOWN?
(JUST LIKE NINA™ DID!)
▶TRY TO MAKE FRIENDS WITH PEOPLE YOU DON'T LIKE!
BLAH BLAH BLAH WASTED BLAH BLAH BLAH SUCH A BITCH BLAH BLAH BLAH MY NEW OUTFIT BLAH BLAH BLAH BLAH BLAH
WHAT A JERK!
I HOPE SHE LIKES ME!
▶FIND NEW PROFUNDITY IN LYRICS OF SONGS ABOUT MOVING!
AND COME THE DAY YOU'LL HEAR THEM SAYIN' THEY'RE THROWIN' IT ALL AWAY NOTHING LEFT TO SAY JUST THROWIN' IT ALL AWAY*...
SOB
*"LORD GRENVILLE" BY AL STEWART
▶ENTERTAIN ROMANTIC ILLUSIONS ABOUT YOUR FORMER TOWN!
I WISH I WERE BACK IN SANTA CRUZ WHERE LIFE WAS PERFECT AND EVERYONE LOVED ME.
▶DESPERATELY SEARCH FOR A CHEAP FLIGHT "HOME"!
$900?! THAT'S THE CHEAPEST YOU'VE GOT?!
IF YOU CAN WAIT 2 WEEKS WE CAN GET YOU A CHEAPER TICKET, MA'AM.
2 WEEKS?! THIS IS AN EMERGENCY!
▶FREAK OUT!
I WANNA GO HOME!!

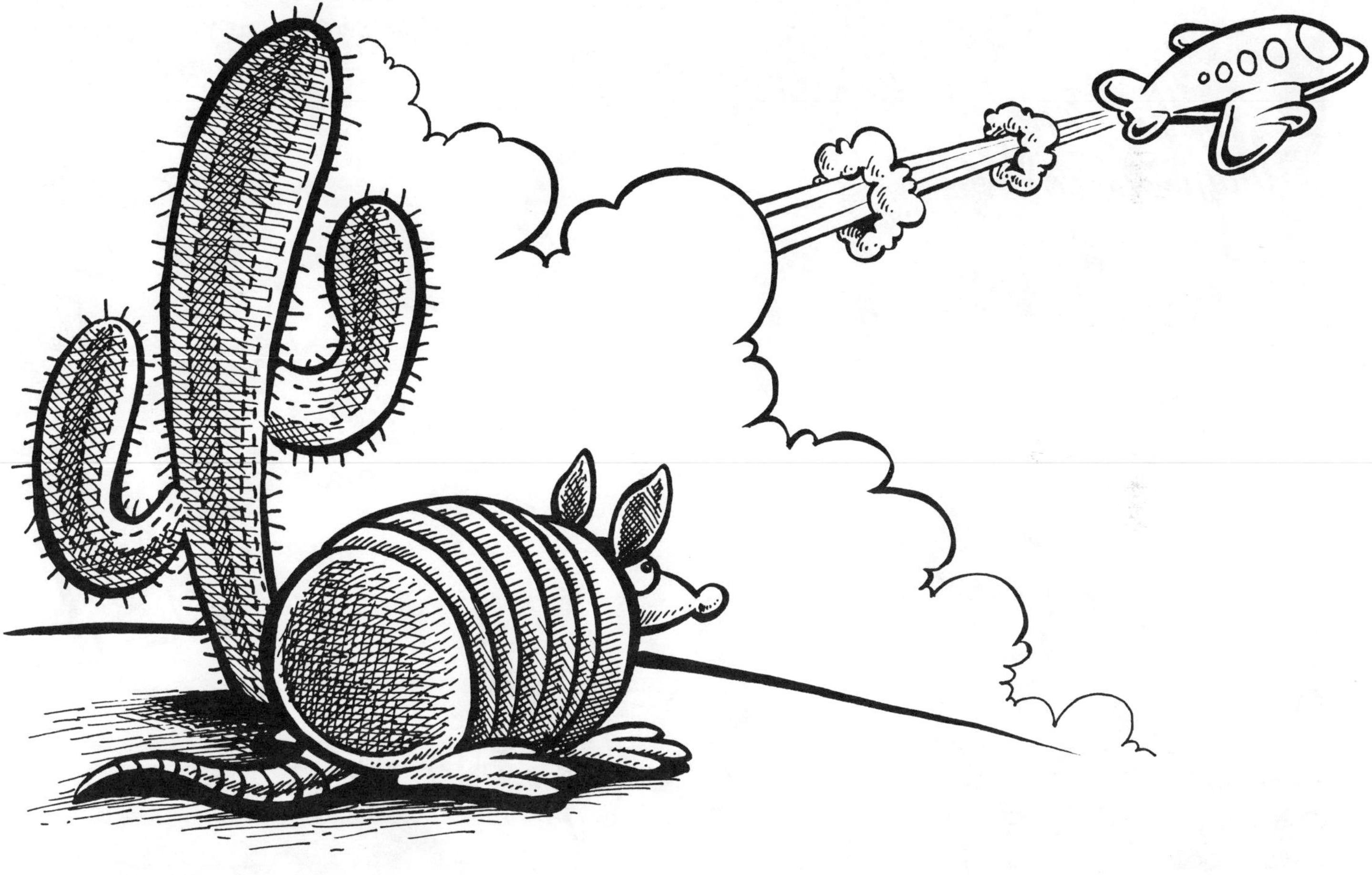

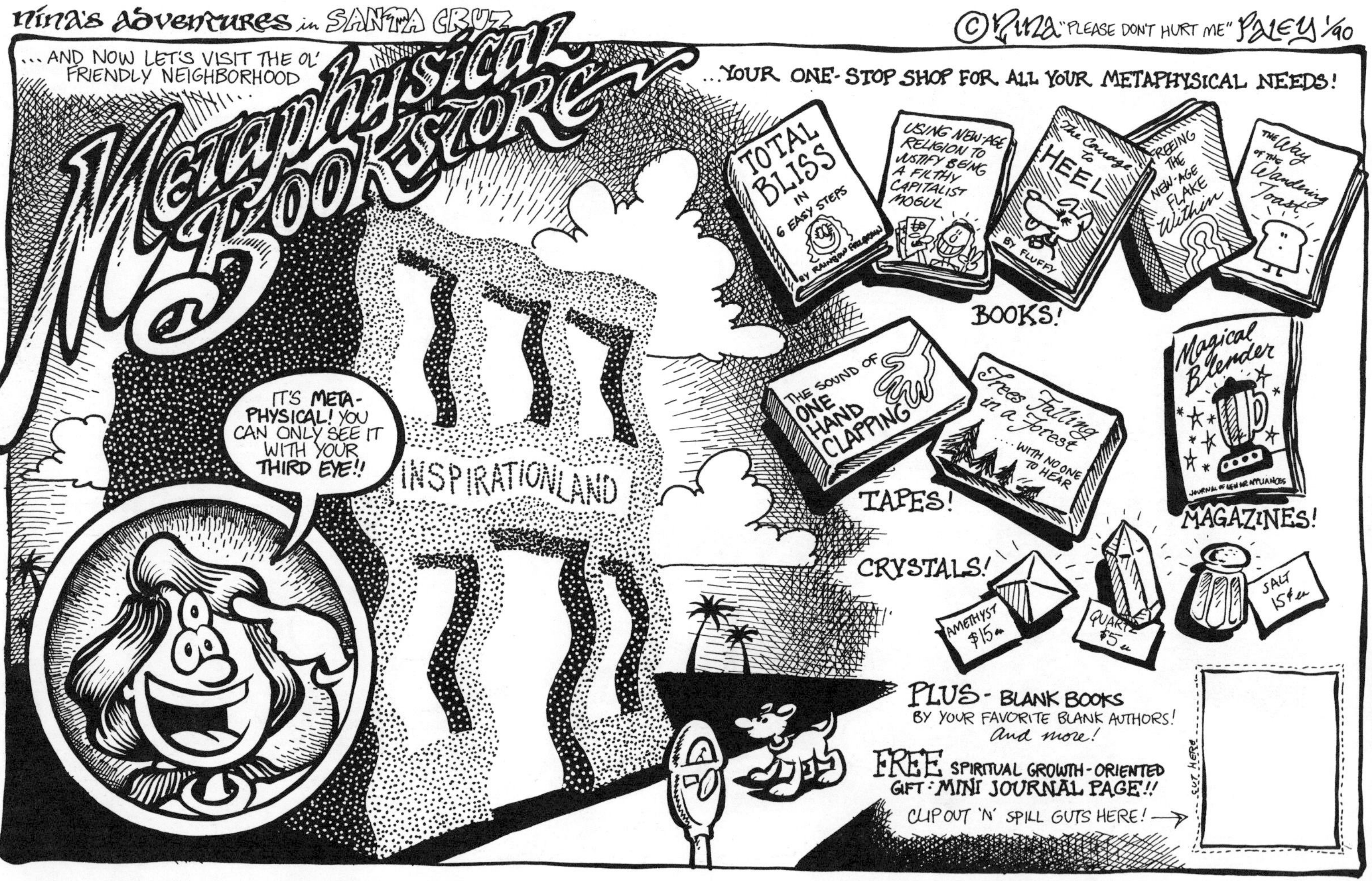

Nina's Adventures in SANTA CRUZ
© Nina "PLEASE DON'T HURT ME" Paley 1/90
...AND NOW LET'S VISIT THE OL' FRIENDLY NEIGHBORHOOD
Metaphysical Bookstore
...YOUR ONE-STOP SHOP FOR ALL YOUR METAPHYSICAL NEEDS!
TOTAL BLISS IN 6 EASY STEPS BY RAINBOW FREEBORN
USING NEW-AGE RELIGION TO JUSTIFY BEING A FILTHY CAPITALIST MOGUL
The Courage to HEEL BY FLUFFY
FREEING THE NEW-AGE FLAKE Within
The Way of the Wandering Toast
BOOKS!
THE SOUND OF ONE HAND CLAPPING
Trees Falling in a Forest ...WITH NO ONE TO HEAR
TAPES!
Magical Blender
JOURNAL OF NEW AGE APPLIANCES
MAGAZINES!
IT'S META-PHYSICAL! YOU CAN ONLY SEE IT WITH YOUR THIRD EYE!!
INSPIRATIONLAND
CRYSTALS!
AMETHYST $15 ea
QUARTZ $5 ea
SALT 15¢ ea
PLUS - BLANK BOOKS BY YOUR FAVORITE BLANK AUTHORS! And more!
FREE SPIRITUAL GROWTH-ORIENTED GIFT: MINI JOURNAL PAGE!!
CLIP OUT 'N' SPILL GUTS HERE!
CUT HERE

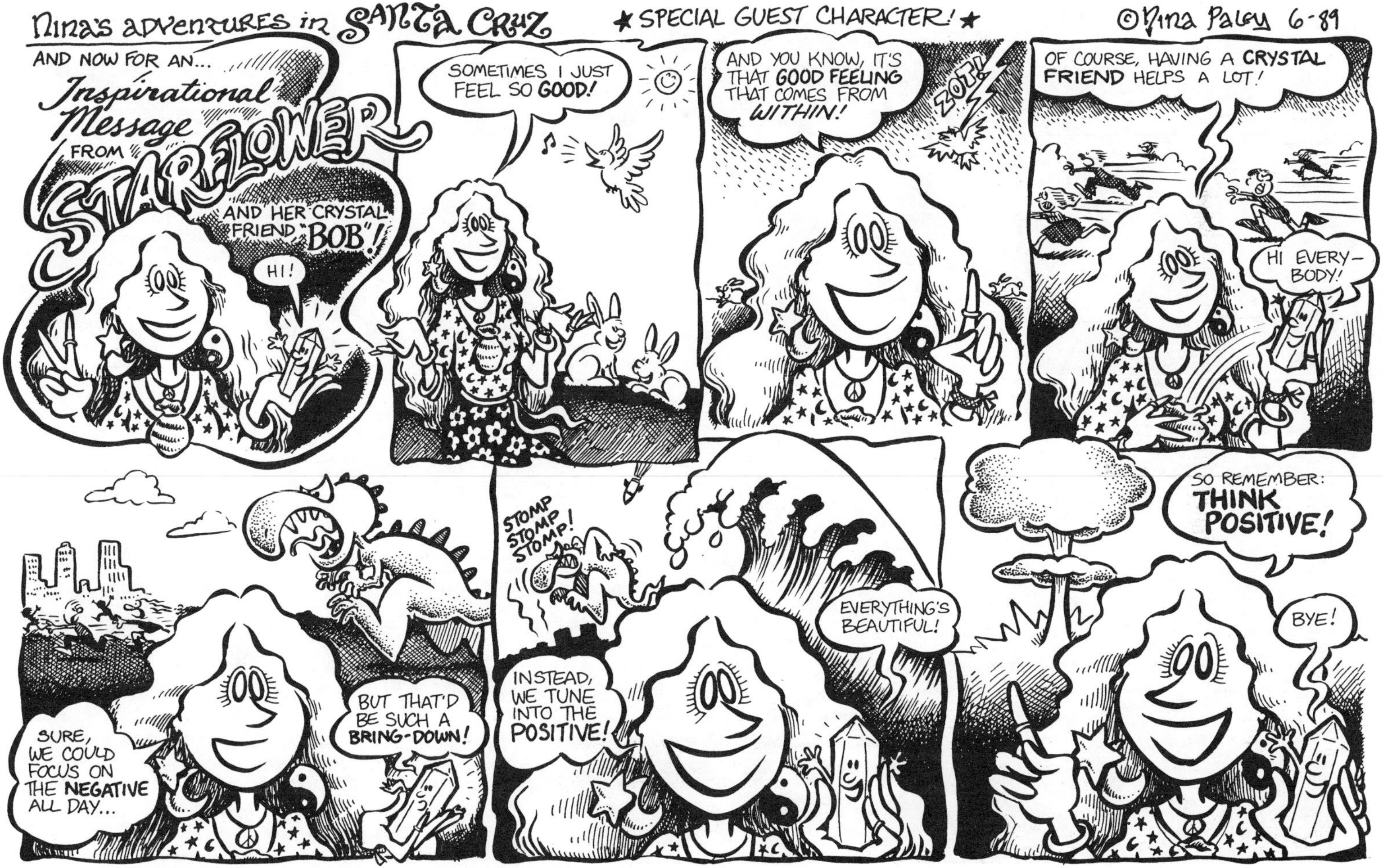
Nina's adventures in SANTA CRUZ
★ SPECIAL GUEST CHARACTER! ★
©Nina Paley 6-89
AND NOW FOR AN...
Inspirational Message
FROM STARFLOWER
AND HER CRYSTAL FRIEND "BOB"!
HI!
SOMETIMES I JUST FEEL SO GOOD!
AND YOU KNOW, IT'S THAT GOOD FEELING THAT COMES FROM WITHIN!
ZOT!
OF COURSE, HAVING A CRYSTAL FRIEND HELPS A LOT!
HI EVERY-BODY!
SURE, WE COULD FOCUS ON THE NEGATIVE ALL DAY...
BUT THAT'D BE SUCH A BRING-DOWN!
STOMP STOMP STOMP!
INSTEAD, WE TUNE INTO THE POSITIVE!
EVERYTHING'S BEAUTIFUL!
SO REMEMBER: THINK POSITIVE!
BYE!

Nina's Adventures in SANTA CRUZ

© Nina Paley 12/90

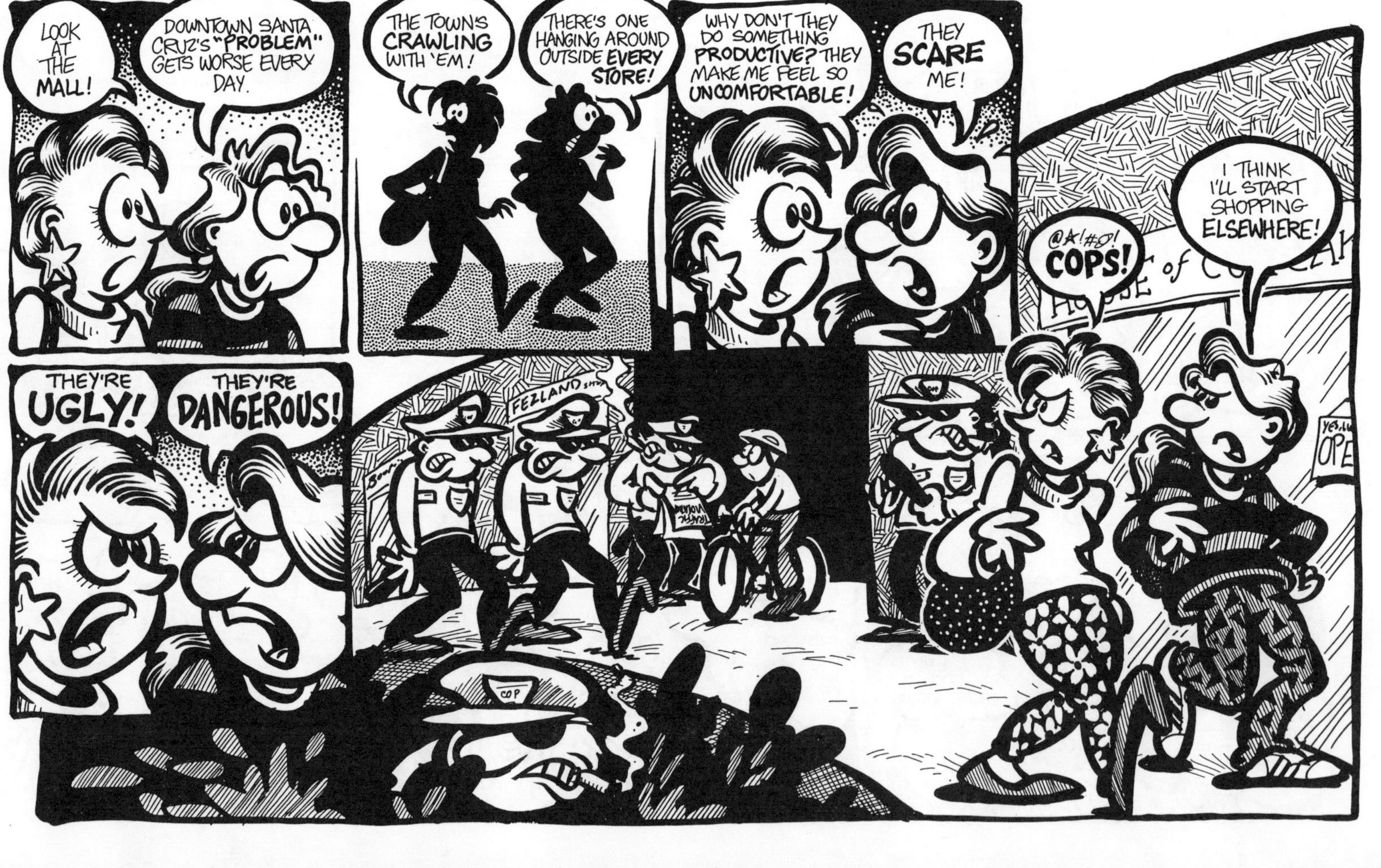

LOOK AT THE MALL!
DOWNTOWN SANTA CRUZ'S "PROBLEM" GETS WORSE EVERY DAY.
THE TOWN'S CRAWLING WITH 'EM!
THERE'S ONE HANGING AROUND OUTSIDE EVERY STORE!
WHY DON'T THEY DO SOMETHING PRODUCTIVE? THEY MAKE ME FEEL SO UNCOMFORTABLE!
THEY SCARE ME!
THEY'RE UGLY!
THEY'RE DANGEROUS!
FEZLAND
COP
@★!#⊘! COPS!
I THINK I'LL START SHOPPING ELSEWHERE!

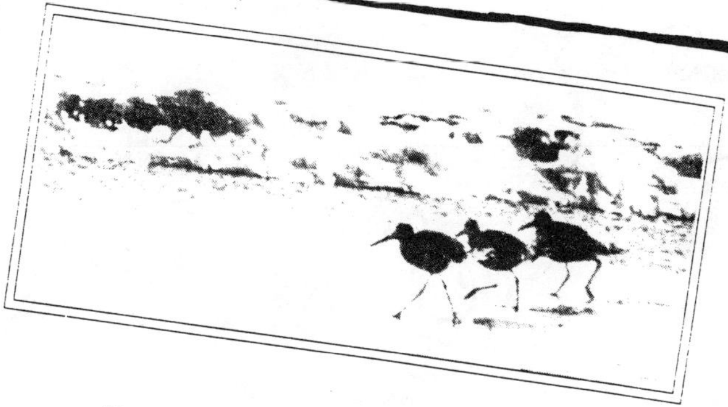

City of Santa Cruz

CITY HALL - 809 CENTER STREET - ROOM 27
SANTA CRUZ, CALIFORNIA 95060 - 3865
OFFICE OF THE CHIEF OF POLICE

(408) 429-[redacted]
DIRECT TELEPHONE NUMBER

February 7, 1991

Ms. Nina Paley
c/o Mr. Thom Zajak
P.O. Box 8543
Santa Cruz, California 95061

Dear Ms. Paley:

It was with great sadness that I observed your comic, for the first time, from the Comic News Issue 154. The comic, "Nina's Adventures in Santa Cruz", depicts two women walking down the mall and speaking in derogatory tones about certain people. When the punch line is delivered, we discover that they were speaking about the "cops" on the mall.

I doubt that your sense of humor would have been well received had you directed your punch line at any other minority group. Police officers in Santa Cruz are a minority group. Granted, most of didn't have to grow up with hatred and discriminati[...] take our uniforms off every day (usually) [...] it twenty-four hours of ever[...] are largely th[...]

Nina's Adventures

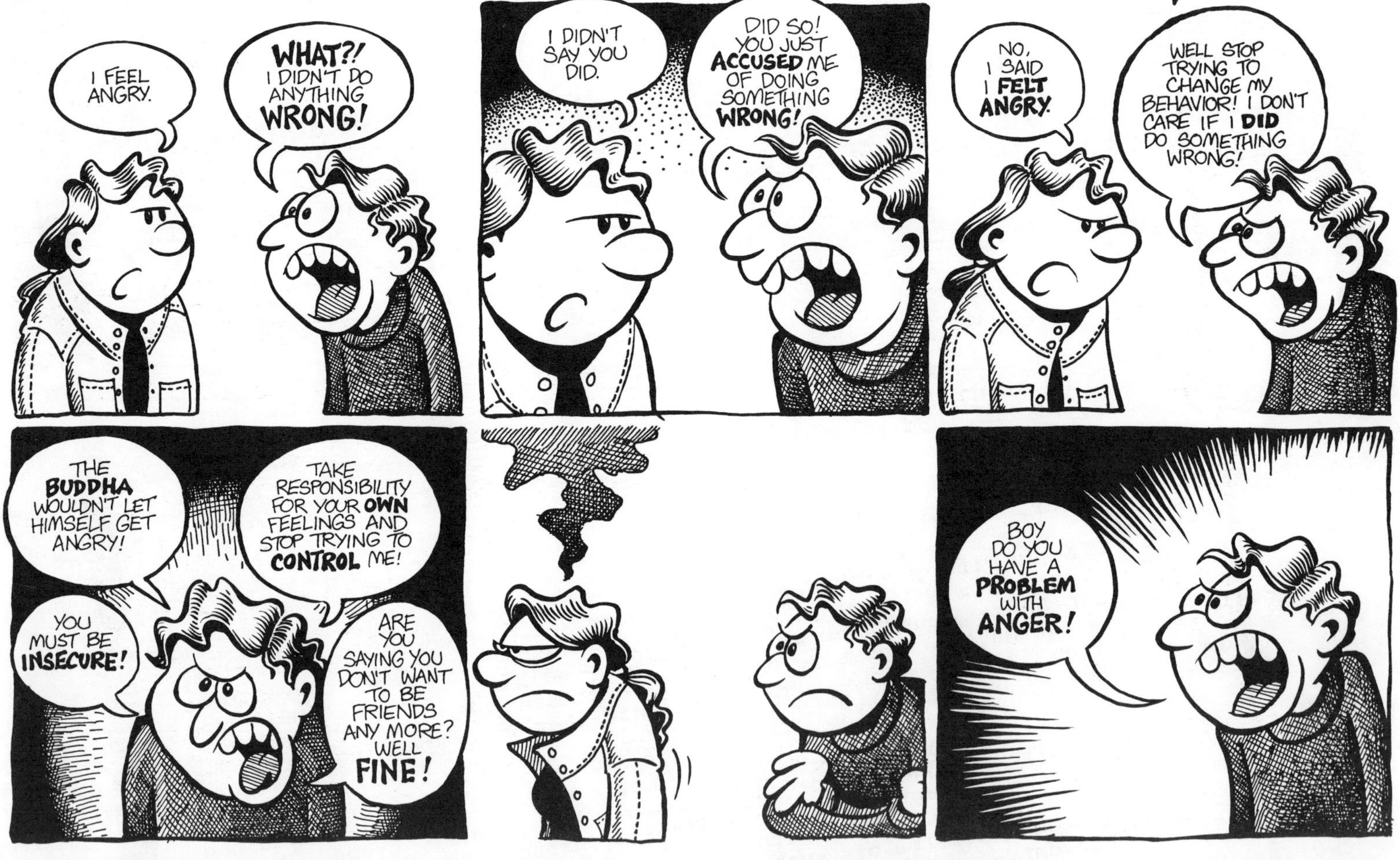
I FEEL ANGRY.
WHAT?! I DIDN'T DO ANYTHING WRONG!
I DIDN'T SAY YOU DID.
DID SO! YOU JUST ACCUSED ME OF DOING SOMETHING WRONG!
NO, I SAID I FELT ANGRY.
WELL STOP TRYING TO CHANGE MY BEHAVIOR! I DON'T CARE IF I DID DO SOMETHING WRONG!
THE BUDDHA WOULDN'T LET HIMSELF GET ANGRY!
TAKE RESPONSIBILITY FOR YOUR OWN FEELINGS AND STOP TRYING TO CONTROL ME!
YOU MUST BE INSECURE!
ARE YOU SAYING YOU DON'T WANT TO BE FRIENDS ANY MORE? WELL FINE!
BOY DO YOU HAVE A PROBLEM WITH ANGER!

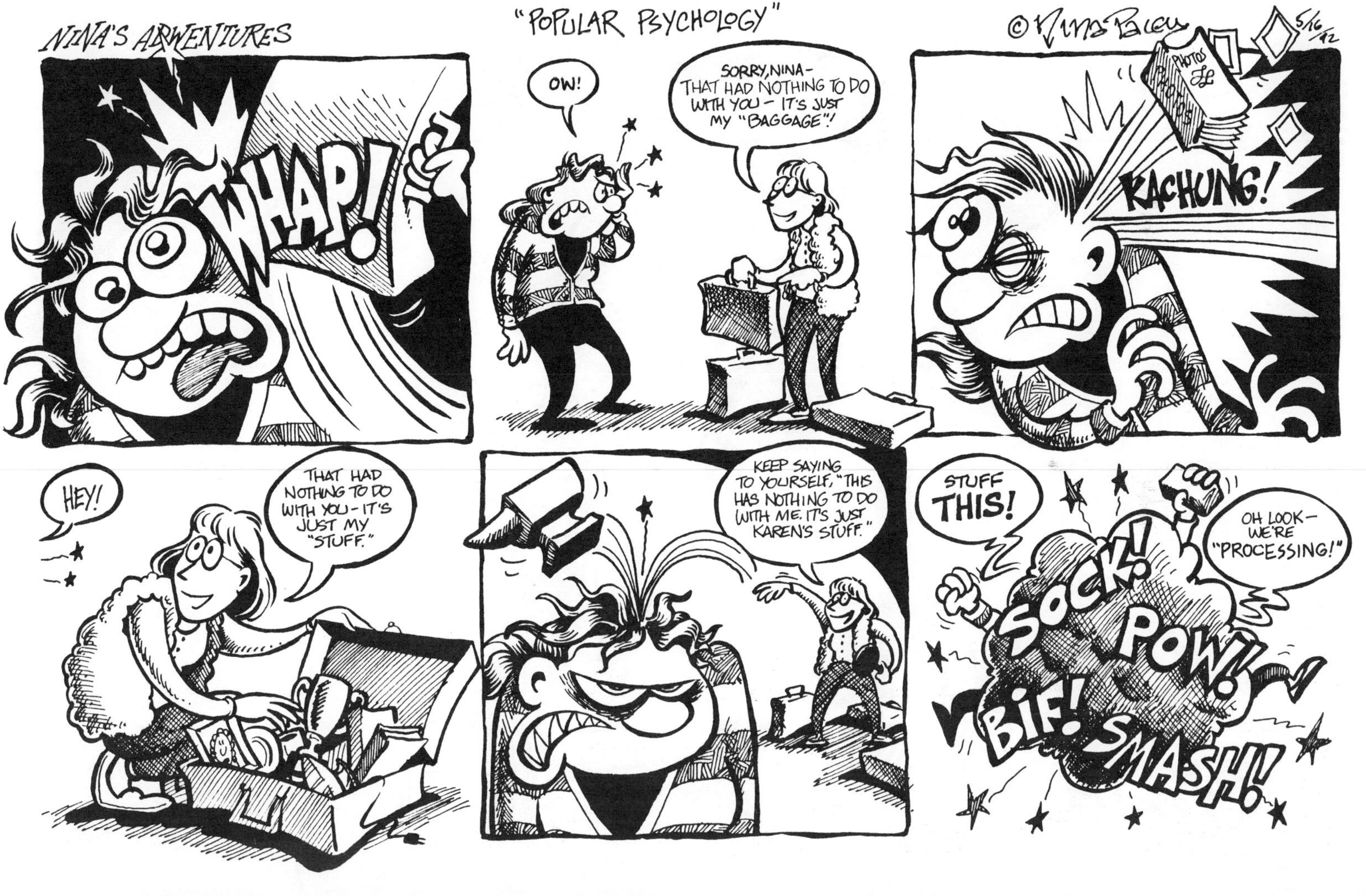
NINA'S ADVENTURES
"POPULAR PSYCHOLOGY"
© Nina Paley 5/16/92
WHAP!
OW!
SORRY, NINA- THAT HAD NOTHING TO DO WITH YOU - IT'S JUST MY "BAGGAGE"!
PHOTOS
KACHUNG!
HEY!
THAT HAD NOTHING TO DO WITH YOU - IT'S JUST MY "STUFF."
KEEP SAYING TO YOURSELF, "THIS HAS NOTHING TO DO WITH ME. IT'S JUST KAREN'S STUFF."
STUFF THIS!
OH LOOK- WE'RE "PROCESSING!"
SOCK! POW! BIF! SMASH!

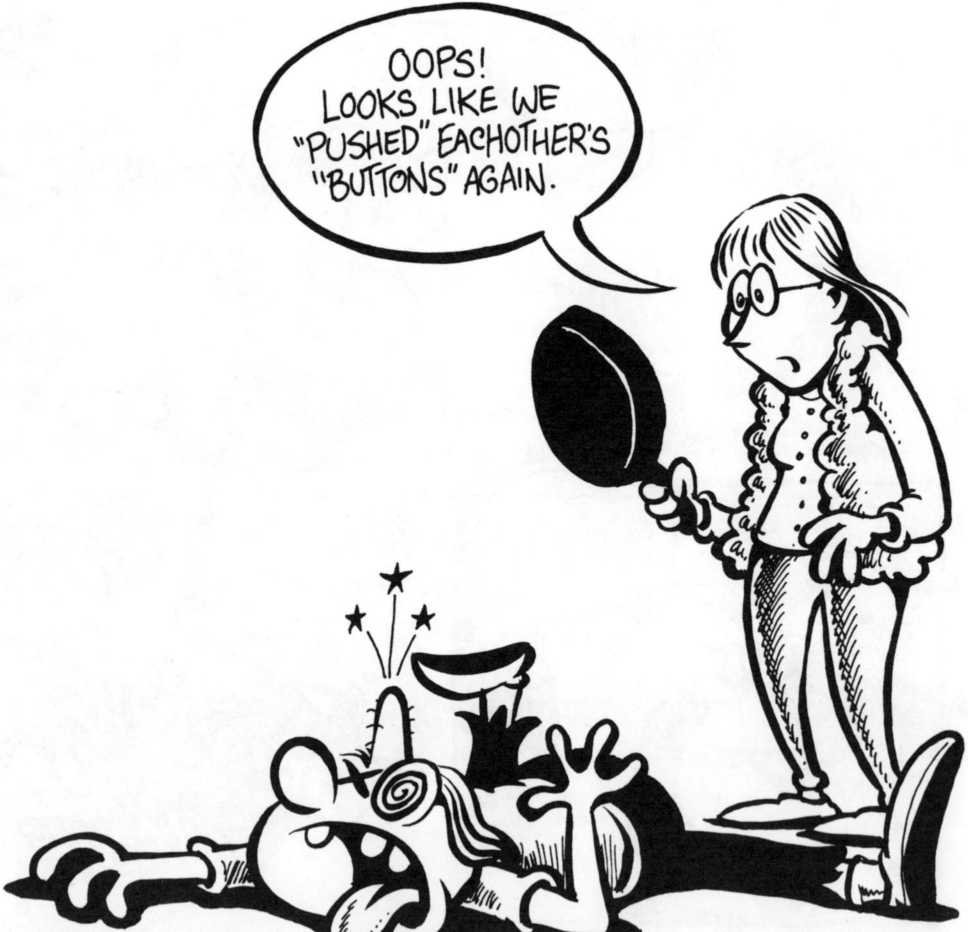
OOPS! LOOKS LIKE WE "PUSHED" EACHOTHER'S "BUTTONS" AGAIN.

nina's adventures

My Best Friend

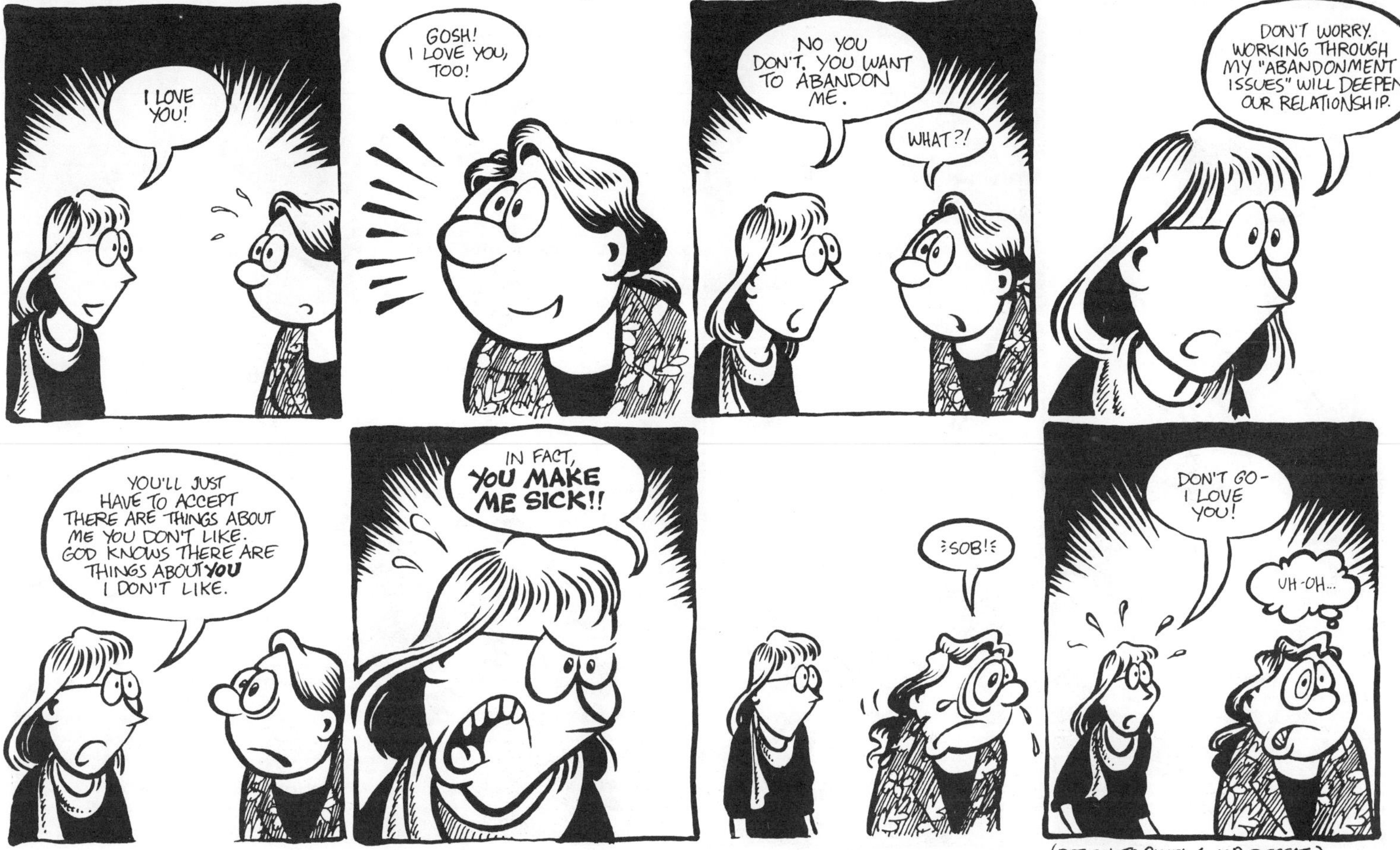
I LOVE YOU!
GOSH! I LOVE YOU, TOO!
NO YOU DON'T. YOU WANT TO ABANDON ME.
WHAT?!
DON'T WORRY. WORKING THROUGH MY "ABANDONMENT ISSUES" WILL DEEPEN OUR RELATIONSHIP.
YOU'LL JUST HAVE TO ACCEPT THERE ARE THINGS ABOUT ME YOU DON'T LIKE. GOD KNOWS THERE ARE THINGS ABOUT **YOU** I DON'T LIKE.
IN FACT, **YOU MAKE ME SICK!!**
SOB!
DON'T GO- I LOVE YOU!
UH-OH...

(RETURN TO PANEL 1 AND REPEAT)

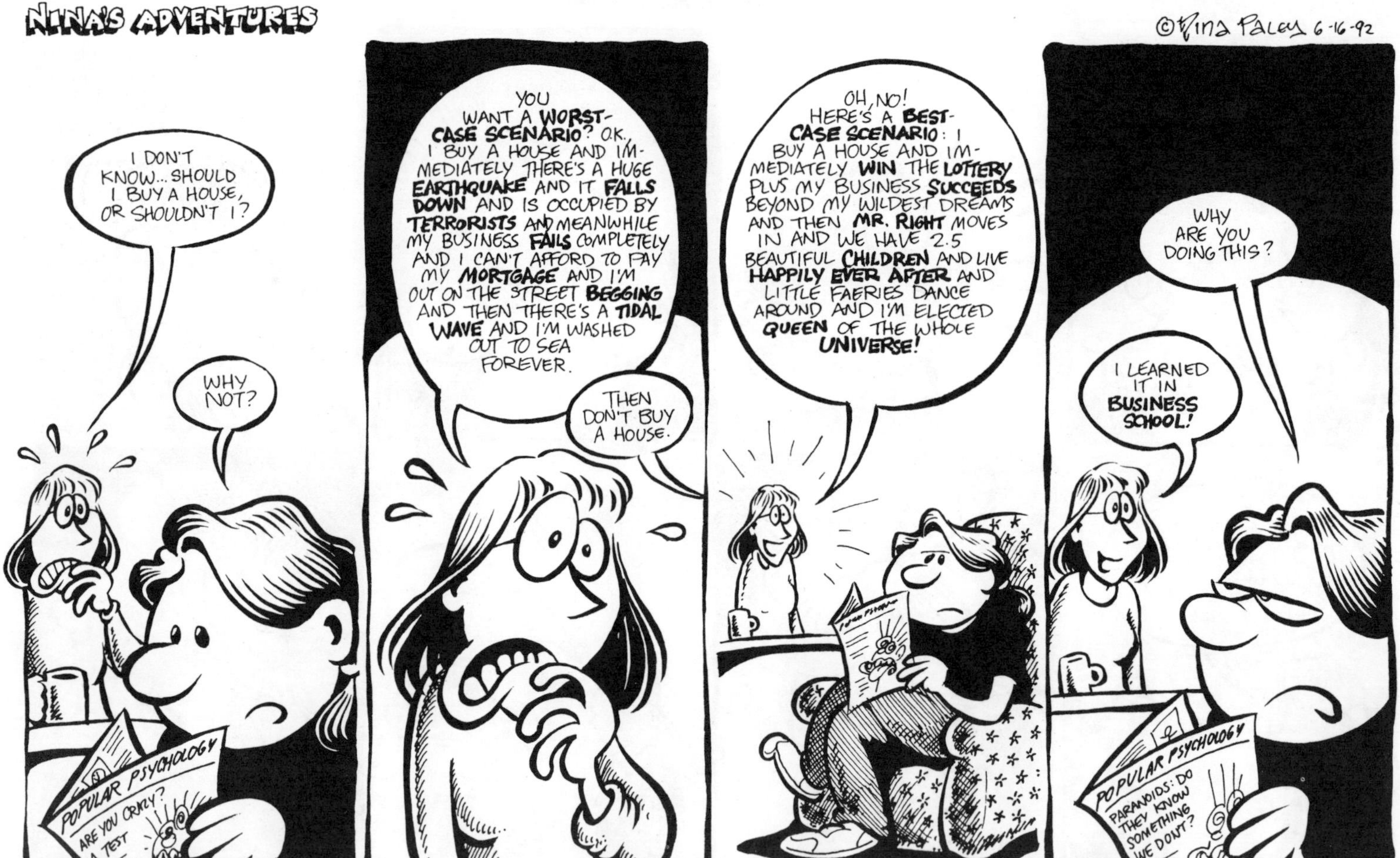
NINA'S ADVENTURES
©Nina Paley 6-16-92
I DON'T KNOW... SHOULD I BUY A HOUSE, OR SHOULDN'T I?
WHY NOT?
POPULAR PSYCHOLOGY
ARE YOU CRAZY? A TEST
YOU WANT A WORST-CASE SCENARIO? O.K. I BUY A HOUSE AND IMMEDIATELY THERE'S A HUGE EARTHQUAKE AND IT FALLS DOWN AND IS OCCUPIED BY TERRORISTS AND MEANWHILE MY BUSINESS FAILS COMPLETELY AND I CAN'T AFFORD TO PAY MY MORTGAGE AND I'M OUT ON THE STREET BEGGING AND THEN THERE'S A TIDAL WAVE AND I'M WASHED OUT TO SEA FOREVER.
THEN DON'T BUY A HOUSE.
OH, NO! HERE'S A BEST-CASE SCENARIO: I BUY A HOUSE AND IMMEDIATELY WIN THE LOTTERY PLUS MY BUSINESS SUCCEEDS BEYOND MY WILDEST DREAMS AND THEN MR. RIGHT MOVES IN AND WE HAVE 2.5 BEAUTIFUL CHILDREN AND LIVE HAPPILY EVER AFTER AND LITTLE FAERIES DANCE AROUND AND I'M ELECTED QUEEN OF THE WHOLE UNIVERSE!
WHY ARE YOU DOING THIS?
I LEARNED IT IN BUSINESS SCHOOL!
POPULAR PSYCHOLOGY
PARANOIDS: DO THEY KNOW SOMETHING WE DON'T?

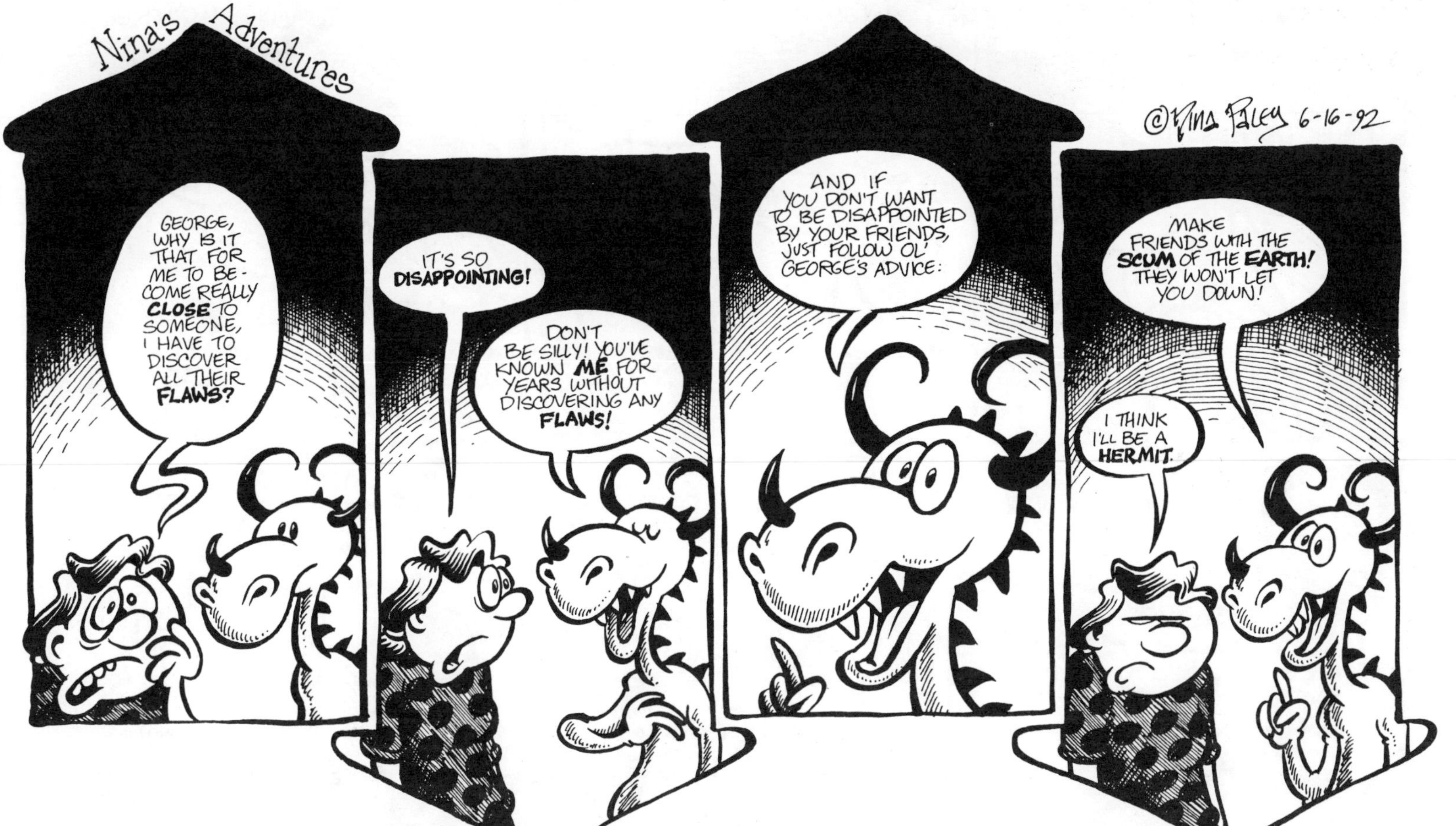

Nina's Adventures
©Nina Paley 6-16-92
GEORGE, WHY IS IT THAT FOR ME TO BECOME REALLY **CLOSE** TO SOMEONE, I HAVE TO DISCOVER ALL THEIR **FLAWS**?
IT'S SO **DISAPPOINTING**!
DON'T BE SILLY! YOU'VE KNOWN **ME** FOR YEARS WITHOUT DISCOVERING ANY **FLAWS**!
AND IF YOU DON'T WANT TO BE DISAPPOINTED BY YOUR FRIENDS, JUST FOLLOW OL' GEORGE'S ADVICE:
MAKE FRIENDS WITH THE **SCUM** OF THE **EARTH**! THEY WON'T LET YOU DOWN!
I THINK I'LL BE A **HERMIT**.

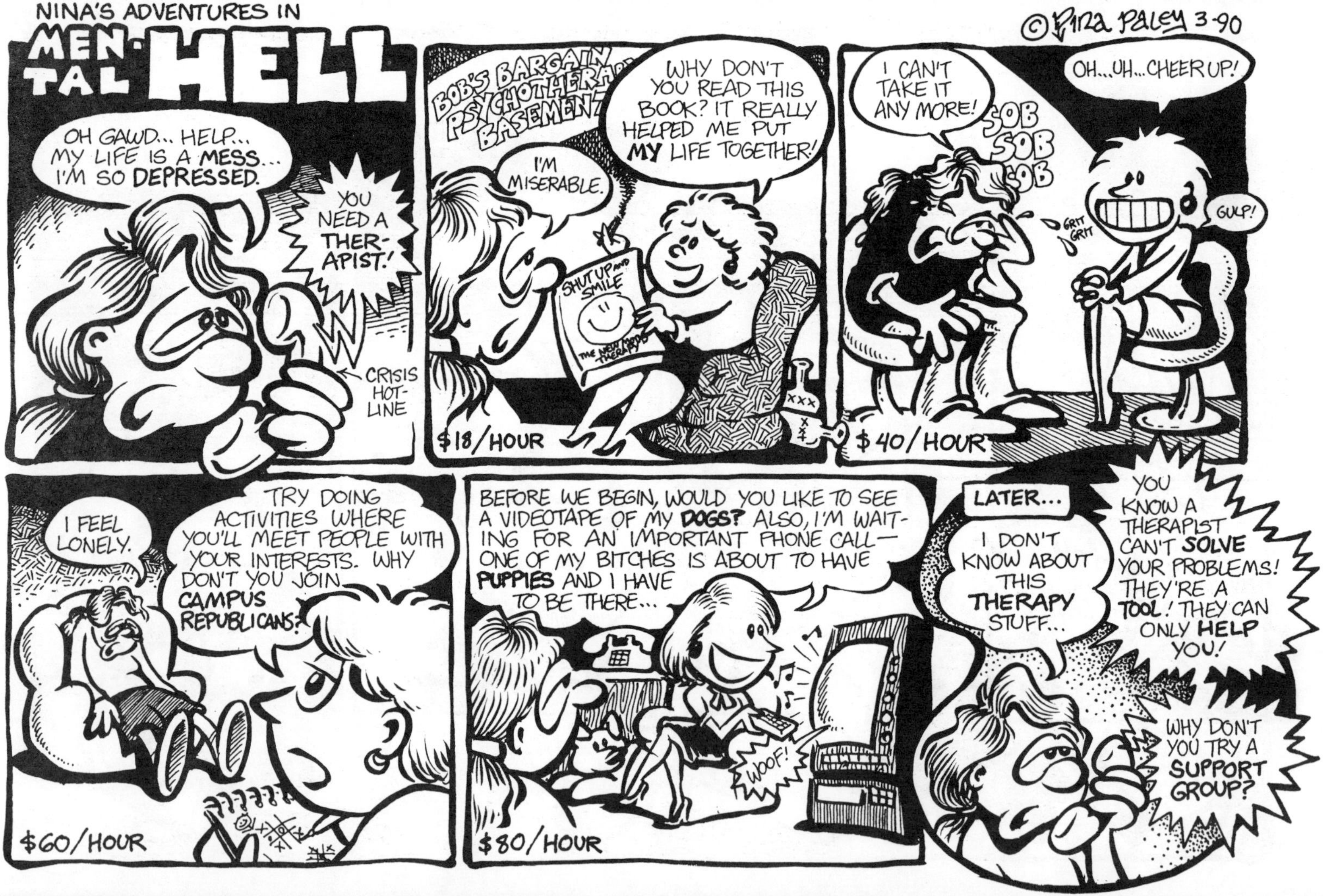
NINA'S ADVENTURES IN
MEN-TAL HELL
© Nina Paley 3-90
OH GAWD... HELP... MY LIFE IS A MESS... I'M SO DEPRESSED.
YOU NEED A THER-APIST!
CRISIS HOT-LINE
BOB'S BARGAIN PSYCHOTHERAPY BASEMENT
I'M MISERABLE.
WHY DON'T YOU READ THIS BOOK? IT REALLY HELPED ME PUT MY LIFE TOGETHER!
SHUT UP AND SMILE
THE NEW MOOD THERAPY
XXX
$18/HOUR
I CAN'T TAKE IT ANY MORE!
SOB SOB SOB
OH... UH... CHEER UP!
GRIT GRIT
GULP!
$40/HOUR
I FEEL LONELY.
TRY DOING ACTIVITIES WHERE YOU'LL MEET PEOPLE WITH YOUR INTERESTS. WHY DON'T YOU JOIN CAMPUS REPUBLICANS?
$60/HOUR
BEFORE WE BEGIN, WOULD YOU LIKE TO SEE A VIDEOTAPE OF MY DOGS? ALSO, I'M WAIT-ING FOR AN IMPORTANT PHONE CALL— ONE OF MY BITCHES IS ABOUT TO HAVE PUPPIES AND I HAVE TO BE THERE...
WOOF!
$80/HOUR
LATER...
I DON'T KNOW ABOUT THIS THERAPY STUFF...
YOU KNOW A THERAPIST CAN'T SOLVE YOUR PROBLEMS! THEY'RE A TOOL! THEY CAN ONLY HELP YOU!
WHY DON'T YOU TRY A SUPPORT GROUP?

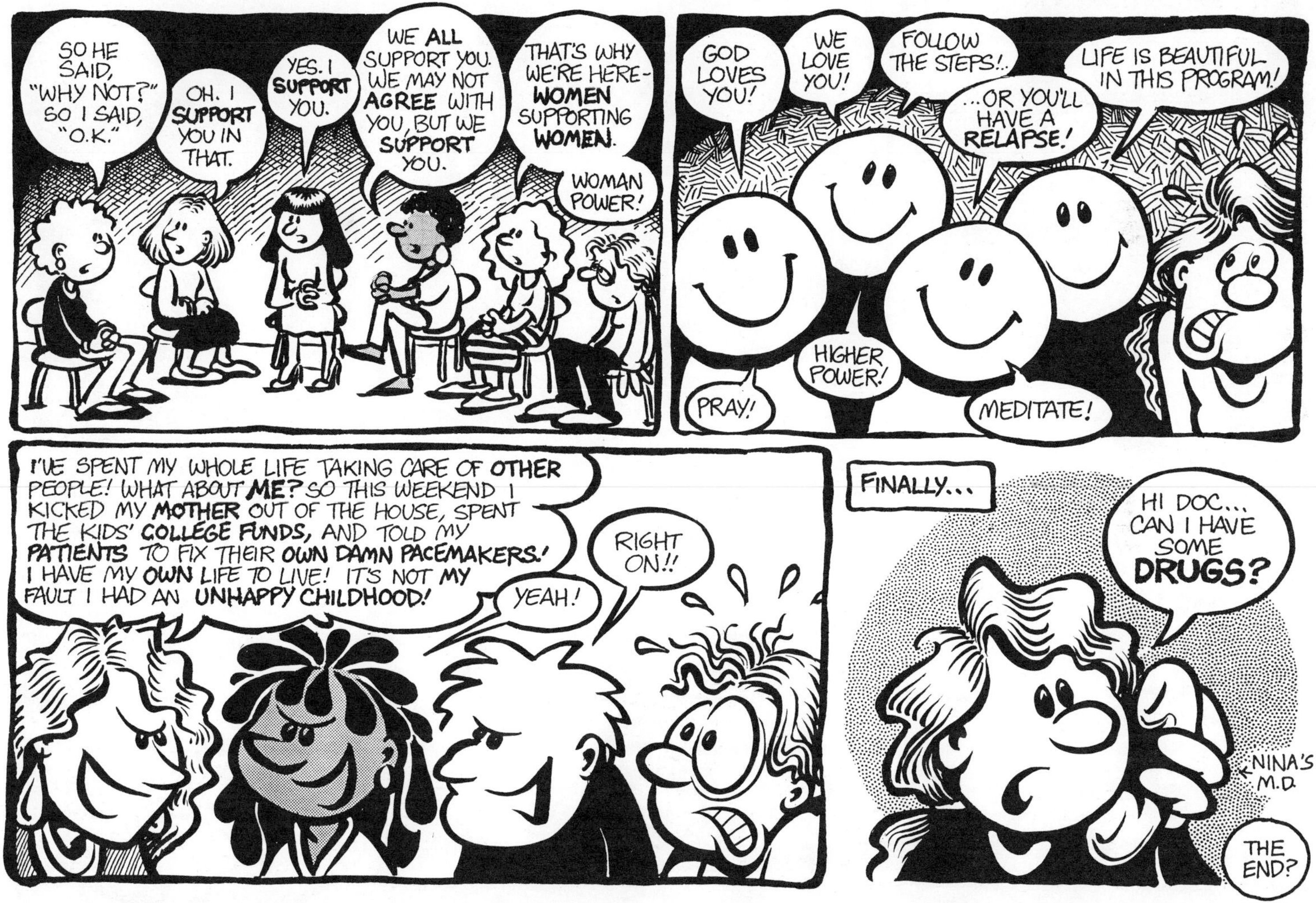
SO HE SAID, "WHY NOT?" SO I SAID, "O.K."
OH. I SUPPORT YOU IN THAT.
YES. I SUPPORT YOU.
WE ALL SUPPORT YOU. WE MAY NOT AGREE WITH YOU, BUT WE SUPPORT YOU.
THAT'S WHY WE'RE HERE- WOMEN SUPPORTING WOMEN.
WOMAN POWER!
GOD LOVES YOU!
WE LOVE YOU!
FOLLOW THE STEPS!..
...OR YOU'LL HAVE A RELAPSE!
LIFE IS BEAUTIFUL IN THIS PROGRAM!
HIGHER POWER!
PRAY!
MEDITATE!
I'VE SPENT MY WHOLE LIFE TAKING CARE OF OTHER PEOPLE! WHAT ABOUT ME? SO THIS WEEKEND I KICKED MY MOTHER OUT OF THE HOUSE, SPENT THE KIDS' COLLEGE FUNDS, AND TOLD MY PATIENTS TO FIX THEIR OWN DAMN PACEMAKERS! I HAVE MY OWN LIFE TO LIVE! IT'S NOT MY FAULT I HAD AN UNHAPPY CHILDHOOD!
YEAH!
RIGHT ON!!
FINALLY...
HI DOC... CAN I HAVE SOME DRUGS?
NINA'S M.D.
THE END?

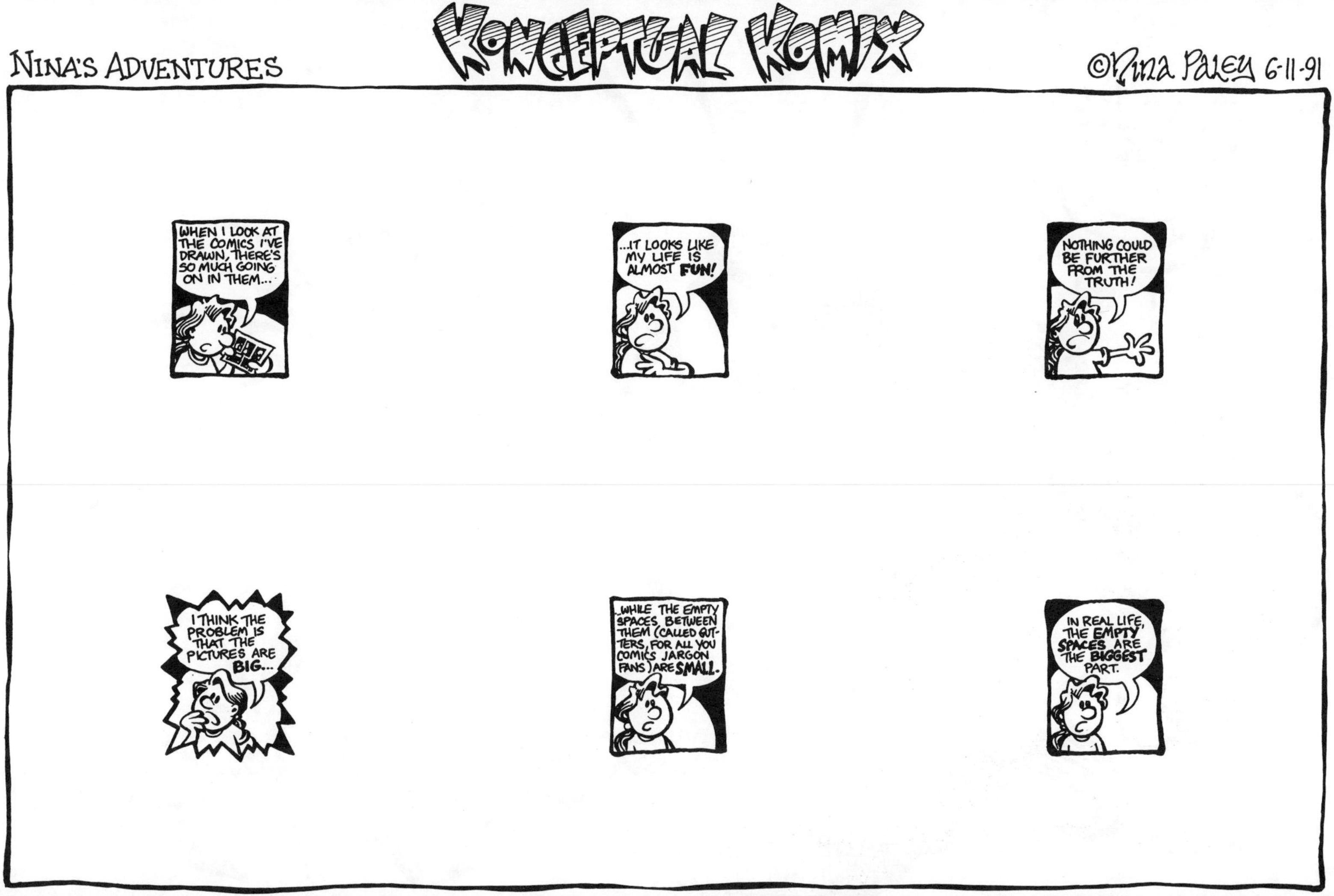
NINA'S ADVENTURES
KONCEPTUAL KOMIX
©Nina Paley 6-11-91
WHEN I LOOK AT THE COMICS I'VE DRAWN, THERE'S SO MUCH GOING ON IN THEM...
...IT LOOKS LIKE MY LIFE IS ALMOST FUN!
NOTHING COULD BE FURTHER FROM THE TRUTH!
I THINK THE PROBLEM IS THAT THE PICTURES ARE BIG...
...WHILE THE EMPTY SPACES BETWEEN THEM (CALLED GUTTERS, FOR ALL YOU COMICS JARGON FANS) ARE SMALL.
IN REAL LIFE, THE EMPTY SPACES ARE THE BIGGEST PART.

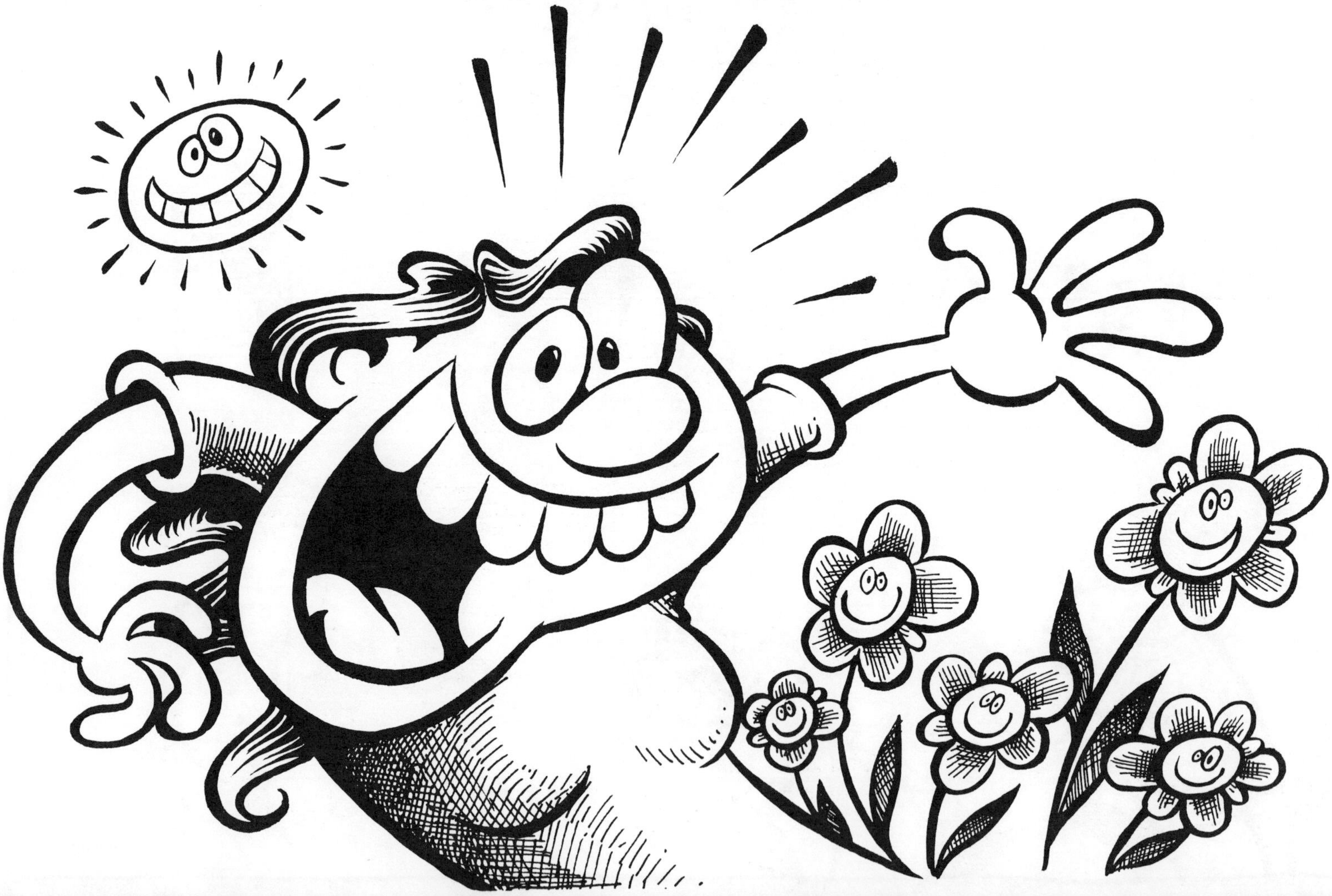

CHAPTER TWO: FUN

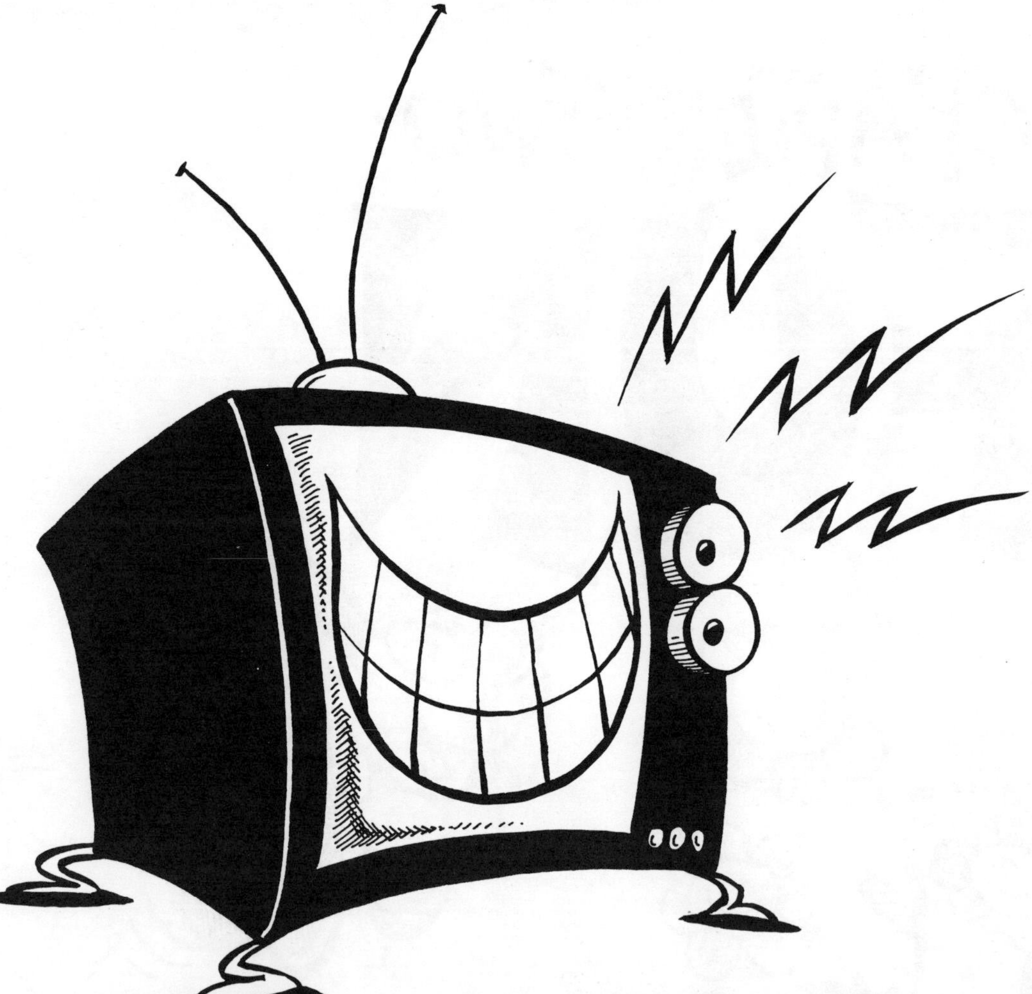

and now for an **anti-drug message** from NINA™:

© Nina Paley 8-23-91

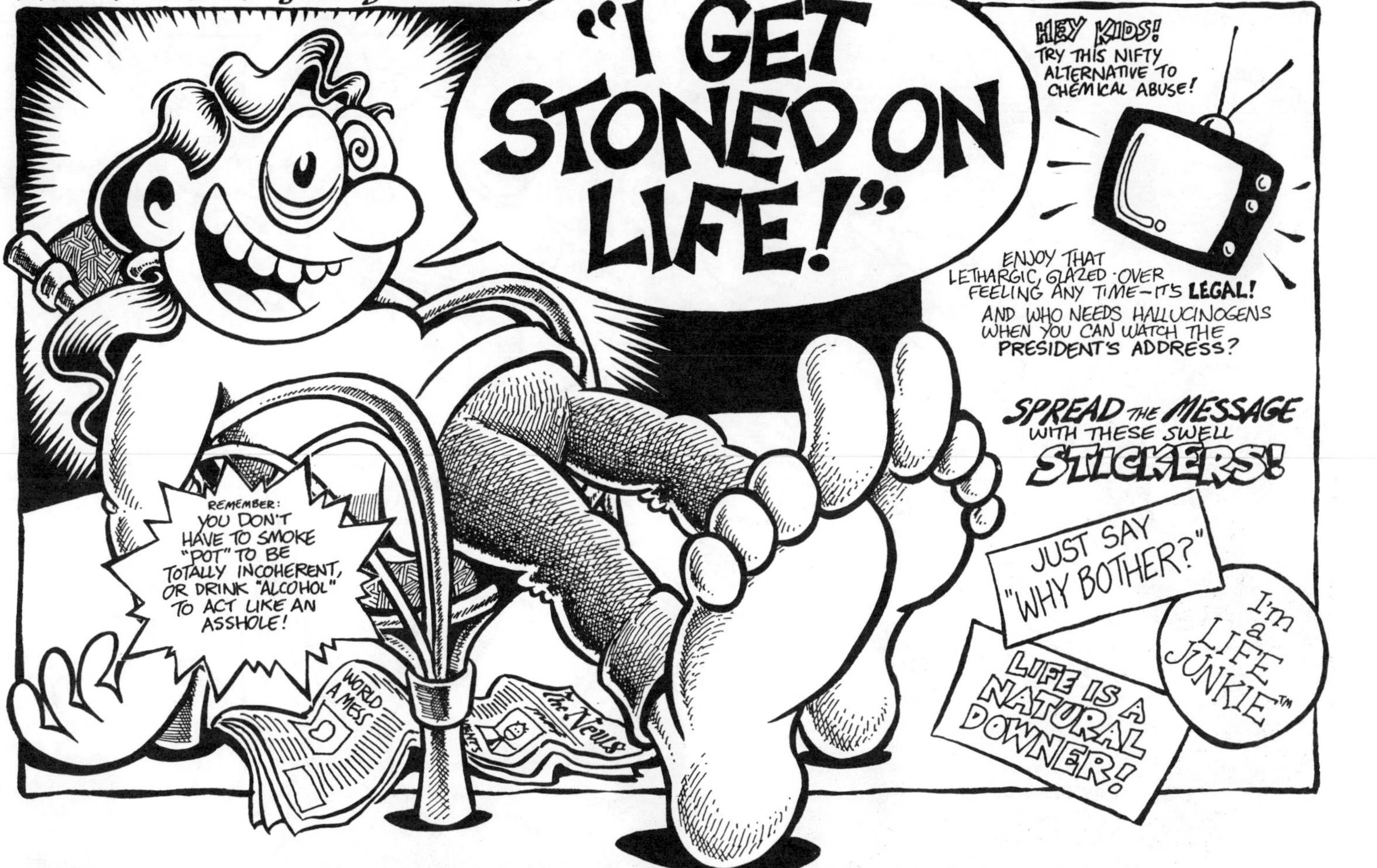
"I GET STONED ON LIFE!"
HEY KIDS! TRY THIS NIFTY ALTERNATIVE TO CHEMICAL ABUSE!
ENJOY THAT LETHARGIC, GLAZED-OVER FEELING ANY TIME—IT'S LEGAL!
AND WHO NEEDS HALLUCINOGENS WHEN YOU CAN WATCH THE PRESIDENT'S ADDRESS?
SPREAD THE MESSAGE WITH THESE SWELL STICKERS!
JUST SAY "WHY BOTHER?"
I'm a LIFE JUNKIE™
LIFE IS A NATURAL DOWNER!
REMEMBER: YOU DON'T HAVE TO SMOKE "POT" TO BE TOTALLY INCOHERENT, OR DRINK "ALCOHOL" TO ACT LIKE AN ASSHOLE!
WORLD A MESS
The News

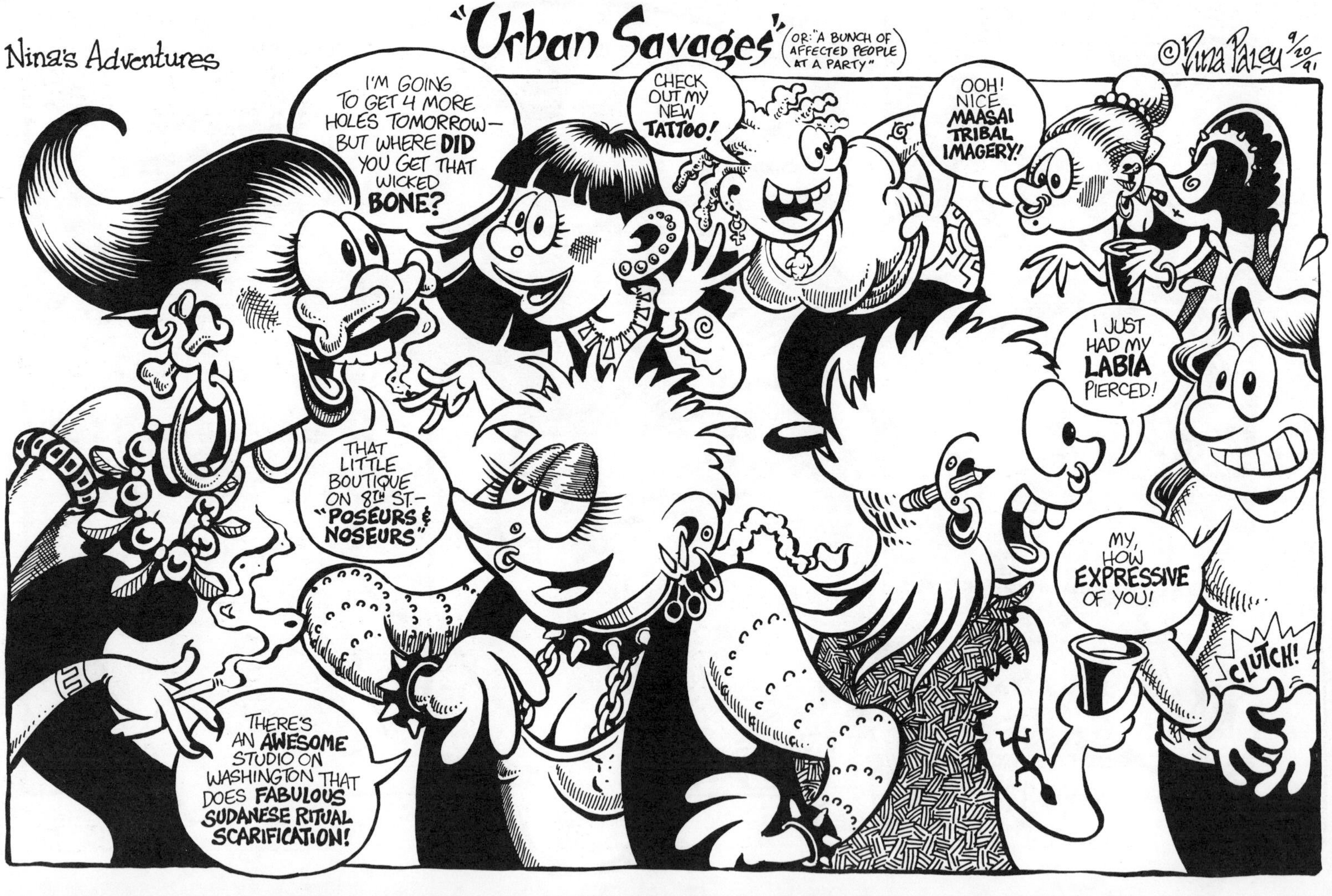
Nina's Adventures
"Urban Savages" (OR: "A BUNCH OF AFFECTED PEOPLE AT A PARTY")
©Nina Paley 9/20/91
I'M GOING TO GET 4 MORE HOLES TOMORROW— BUT WHERE DID YOU GET THAT WICKED BONE?
THAT LITTLE BOUTIQUE ON 8TH ST.— "POSEURS & NOSEURS"
CHECK OUT MY NEW TATTOO!
OOH! NICE MAASAI TRIBAL IMAGERY!
I JUST HAD MY LABIA PIERCED!
MY, HOW EXPRESSIVE OF YOU!
THERE'S AN AWESOME STUDIO ON WASHINGTON THAT DOES FABULOUS SUDANESE RITUAL SCARIFICATION!
CLUTCH!

Nina's Adventures

"CHEMISTRY"

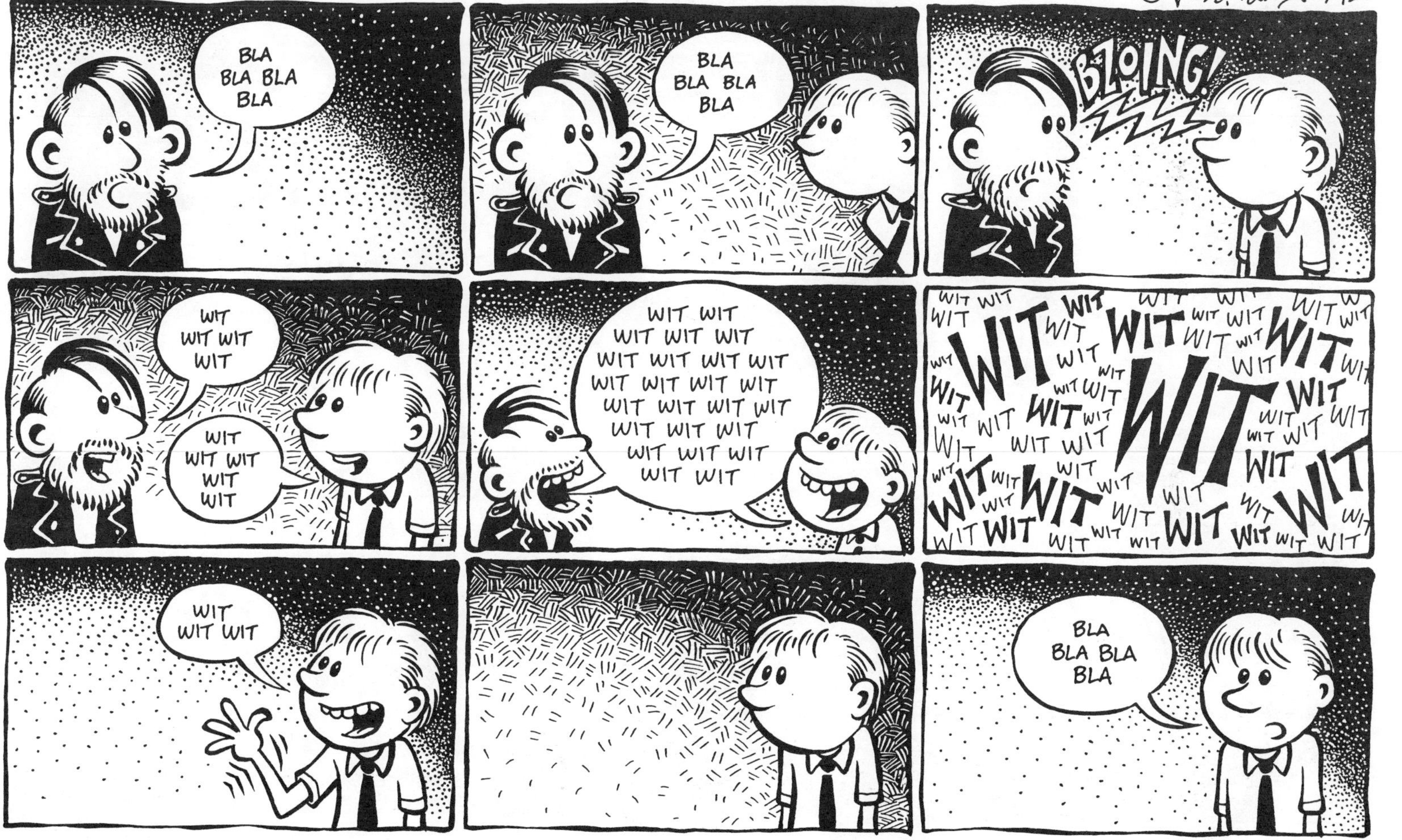
BLA BLA BLA BLA
BLA BLA BLA BLA
BZOING!
WIT WIT WIT WIT
WIT WIT WIT WIT WIT
WIT WIT WIT WIT WIT WIT WIT WIT WIT WIT WIT WIT WIT WIT WIT WIT WIT WIT WIT WIT WIT WIT WIT
WIT WIT WIT
BLA BLA BLA BLA

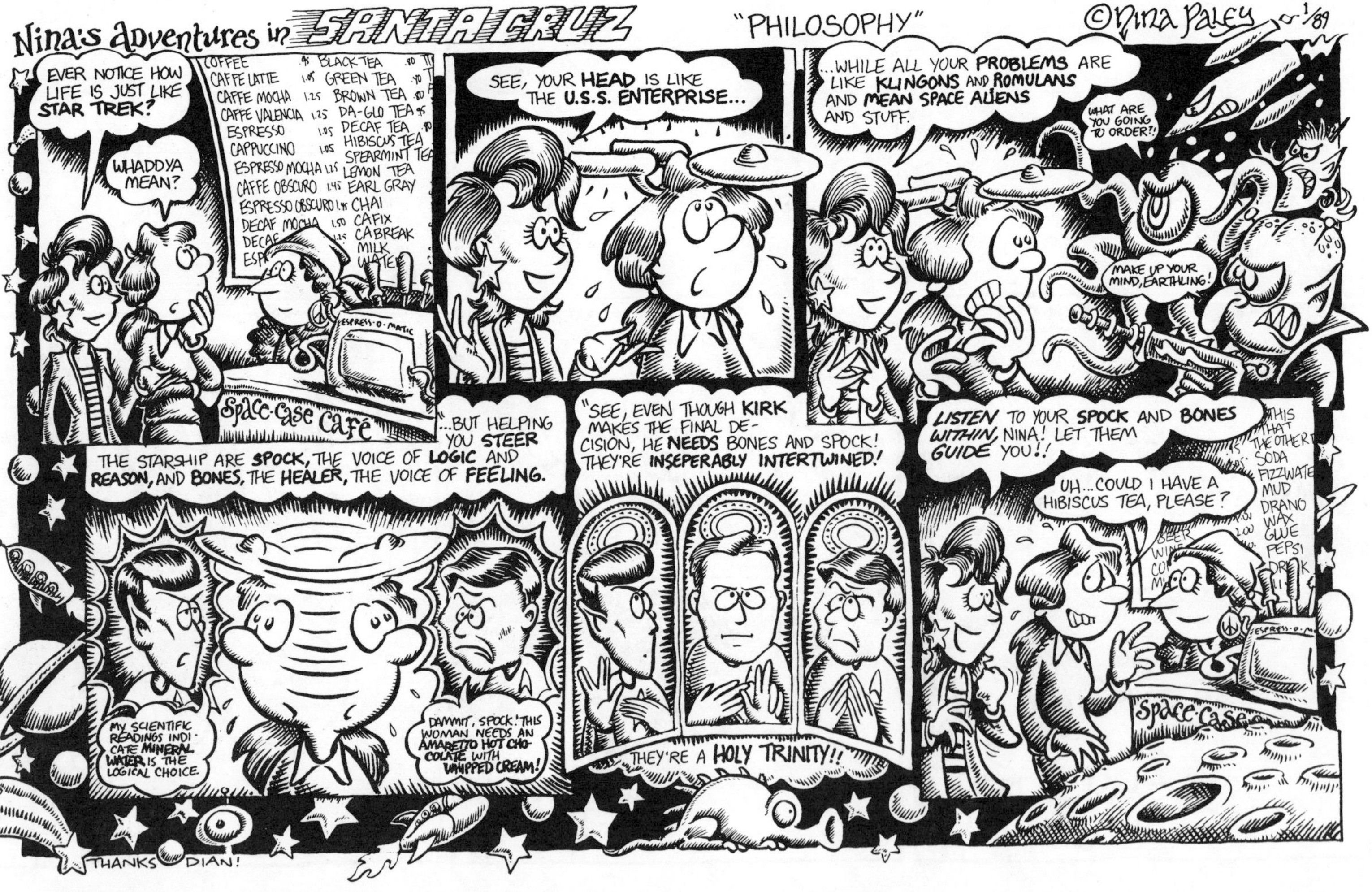
Nina's Adventures in SANTA CRUZ
"PHILOSOPHY"
©Nina Paley 1/89
EVER NOTICE HOW LIFE IS JUST LIKE STAR TREK?
WHADDYA MEAN?
COFFEE .95 BLACK TEA .80
CAFFE LATTE 1.05 GREEN TEA .90
CAFFE MOCHA 1.25 BROWN TEA .80
CAFFE VALENCIA 1.25 DA-GLO TEA .95
ESPRESSO 1.05 DECAF TEA .80
CAPPUCCINO 1.05 HIBISCUS TEA
ESPRESSO MOCHA 1.25 SPEARMINT TEA
CAFFE OBSCURO 1.45 LEMON TEA
ESPRESSO OBSCURO 1.95 EARL GRAY
DECAF MOCHA 1.50 CHAI
CAFIX
CABREAK
MILK
ESPRESS-O-MATIC
Space-Case Café
SEE, YOUR HEAD IS LIKE THE U.S.S. ENTERPRISE...
...WHILE ALL YOUR PROBLEMS ARE LIKE KLINGONS AND ROMULANS AND MEAN SPACE ALIENS AND STUFF.
WHAT ARE YOU GOING TO ORDER?!
MAKE UP YOUR MIND, EARTHLING!
...BUT HELPING YOU STEER THE STARSHIP ARE SPOCK, THE VOICE OF LOGIC AND REASON, AND BONES, THE HEALER, THE VOICE OF FEELING.
MY SCIENTIFIC READINGS INDICATE MINERAL WATER IS THE LOGICAL CHOICE.
DAMMIT, SPOCK! THIS WOMAN NEEDS AN AMARETTO HOT CHOCOLATE WITH WHIPPED CREAM!
"SEE, EVEN THOUGH KIRK MAKES THE FINAL DECISION, HE NEEDS BONES AND SPOCK! THEY'RE INSEPERABLY INTERTWINED!
THEY'RE A HOLY TRINITY!!
LISTEN TO YOUR SPOCK AND BONES WITHIN, NINA! LET THEM GUIDE YOU!!
THIS
THAT
THE OTHER
SODA
FIZZWATE
MUD
DRANO
WAX
GLUE
PEPSI
UH...COULD I HAVE A HIBISCUS TEA, PLEASE?
SPACE-CASE
THANKS DIAN!

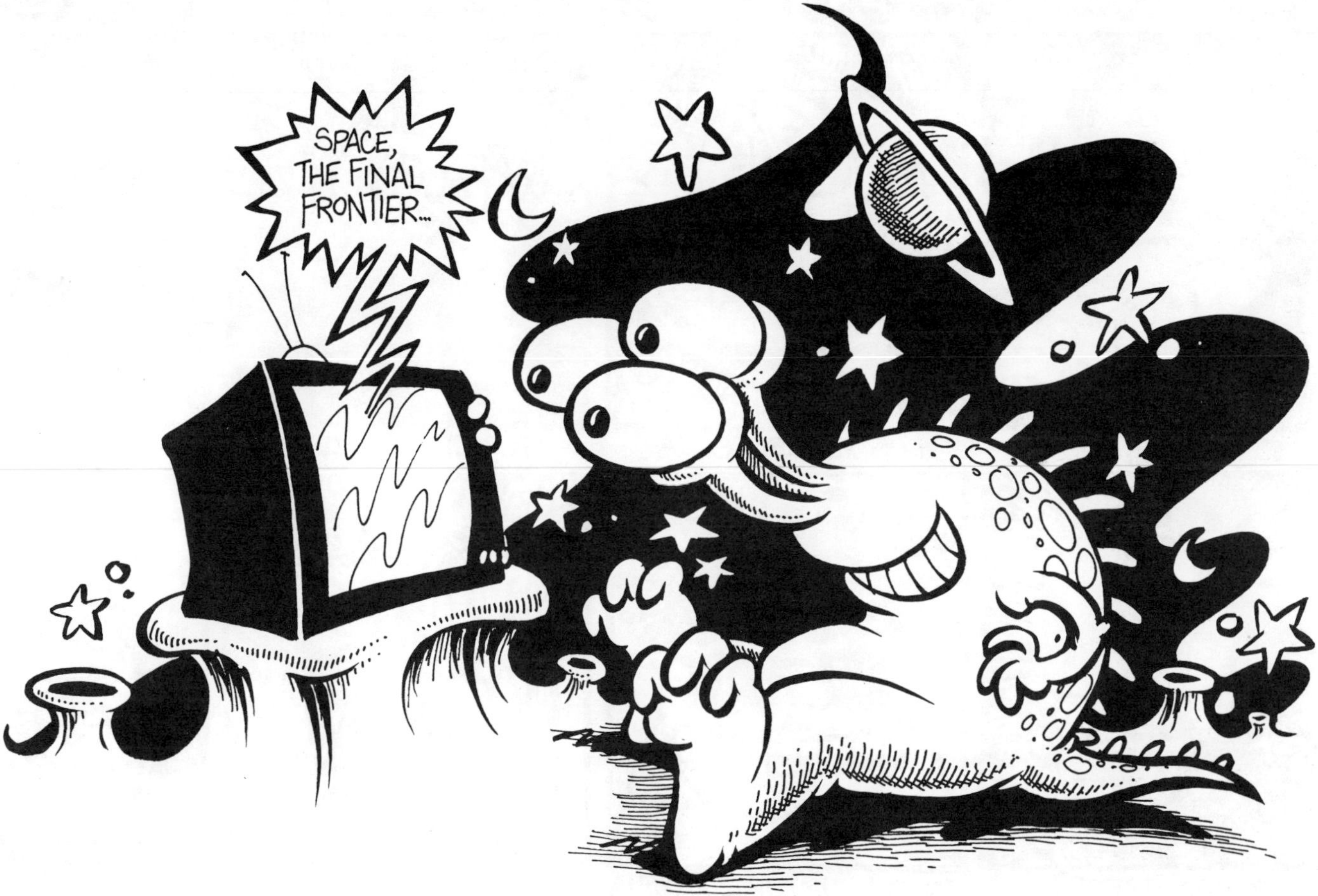
SPACE,
THE FINAL
FRONTIER...

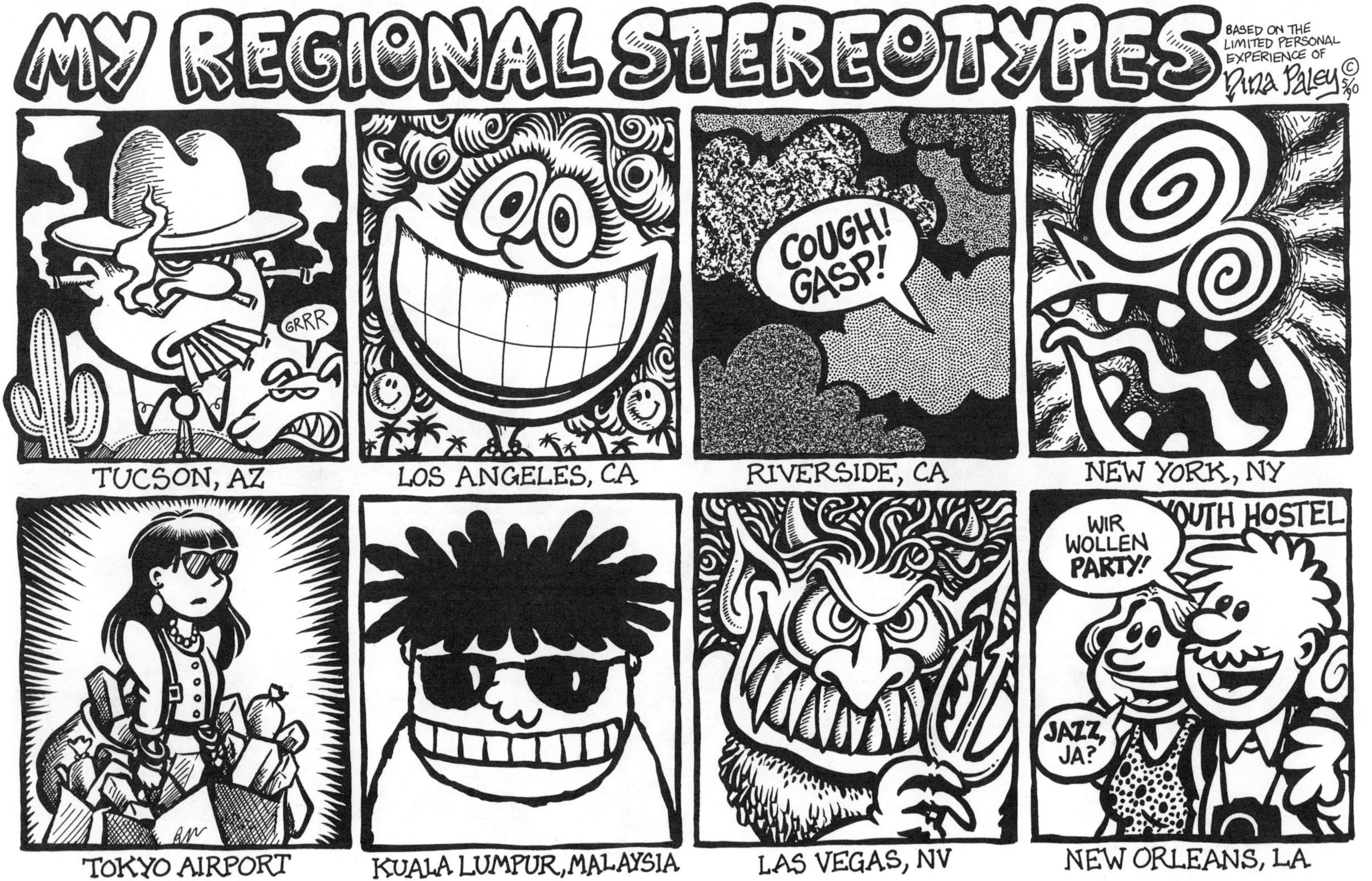
MY REGIONAL STEREOTYPES
BASED ON THE LIMITED PERSONAL EXPERIENCE OF
Nina Paley © 5/90
GRRR
TUCSON, AZ
LOS ANGELES, CA
COUGH! GASP!
RIVERSIDE, CA
NEW YORK, NY
TOKYO AIRPORT
KUALA LUMPUR, MALAYSIA
LAS VEGAS, NV
YOUTH HOSTEL
WIR WOLLEN PARTY!
JAZZ, JA?
NEW ORLEANS, LA

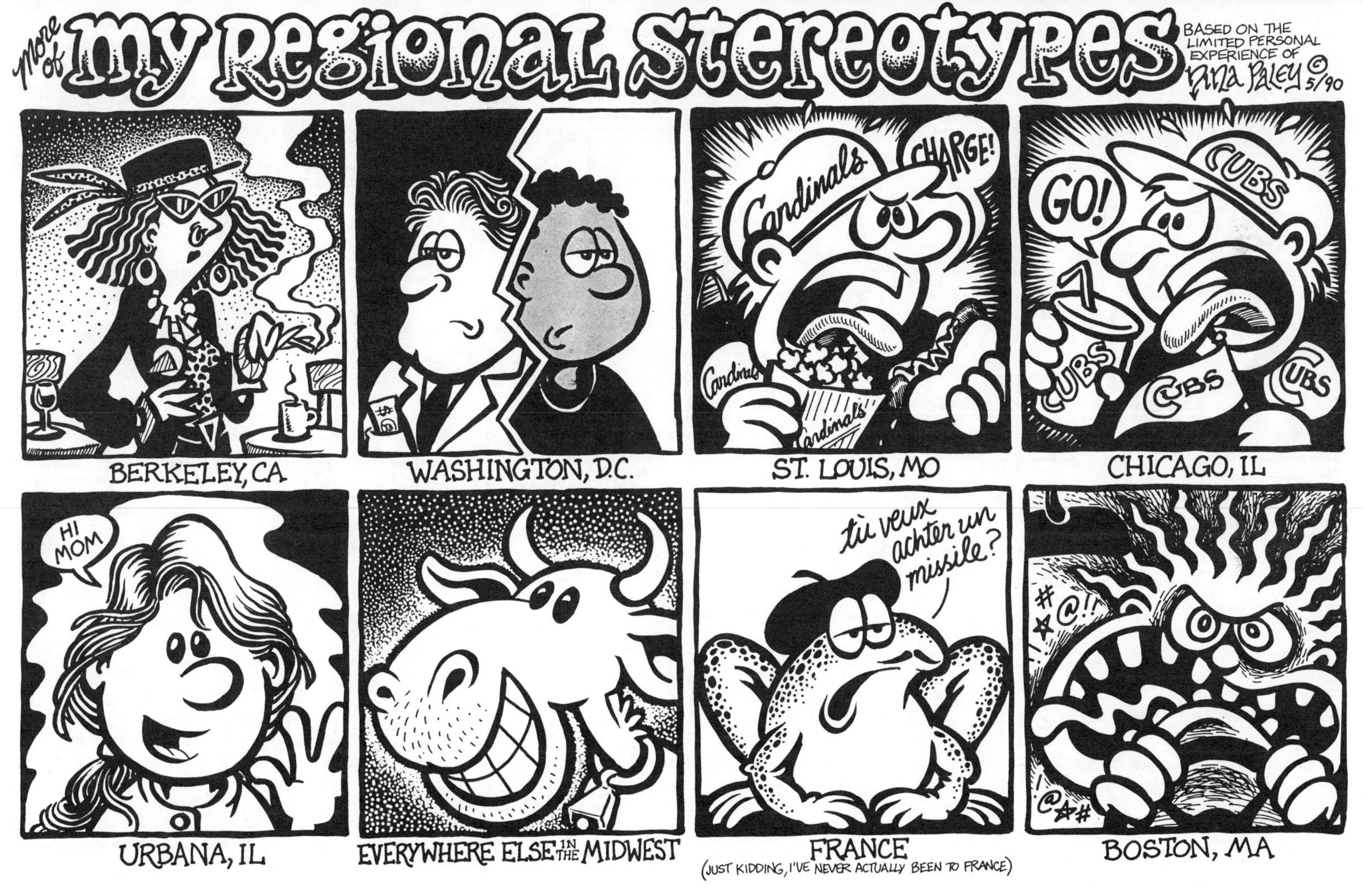
more of My Regional Stereotypes
BASED ON THE LIMITED PERSONAL EXPERIENCE OF
Nina Paley © 5/90
BERKELEY, CA
WASHINGTON, D.C.
Cardinals
CHARGE!
Cardinals
Cardinals
ST. LOUIS, MO
GO!
CUBS
CUBS
CUBS
CUBS
CHICAGO, IL
HI MOM
URBANA, IL
EVERYWHERE ELSE IN THE MIDWEST
tu veux achter un missile?
FRANCE
(JUST KIDDING, I'VE NEVER ACTUALLY BEEN TO FRANCE)
#@!!
@☆#
BOSTON, MA

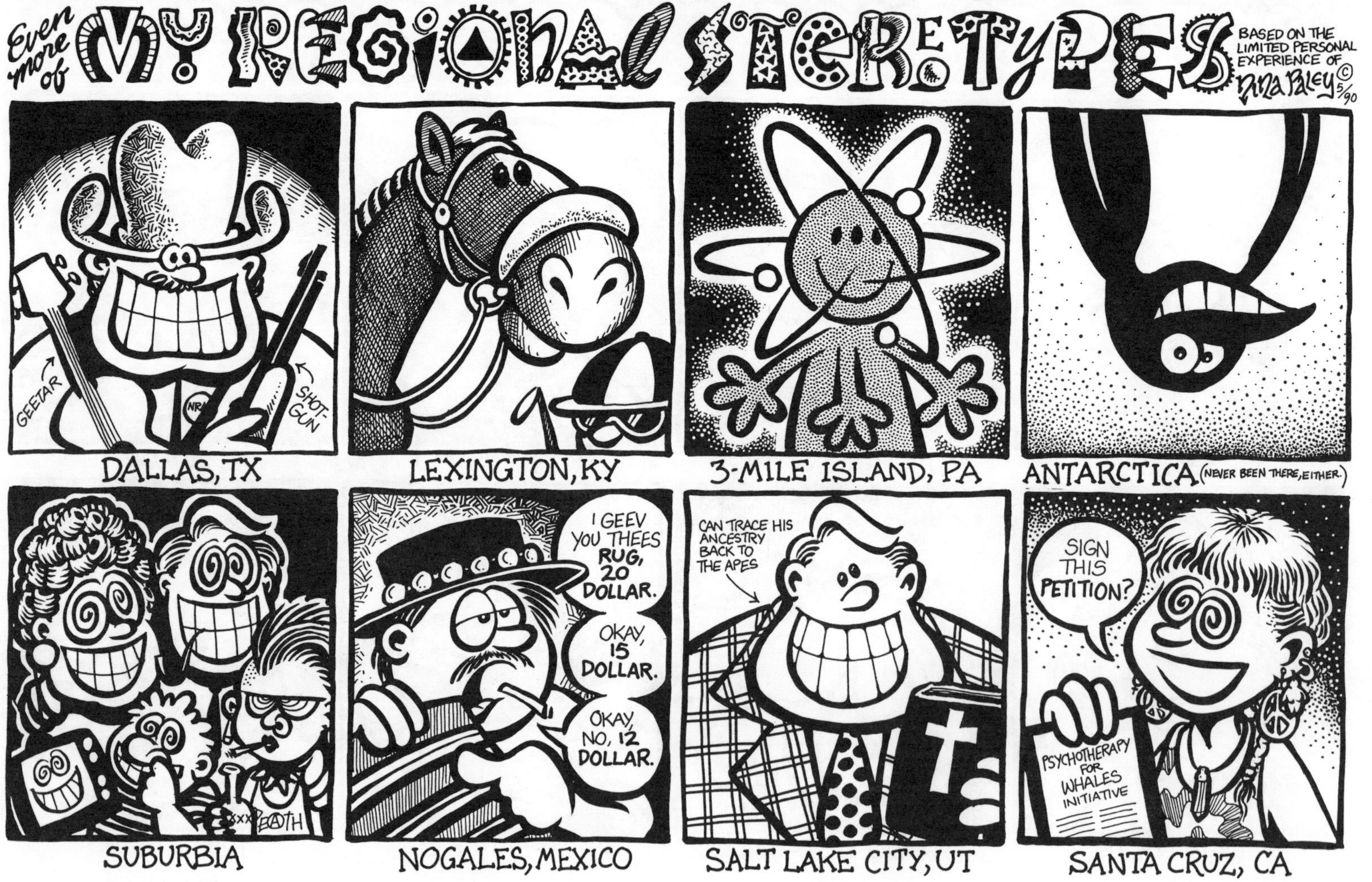
Even more of MY REGIONAL STEREOTYPES
BASED ON THE LIMITED PERSONAL EXPERIENCE OF Nina Paley © 5/90
GEETAR
NRA
SHOT-GUN
DALLAS, TX
LEXINGTON, KY
3-MILE ISLAND, PA
ANTARCTICA (NEVER BEEN THERE, EITHER.)
XXX DEATH
SUBURBIA
I GEEV YOU THEES RUG, 20 DOLLAR.
OKAY, 15 DOLLAR.
OKAY, NO, 12 DOLLAR.
NOGALES, MEXICO
CAN TRACE HIS ANCESTRY BACK TO THE APES
SALT LAKE CITY, UT
SIGN THIS PETITION?
PSYCHOTHERAPY FOR WHALES INITIATIVE
SANTA CRUZ, CA

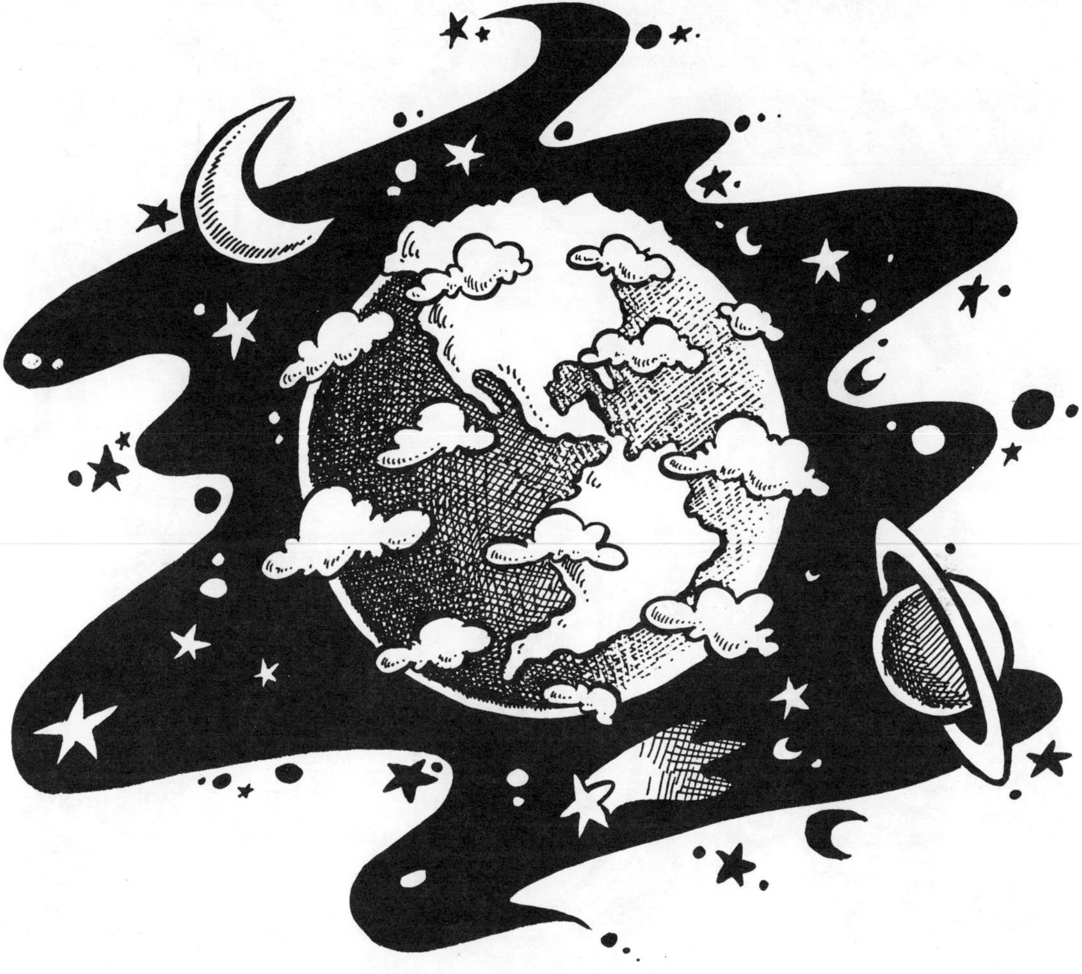

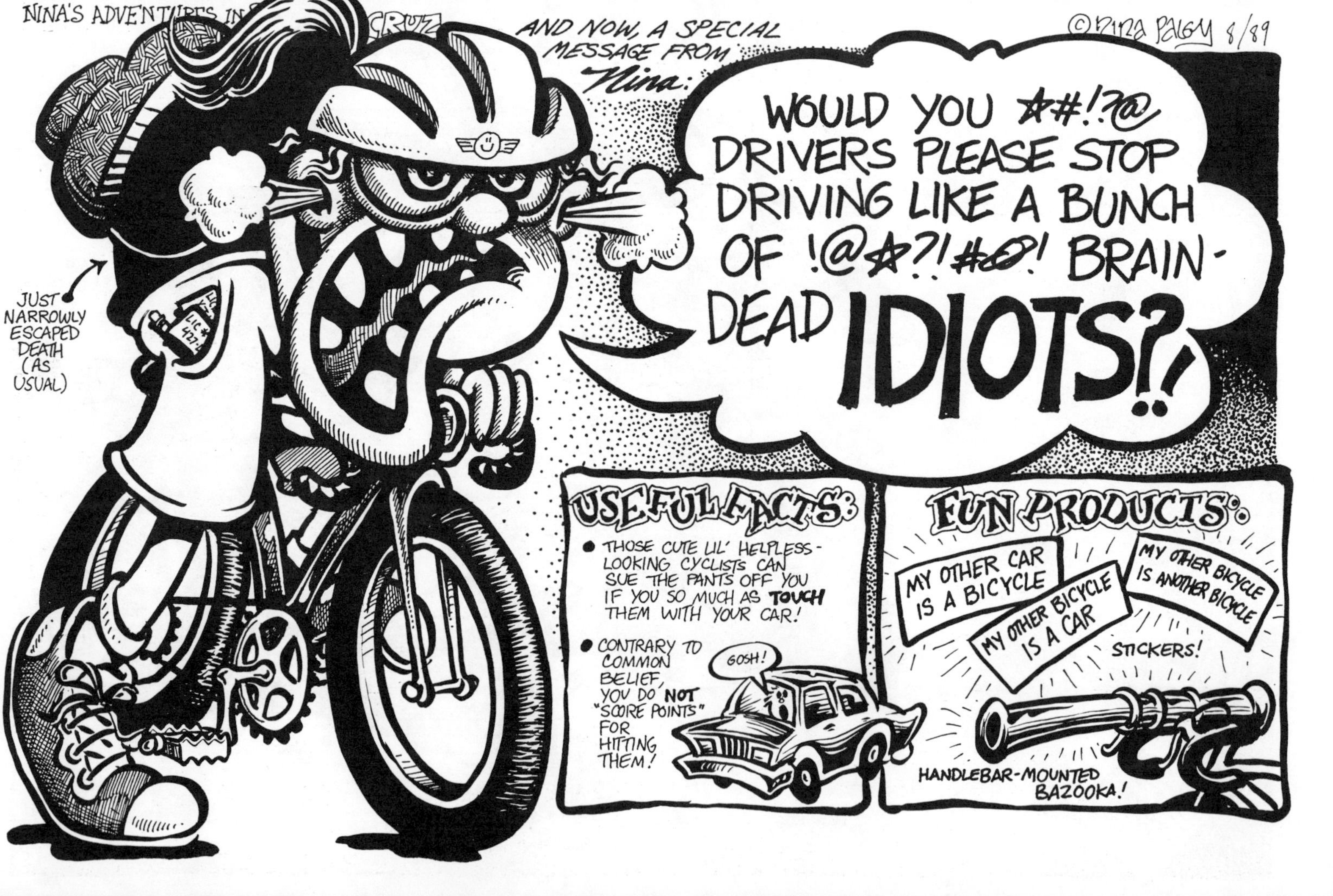

NINA'S ADVENTURES IN S... CRUZ
© Nina Paley 8/89
AND NOW, A SPECIAL MESSAGE FROM Nina:
WOULD YOU ☆#!?@ DRIVERS PLEASE STOP DRIVING LIKE A BUNCH OF !@☆?!#&! BRAIN-DEAD IDIOTS?!!
JUST NARROWLY ESCAPED DEATH (AS USUAL)
LIC 427
USEFUL FACTS:
• THOSE CUTE LIL' HELPLESS-LOOKING CYCLISTS CAN SUE THE PANTS OFF YOU IF YOU SO MUCH AS TOUCH THEM WITH YOUR CAR!
• CONTRARY TO COMMON BELIEF, YOU DO NOT "SCORE POINTS" FOR HITTING THEM!
GOSH!
FUN PRODUCTS:
MY OTHER CAR IS A BICYCLE
MY OTHER BICYCLE IS A CAR
MY OTHER BICYCLE IS ANOTHER BICYCLE
STICKERS!
HANDLEBAR-MOUNTED BAZOOKA!

Nina's Adventures in SANTA CRUZ

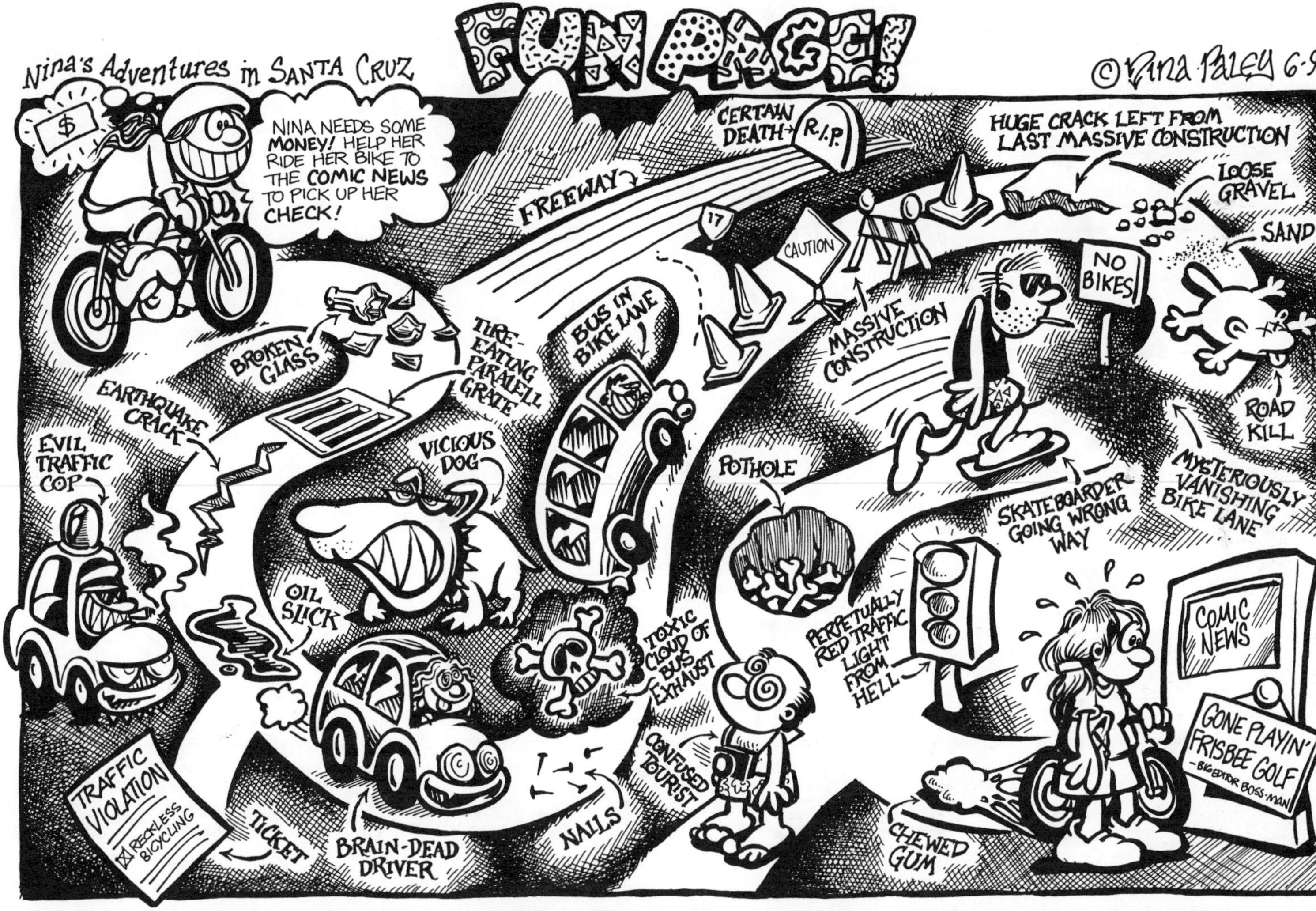

© Nina Paley 6-90

cats i have known

Nina's Adventures in Santa Cruz

©Nina Paley 7-90

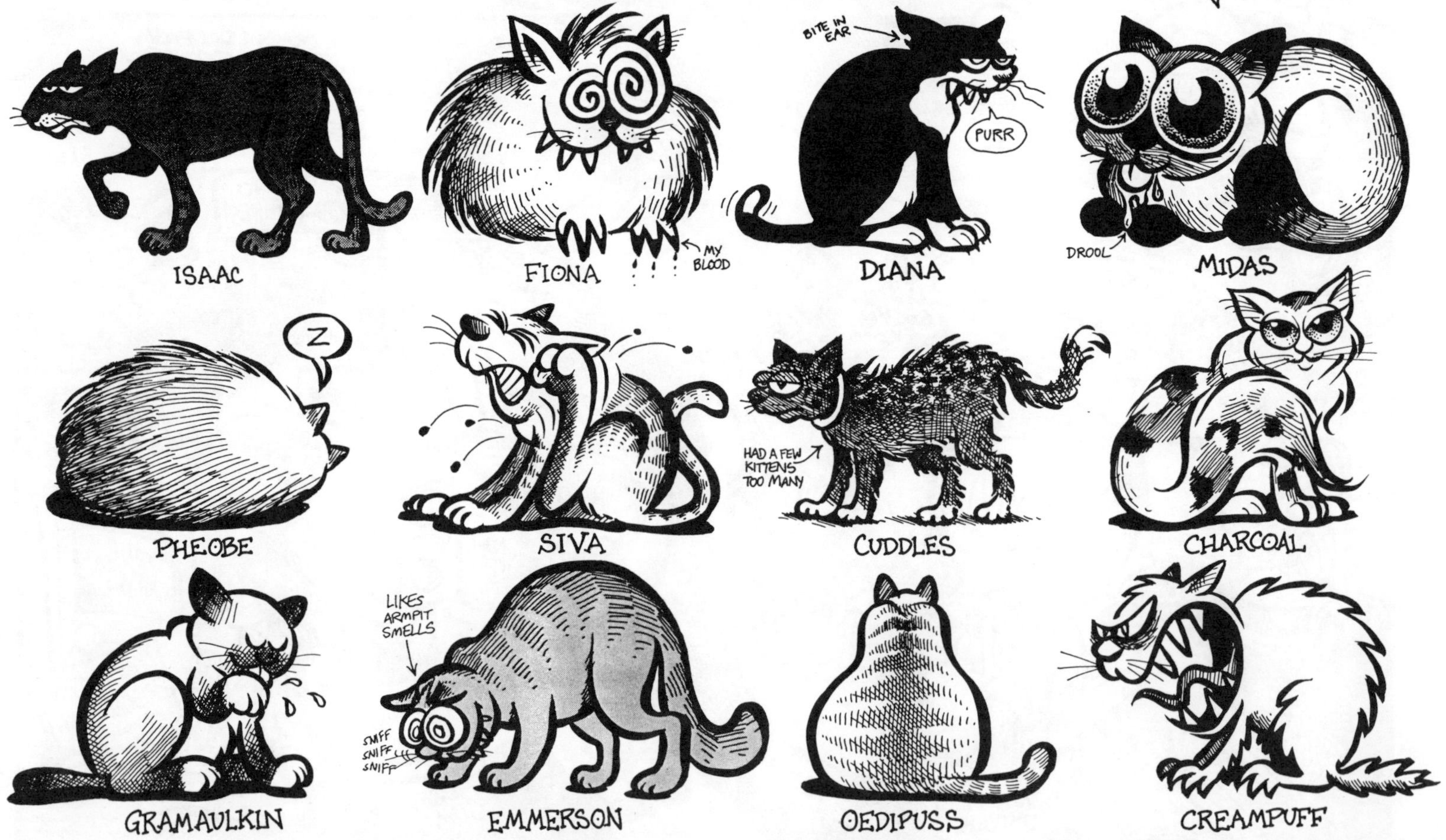

ISAAC
MY BLOOD
FIONA
BITE IN EAR
PURR
DIANA
DROOL
MIDAS
Z
PHEOBE
SIVA
HAD A FEW KITTENS TOO MANY
CUDDLES
CHARCOAL
GRAMAULKIN
LIKES ARMPIT SMELLS
SNIFF
SNIFF
SNIFF
EMMERSON
OEDIPUSS
CREAMPUFF

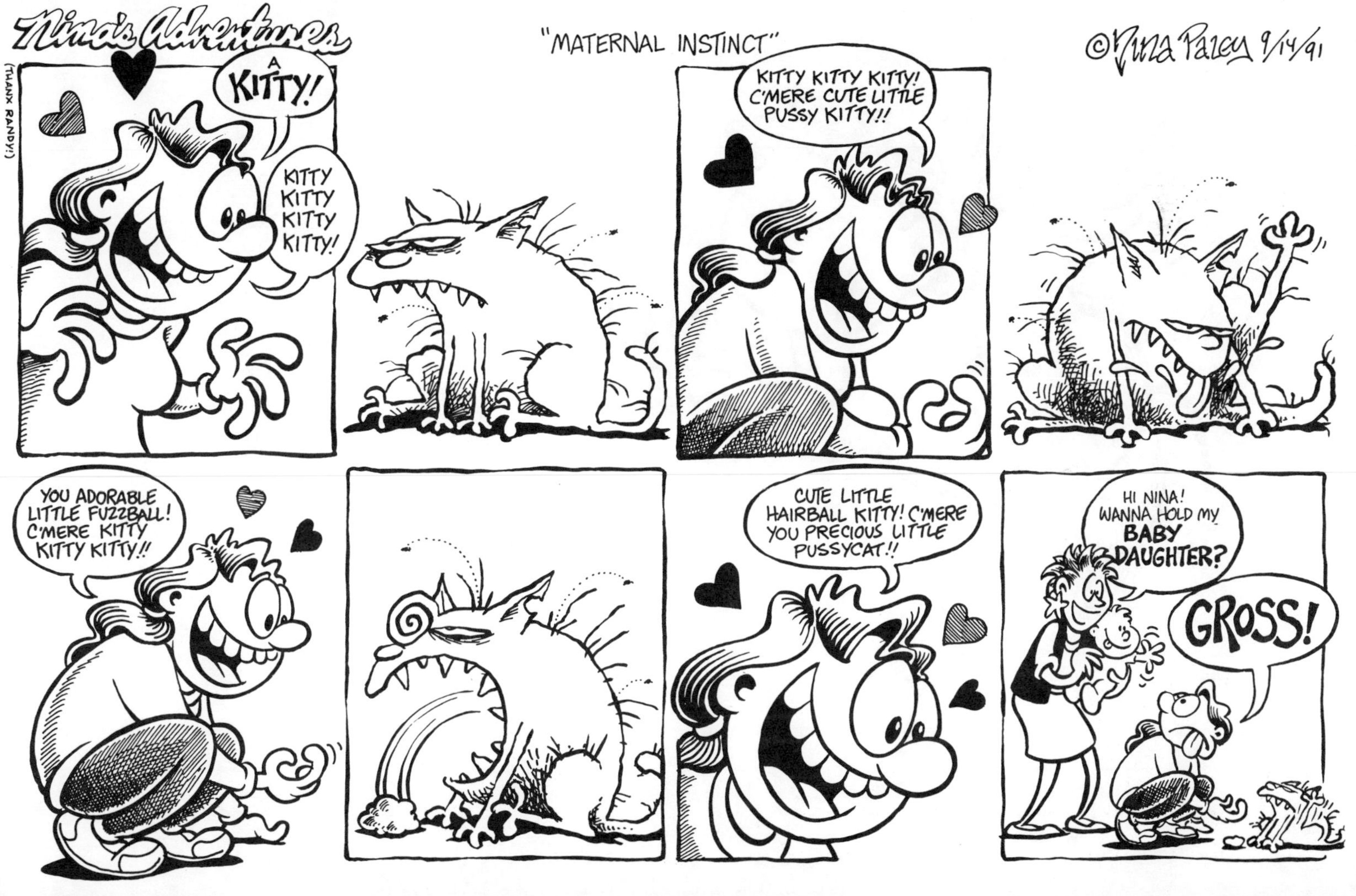

Nina's Adventures
"MATERNAL INSTINCT"
©Nina Paley 9/14/91
(THANX RANDY!)
A KITTY!
KITTY KITTY KITTY KITTY!
KITTY KITTY KITTY! C'MERE CUTE LITTLE PUSSY KITTY!!
YOU ADORABLE LITTLE FUZZBALL! C'MERE KITTY KITTY KITTY!!
CUTE LITTLE HAIRBALL KITTY! C'MERE YOU PRECIOUS LITTLE PUSSYCAT!!
HI NINA! WANNA HOLD MY BABY DAUGHTER?
GROSS!

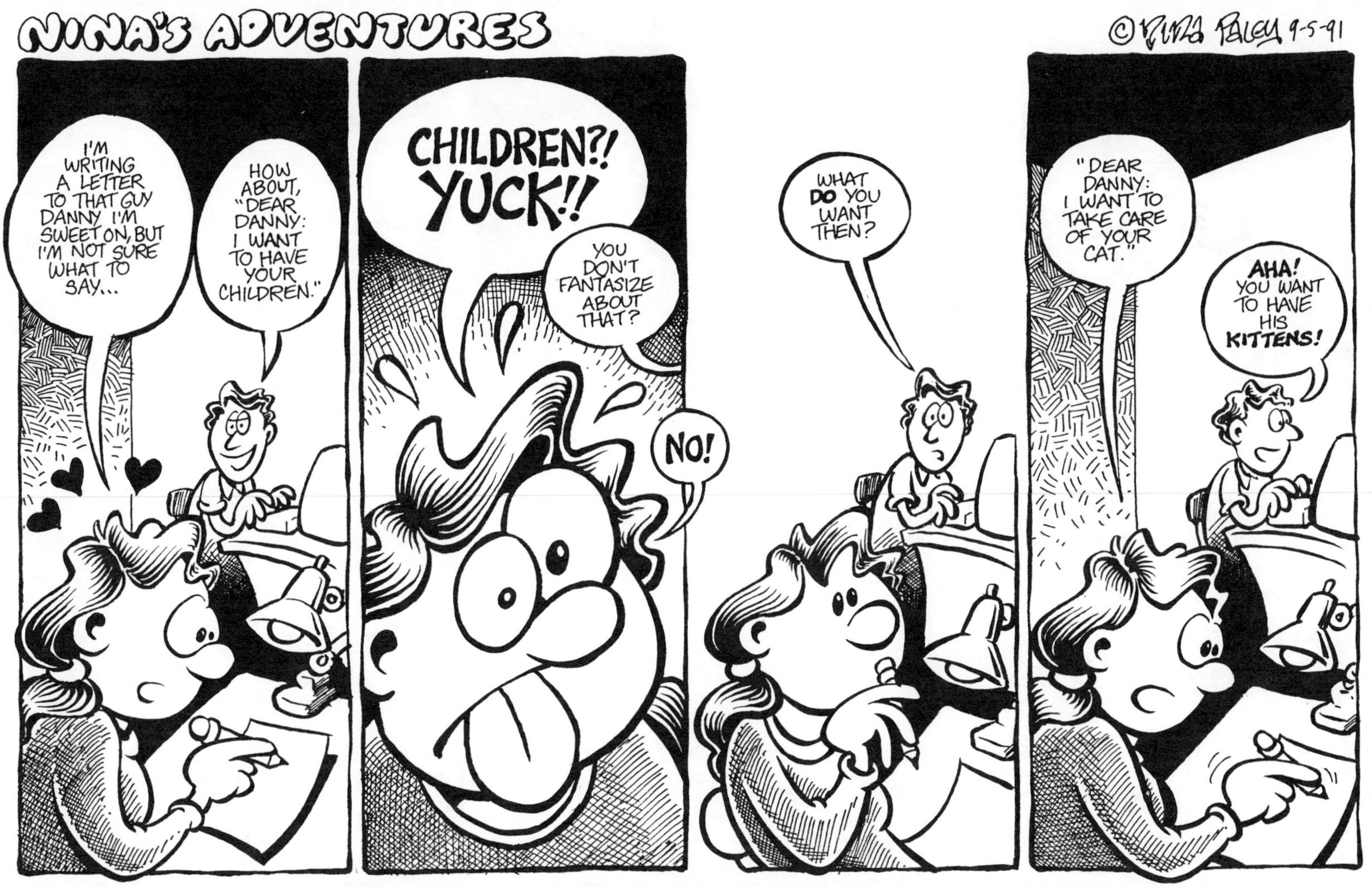
NINA'S ADVENTURES
© Nina Paley 9-5-91
I'M WRITING A LETTER TO THAT GUY DANNY I'M SWEET ON, BUT I'M NOT SURE WHAT TO SAY...
HOW ABOUT, "DEAR DANNY: I WANT TO HAVE YOUR CHILDREN."
CHILDREN?! YUCK!!
YOU DON'T FANTASIZE ABOUT THAT?
NO!
WHAT DO YOU WANT THEN?
"DEAR DANNY: I WANT TO TAKE CARE OF YOUR CAT."
AHA! YOU WANT TO HAVE HIS KITTENS!

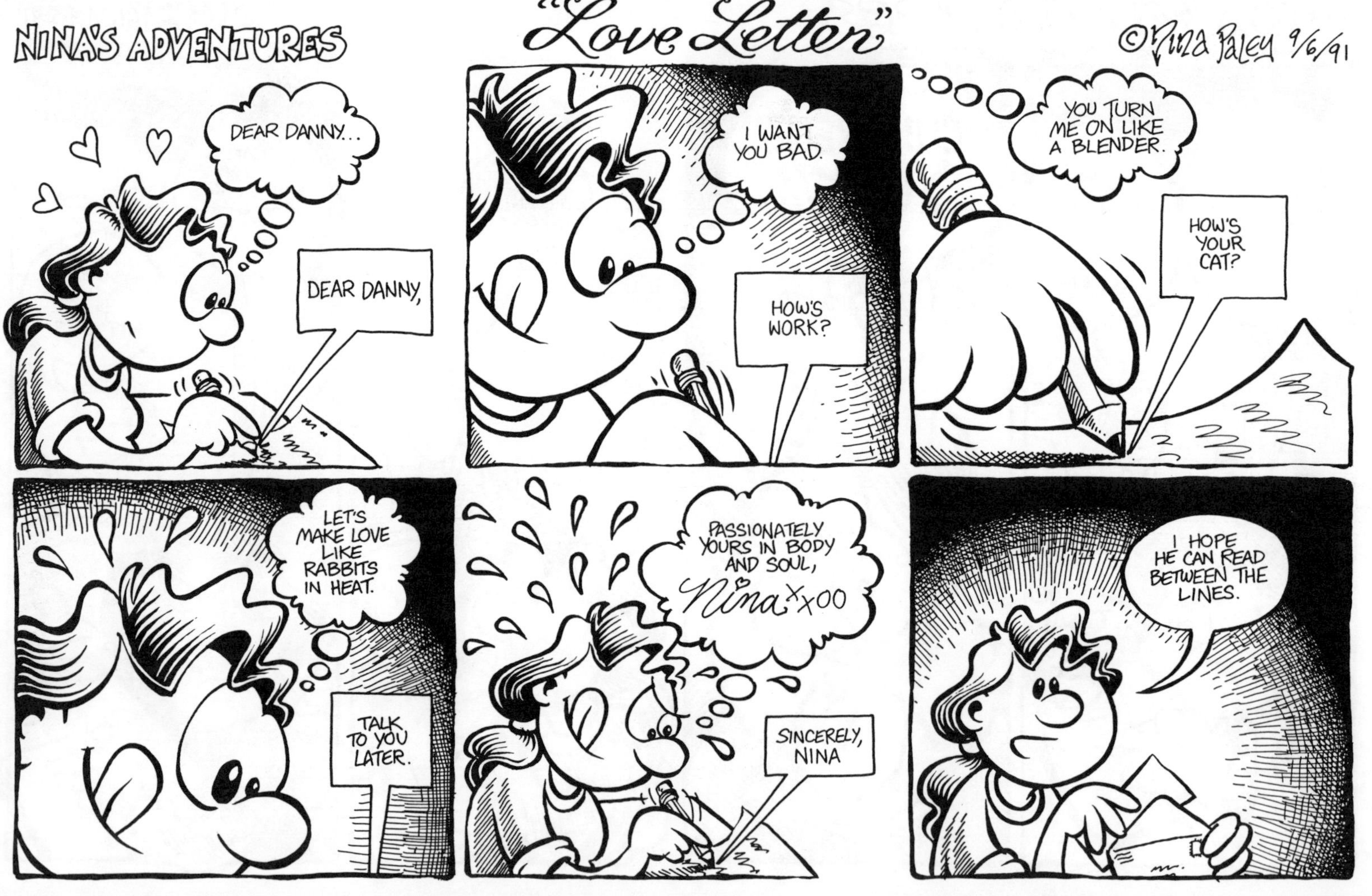
NINA'S ADVENTURES
"Love Letter"
© Nina Paley 9/6/91
DEAR DANNY...
DEAR DANNY,
I WANT YOU BAD.
HOW'S WORK?
YOU TURN ME ON LIKE A BLENDER.
HOW'S YOUR CAT?
LET'S MAKE LOVE LIKE RABBITS IN HEAT.
TALK TO YOU LATER.
PASSIONATELY YOURS IN BODY AND SOUL, Nina xxoo
SINCERELY, NINA
I HOPE HE CAN READ BETWEEN THE LINES.

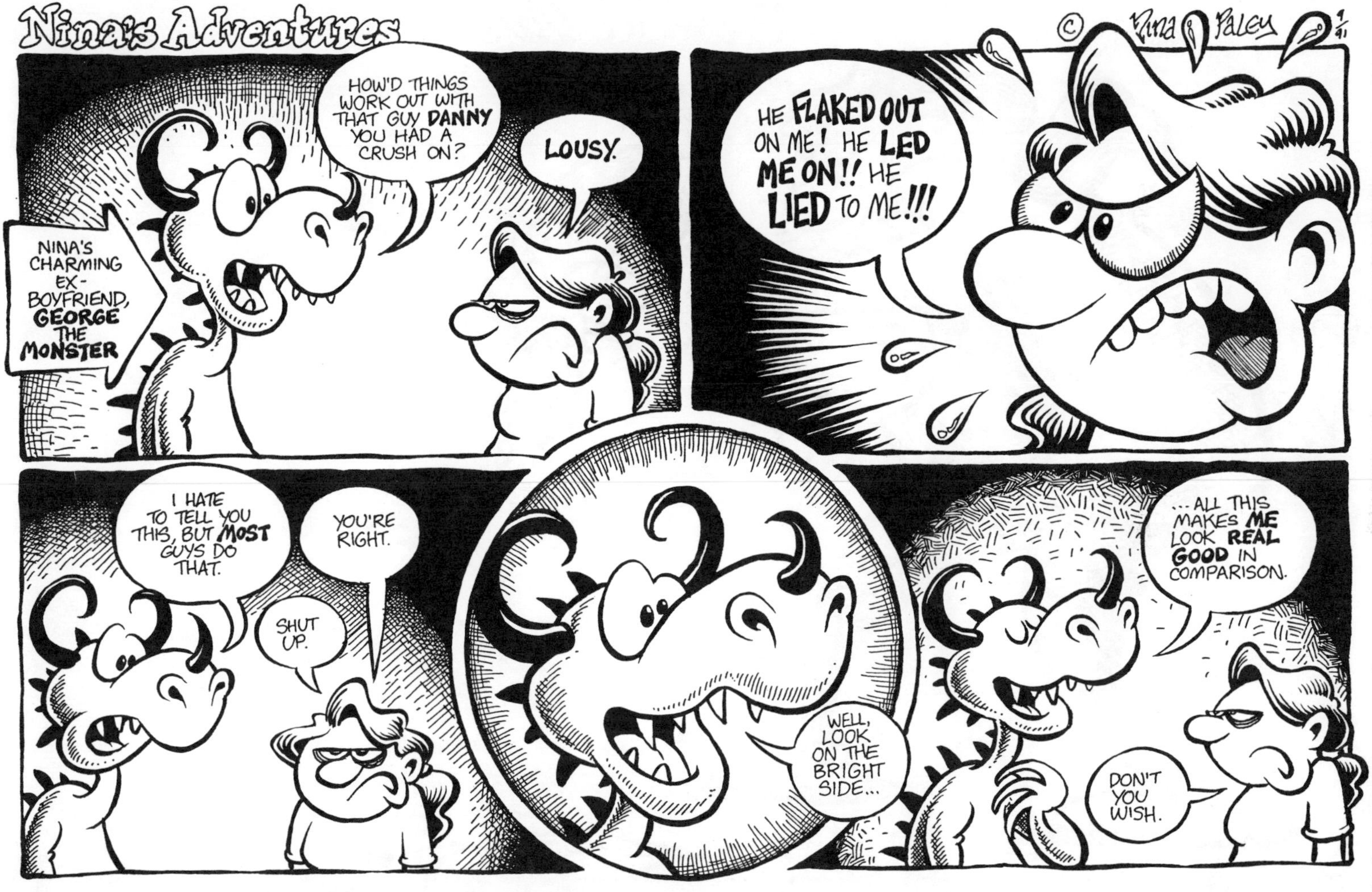
Nina's Adventures
© Nina Paley 9/91
NINA'S CHARMING EX-BOYFRIEND, GEORGE THE MONSTER
HOW'D THINGS WORK OUT WITH THAT GUY DANNY YOU HAD A CRUSH ON?
LOUSY.
HE FLAKED OUT ON ME! HE LED ME ON!! HE LIED TO ME!!!
I HATE TO TELL YOU THIS, BUT MOST GUYS DO THAT.
YOU'RE RIGHT.
SHUT UP.
WELL, LOOK ON THE BRIGHT SIDE...
...ALL THIS MAKES ME LOOK REAL GOOD IN COMPARISON.
DON'T YOU WISH.

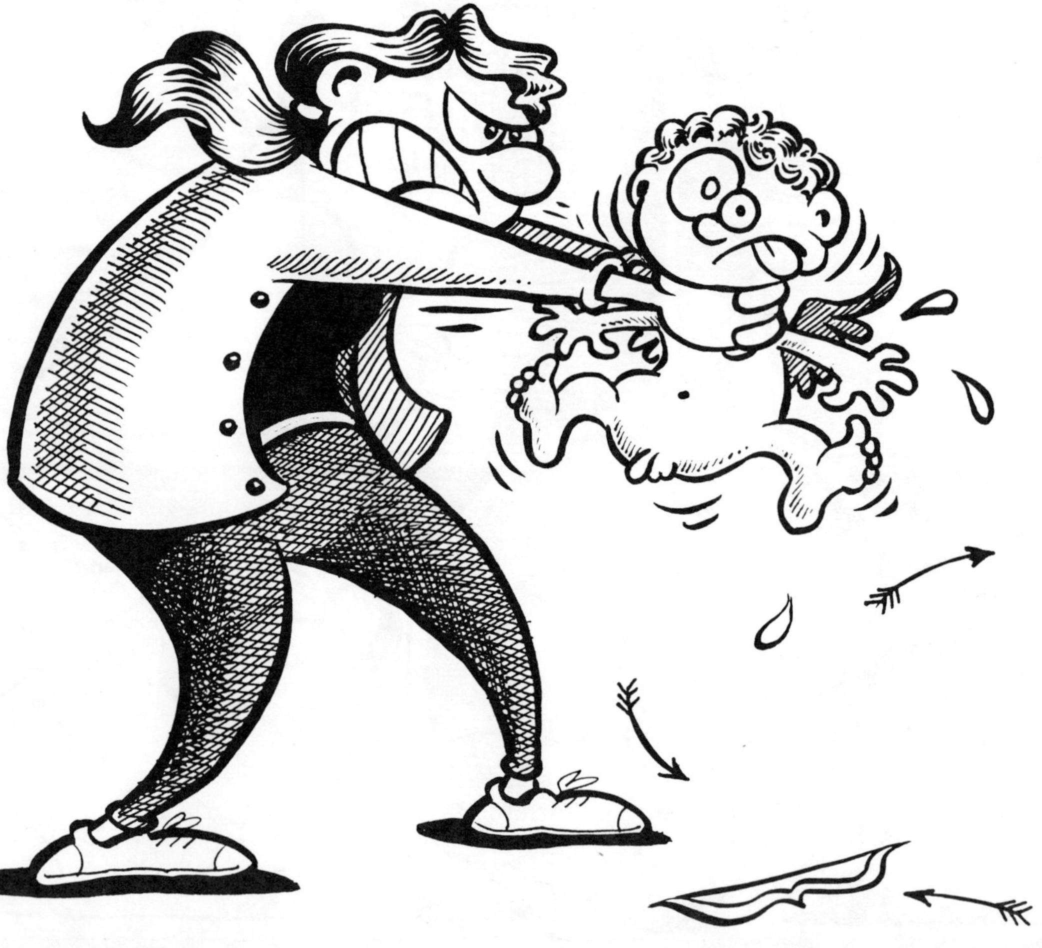

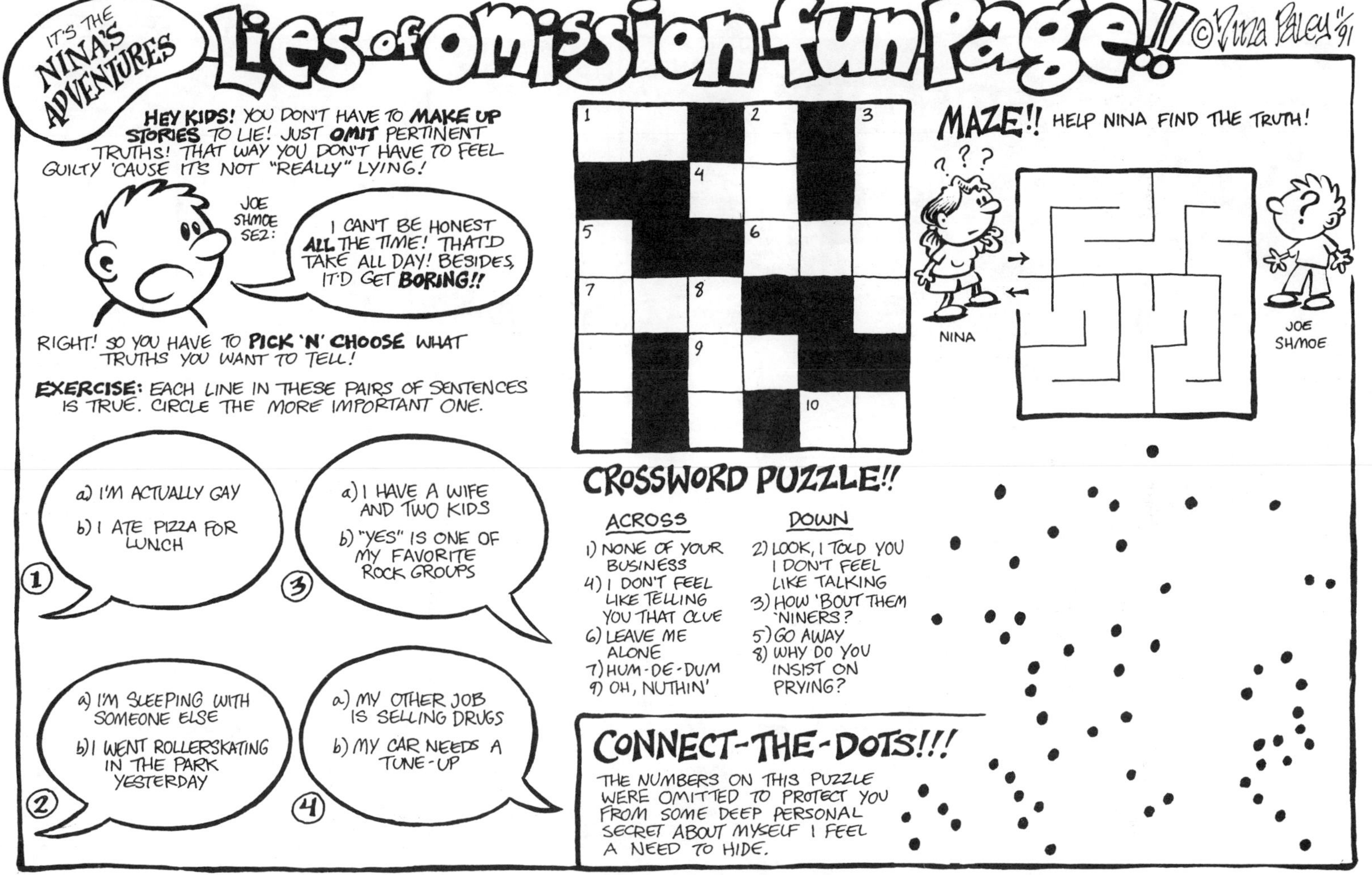

IT'S THE NINA'S ADVENTURES
LIES OF OMISSION FUN PAGE!!
© NINA PALEY '91
HEY KIDS! YOU DON'T HAVE TO MAKE UP STORIES TO LIE! JUST OMIT PERTINENT TRUTHS! THAT WAY YOU DON'T HAVE TO FEEL GUILTY 'CAUSE IT'S NOT "REALLY" LYING!
JOE SHMOE SEZ:
I CAN'T BE HONEST ALL THE TIME! THAT'D TAKE ALL DAY! BESIDES, IT'D GET BORING!!
RIGHT! SO YOU HAVE TO PICK 'N' CHOOSE WHAT TRUTHS YOU WANT TO TELL!
EXERCISE: EACH LINE IN THESE PAIRS OF SENTENCES IS TRUE. CIRCLE THE MORE IMPORTANT ONE.
1
a) I'M ACTUALLY GAY
b) I ATE PIZZA FOR LUNCH
2
a) I'M SLEEPING WITH SOMEONE ELSE
b) I WENT ROLLERSKATING IN THE PARK YESTERDAY
3
a) I HAVE A WIFE AND TWO KIDS
b) "YES" IS ONE OF MY FAVORITE ROCK GROUPS
4
a) MY OTHER JOB IS SELLING DRUGS
b) MY CAR NEEDS A TUNE-UP
1 2 3 4 5 6 7 8 9 10
CROSSWORD PUZZLE!!
ACROSS
1) NONE OF YOUR BUSINESS
4) I DON'T FEEL LIKE TELLING YOU THAT CLUE
6) LEAVE ME ALONE
7) HUM-DE-DUM
9) OH, NUTHIN'
DOWN
2) LOOK, I TOLD YOU I DON'T FEEL LIKE TALKING
3) HOW 'BOUT THEM 'NINERS?
5) GO AWAY
8) WHY DO YOU INSIST ON PRYING?
MAZE!! HELP NINA FIND THE TRUTH!
NINA
JOE SHMOE
CONNECT-THE-DOTS!!!
THE NUMBERS ON THIS PUZZLE WERE OMITTED TO PROTECT YOU FROM SOME DEEP PERSONAL SECRET ABOUT MYSELF I FEEL A NEED TO HIDE.

NINA'S ADVENTURES

© Nina Paley 4-89

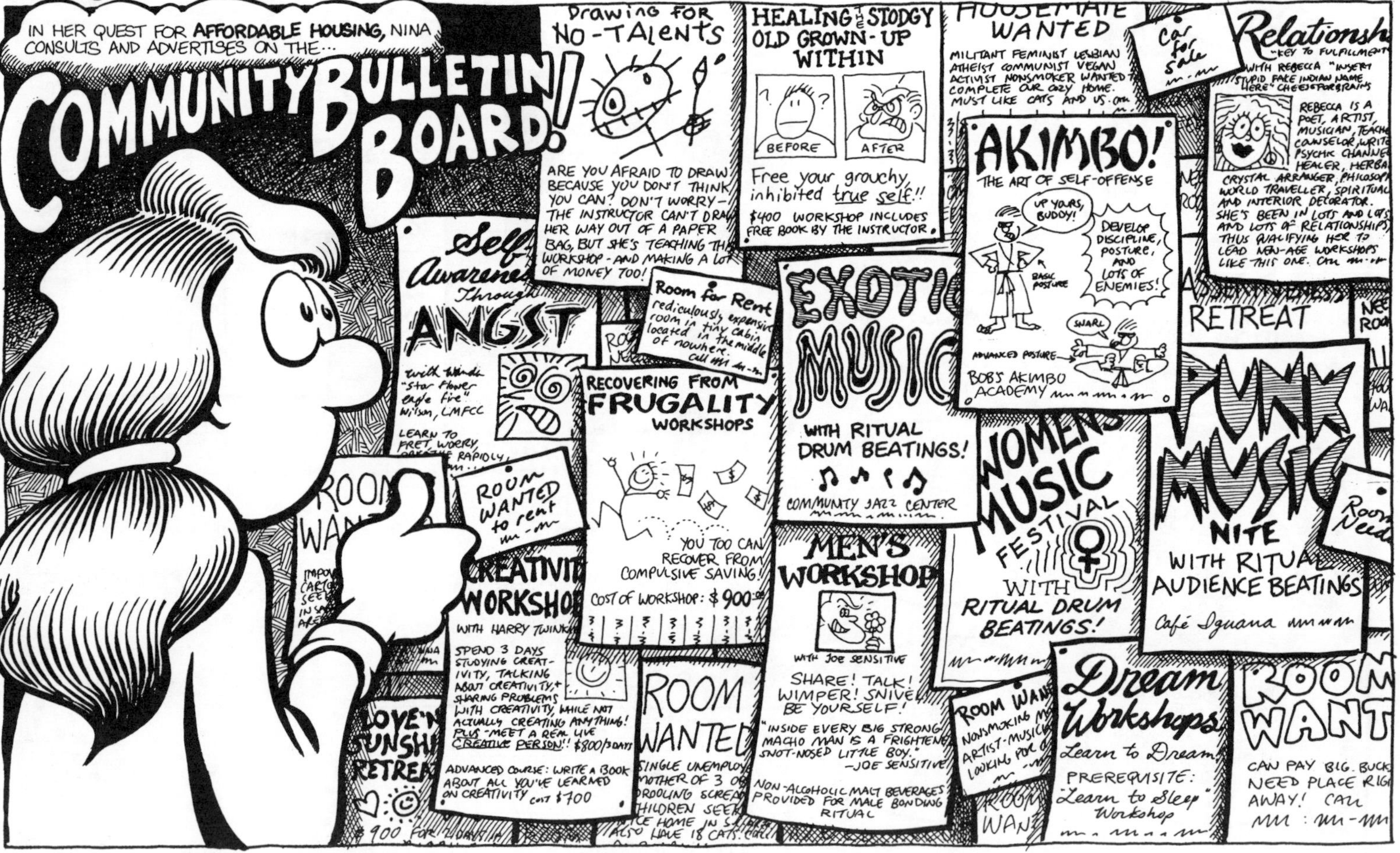

IN HER QUEST FOR AFFORDABLE HOUSING, NINA CONSULTS AND ADVERTISES ON THE...
COMMUNITY BULLETIN BOARD!
Drawing for NO-TALENTS
ARE YOU AFRAID TO DRAW BECAUSE YOU DON'T THINK YOU CAN? DON'T WORRY-- THE INSTRUCTOR CAN'T DRAW HER WAY OUT OF A PAPER BAG, BUT SHE'S TEACHING THIS WORKSHOP - AND MAKING A LOT OF MONEY TOO!
HEALING THE STODGY OLD GROWN-UP WITHIN
BEFORE
AFTER
Free your grouchy, inhibited true self!!
$400 WORKSHOP INCLUDES FREE BOOK BY THE INSTRUCTOR
HOUSEMATE WANTED
MILITANT FEMINIST LESBIAN ATHEIST COMMUNIST VEGAN ACTIVIST NONSMOKER WANTED TO COMPLETE OUR COZY HOME. MUST LIKE CATS AND US.
Car for Sale
Relationsh
KEY TO FULFILLMENT
WITH REBECCA "INSERT STUPID FAKE INDIAN NAME HERE" CHEESEFORBRAINS
REBECCA IS A POET, ARTIST, MUSICIAN, TEACHER, COUNSELOR, WRITER, PSYCHIC CHANNEL, HEALER, HERBAL CRYSTAL ARRANGER, PHILOSOPH WORLD TRAVELLER, SPIRITUAL AND INTERIOR DECORATOR. SHE'S BEEN IN LOTS AND LOTS AND LOTS OF RELATIONSHIPS, THUS QUALIFYING HER TO LEAD NEW-AGE WORKSHOPS LIKE THIS ONE. CALL
AKIMBO!
THE ART OF SELF-OFFENSE
UP YOURS, BUDDY!
BASIC POSTURE
DEVELOP DISCIPLINE, POSTURE, AND LOTS OF ENEMIES!
SNARL
ADVANCED POSTURE
BOB'S AKIMBO ACADEMY
Self Awareness Through ANGST
with Wanda "Star Flower Eagle Fire" Wilson, LMFCC
LEARN TO FRET, WORRY, OBSESS RAPIDLY
Room for Rent
rediculously expensive room in tiny cabin located in the middle of nowhere.
RECOVERING FROM FRUGALITY WORKSHOPS
YOU TOO CAN RECOVER FROM COMPULSIVE SAVING!
COST OF WORKSHOP: $900.00
EXOTIC MUSIC
WITH RITUAL DRUM BEATINGS!
COMMUNITY JAZZ CENTER
RETREAT
ROOM WANTED to rent
ROOM WANTED
CREATIVITY WORKSHOP
WITH HARRY TWINK
SPEND 3 DAYS STUDYING CREATIVITY, TALKING ABOUT CREATIVITY, + SHARING PROBLEMS WITH CREATIVITY, WHILE NOT ACTUALLY CREATING ANYTHING! PLUS - MEET A REAL LIVE CREATIVE PERSON!! $800/3 DAYS
ADVANCED COURSE: WRITE A BOOK ABOUT ALL YOU'VE LEARNED ON CREATIVITY cost $700
LOVE'N SUNSHINE RETREAT
ROOM WANTED
SINGLE UNEMPLOYED MOTHER OF 3 OR DROOLING SCREAMING CHILDREN SEEKS NICE HOME IN SAFE... ALSO HAVE 18 CATS.
$900 FOR 2 DAYS IN
MEN'S WORKSHOP
WITH JOE SENSITIVE
SHARE! TALK! WIMPER! SNIVEL! BE YOURSELF!
"INSIDE EVERY BIG STRONG MACHO MAN IS A FRIGHTENED SNOT-NOSED LITTLE BOY." -JOE SENSITIVE
NON-ALCOHOLIC MALT BEVERAGES PROVIDED FOR MALE BONDING RITUAL
WOMENS MUSIC FESTIVAL
WITH RITUAL DRUM BEATINGS!
PUNK MUSIC NITE
WITH RITUAL AUDIENCE BEATINGS
Café Iguana
Room Needed
ROOM WANTED
NONSMOKING ARTIST-MUSICIAN LOOKING FOR
Dream Workshops
Learn to Dream
PREREQUISITE: "Learn to Sleep" Workshop
ROOM WANTED
CAN PAY BIG BUCKS NEED PLACE RIGHT AWAY! CALL

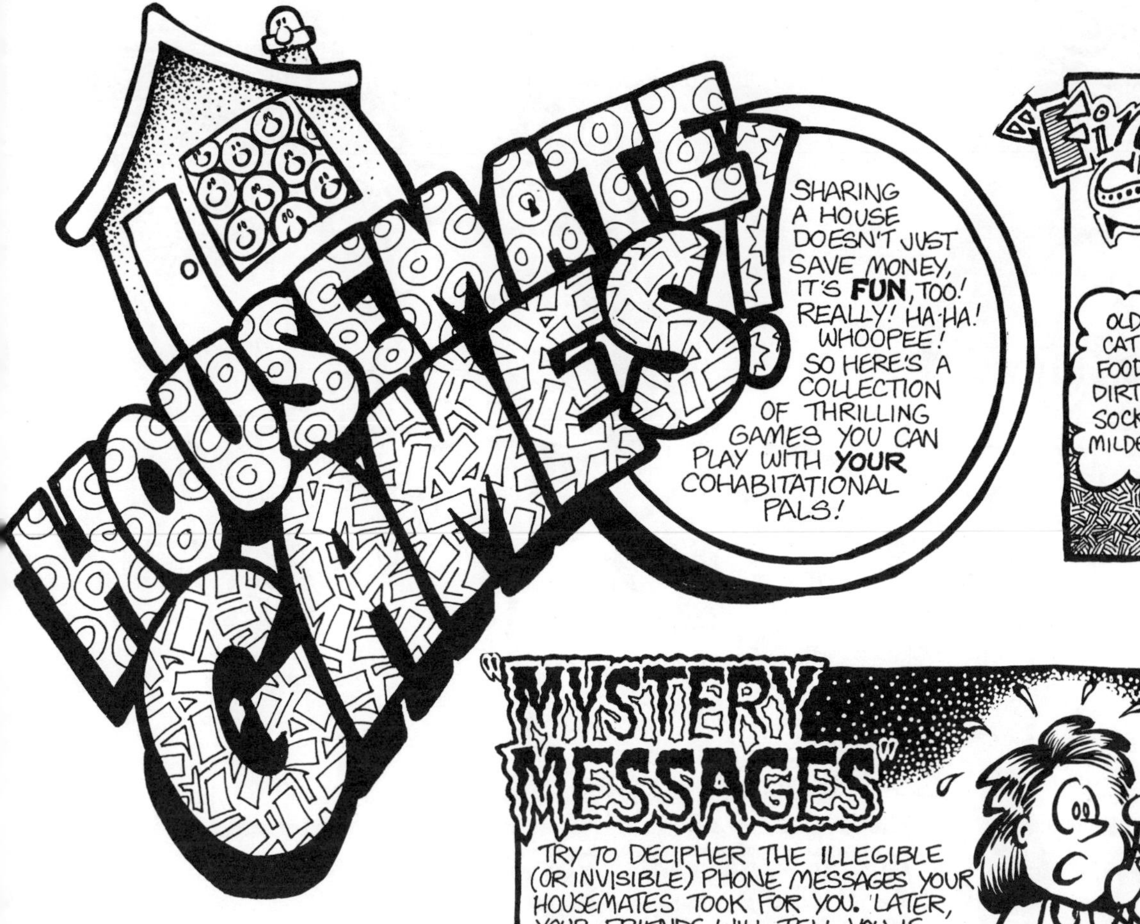
HOUSEMATE GAMES!
SHARING A HOUSE DOESN'T JUST SAVE MONEY, IT'S **FUN**, TOO! REALLY! HA-HA! WHOOPEE! SO HERE'S A COLLECTION OF THRILLING GAMES YOU CAN PLAY WITH **YOUR** COHABITATIONAL PALS!

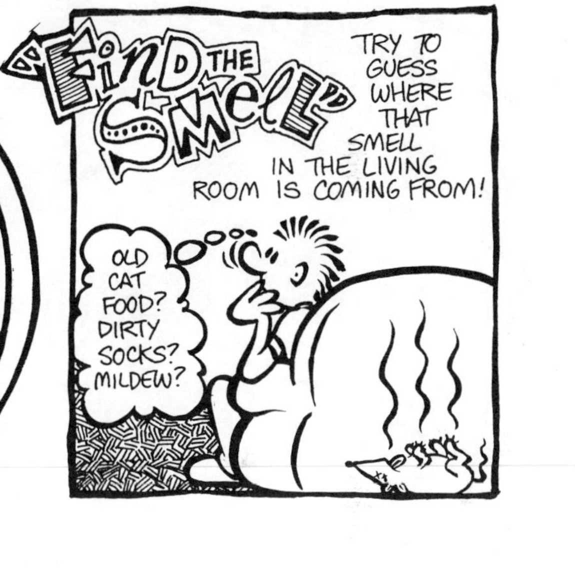
"FIND THE SMELL"
TRY TO GUESS WHERE THAT SMELL IN THE LIVING ROOM IS COMING FROM!
OLD CAT FOOD? DIRTY SOCKS? MILDEW?

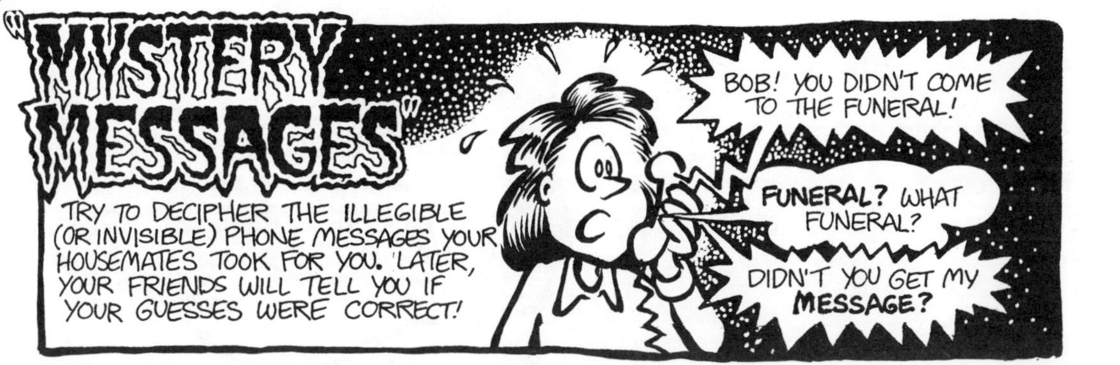
"MYSTERY MESSAGES"
TRY TO DECIPHER THE ILLEGIBLE (OR INVISIBLE) PHONE MESSAGES YOUR HOUSEMATES TOOK FOR YOU. LATER, YOUR FRIENDS WILL TELL YOU IF YOUR GUESSES WERE CORRECT!
BOB! YOU DIDN'T COME TO THE FUNERAL!
FUNERAL? WHAT FUNERAL?
DIDN'T YOU GET MY **MESSAGE?**

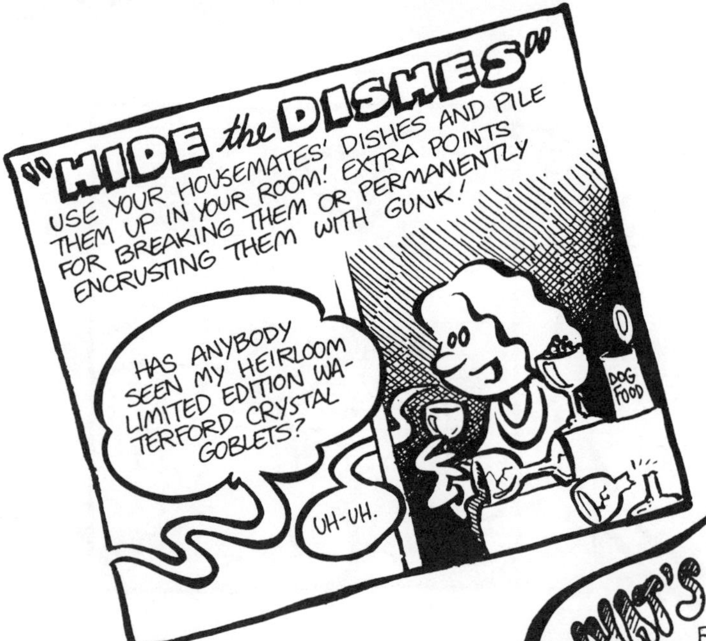
"HIDE the DISHES"
USE YOUR HOUSEMATES' DISHES AND PILE THEM UP IN YOUR ROOM! EXTRA POINTS FOR BREAKING THEM OR PERMANENTLY ENCRUSTING THEM WITH GUNK!
HAS ANYBODY SEEN MY HEIRLOOM LIMITED EDITION WATERFORD CRYSTAL GOBLETS?
UH-UH.
DOG FOOD

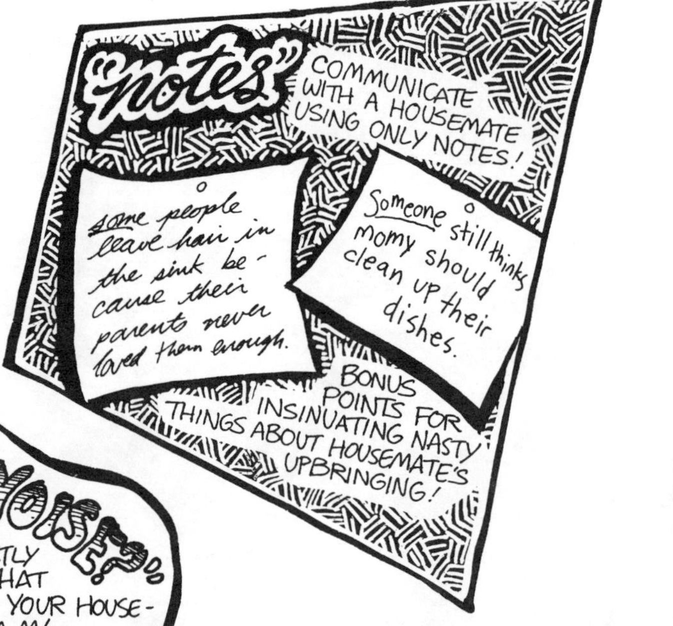
"notes"
COMMUNICATE WITH A HOUSEMATE USING ONLY NOTES!
some people leave hair in the sink because their parents never loved them enough.
Someone still thinks mommy should clean up their dishes.
BONUS POINTS FOR INSINUATING NASTY THINGS ABOUT HOUSEMATE'S UPBRINGING!

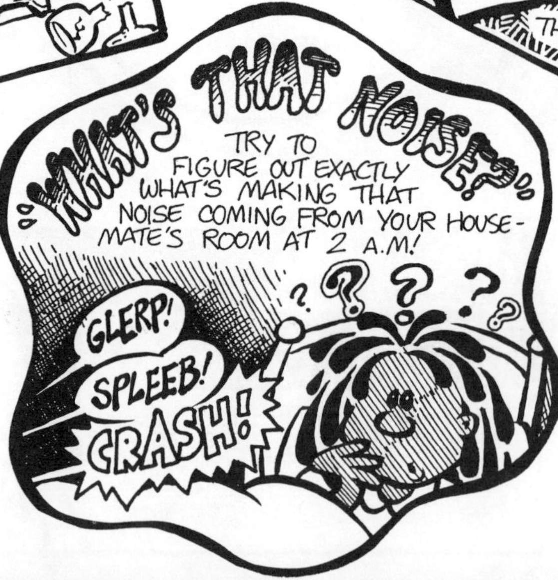
"WHAT'S THAT NOISE?"
TRY TO FIGURE OUT EXACTLY WHAT'S MAKING THAT NOISE COMING FROM YOUR HOUSEMATE'S ROOM AT 2 A.M!
GLERP!
SPLEEB!
CRASH!

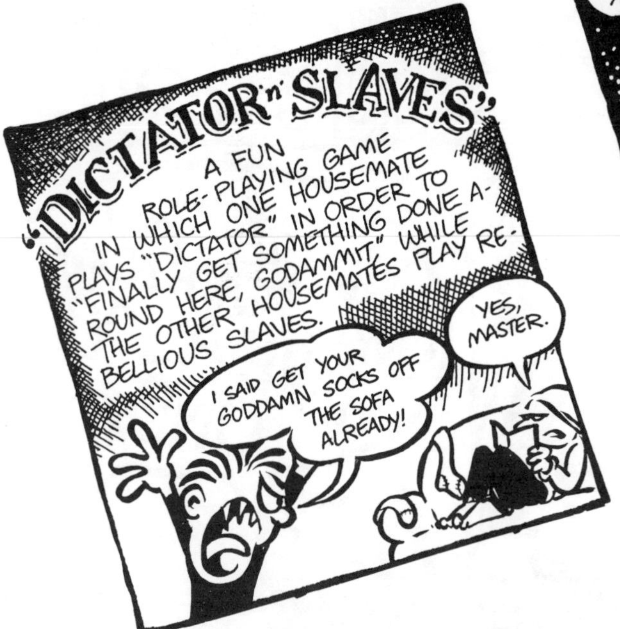
"DICTATOR 'n' SLAVES"
A FUN ROLE-PLAYING GAME IN WHICH ONE HOUSEMATE PLAYS "DICTATOR" IN ORDER TO "FINALLY GET SOMETHING DONE A-ROUND HERE, GODAMMIT," WHILE THE OTHER HOUSEMATES PLAY RE-BELLIOUS SLAVES.
I SAID GET YOUR GODDAMN SOCKS OFF THE SOFA ALREADY!
YES, MASTER.

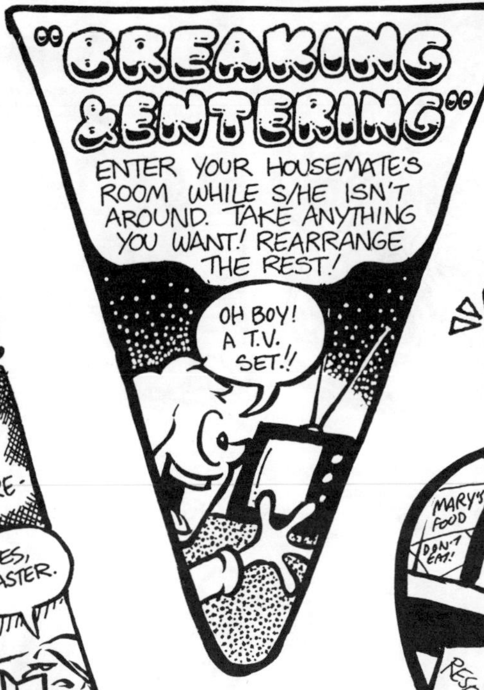
"BREAKING &ENTERING"
ENTER YOUR HOUSEMATE'S ROOM WHILE S/HE ISN'T AROUND. TAKE ANYTHING YOU WANT! REARRANGE THE REST!
OH BOY! A T.V. SET!!

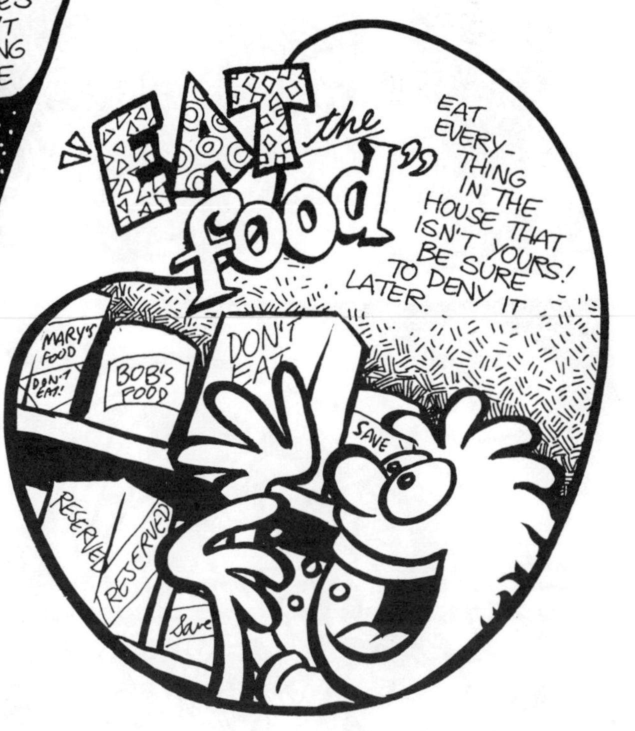
"EAT the food"
EAT EVERY-THING IN THE HOUSE THAT ISN'T YOURS! BE SURE TO DENY IT LATER.
MARY'S FOOD
DON'T EAT!
BOB'S FOOD
DON'T EAT
SAVE
RESERVED
RESERVED
Save

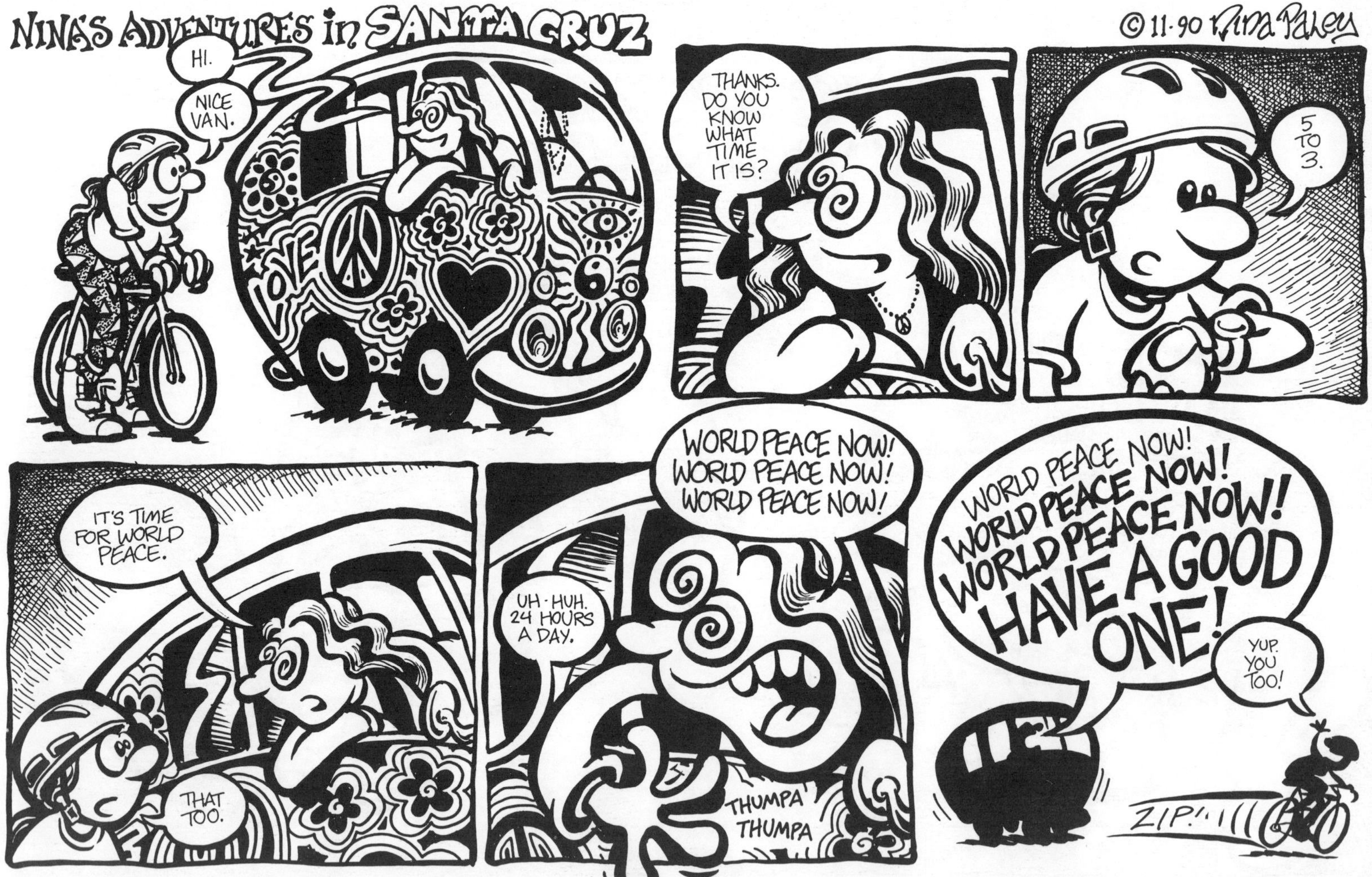
NINA'S ADVENTURES in SANTA CRUZ
© 11·90 Nina Paley
HI.
NICE VAN.
LOVE
THANKS. DO YOU KNOW WHAT TIME IT IS?
5 TO 3.
IT'S TIME FOR WORLD PEACE.
THAT TOO.
UH-HUH. 24 HOURS A DAY.
WORLD PEACE NOW! WORLD PEACE NOW! WORLD PEACE NOW!
THUMPA THUMPA
WORLD PEACE NOW! WORLD PEACE NOW! WORLD PEACE NOW! HAVE A GOOD ONE!
YUP. YOU TOO!
ZIP!

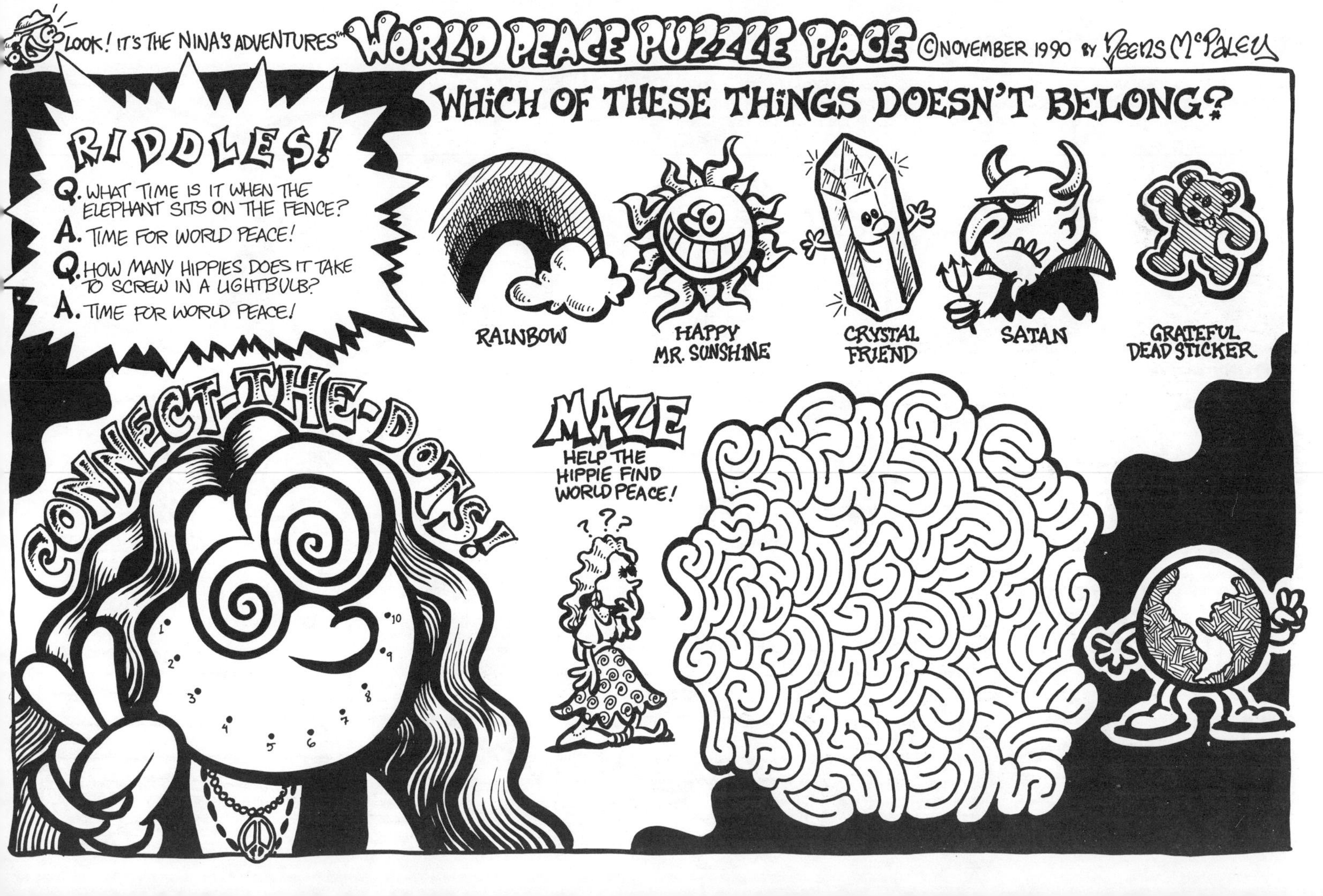

LOOK! IT'S THE NINA'S ADVENTURES™ WORLD PEACE PUZZLE PAGE ©NOVEMBER 1990 BY
WHICH OF THESE THINGS DOESN'T BELONG?
RIDDLES!
Q. WHAT TIME IS IT WHEN THE ELEPHANT SITS ON THE FENCE?
A. TIME FOR WORLD PEACE!
Q. HOW MANY HIPPIES DOES IT TAKE TO SCREW IN A LIGHTBULB?
A. TIME FOR WORLD PEACE!
RAINBOW
HAPPY MR. SUNSHINE
CRYSTAL FRIEND
SATAN
GRATEFUL DEAD STICKER
CONNECT-THE-DOTS!
MAZE
HELP THE HIPPIE FIND WORLD PEACE!
? ? ?
1
2
3
4
5
6
7
8
9
10

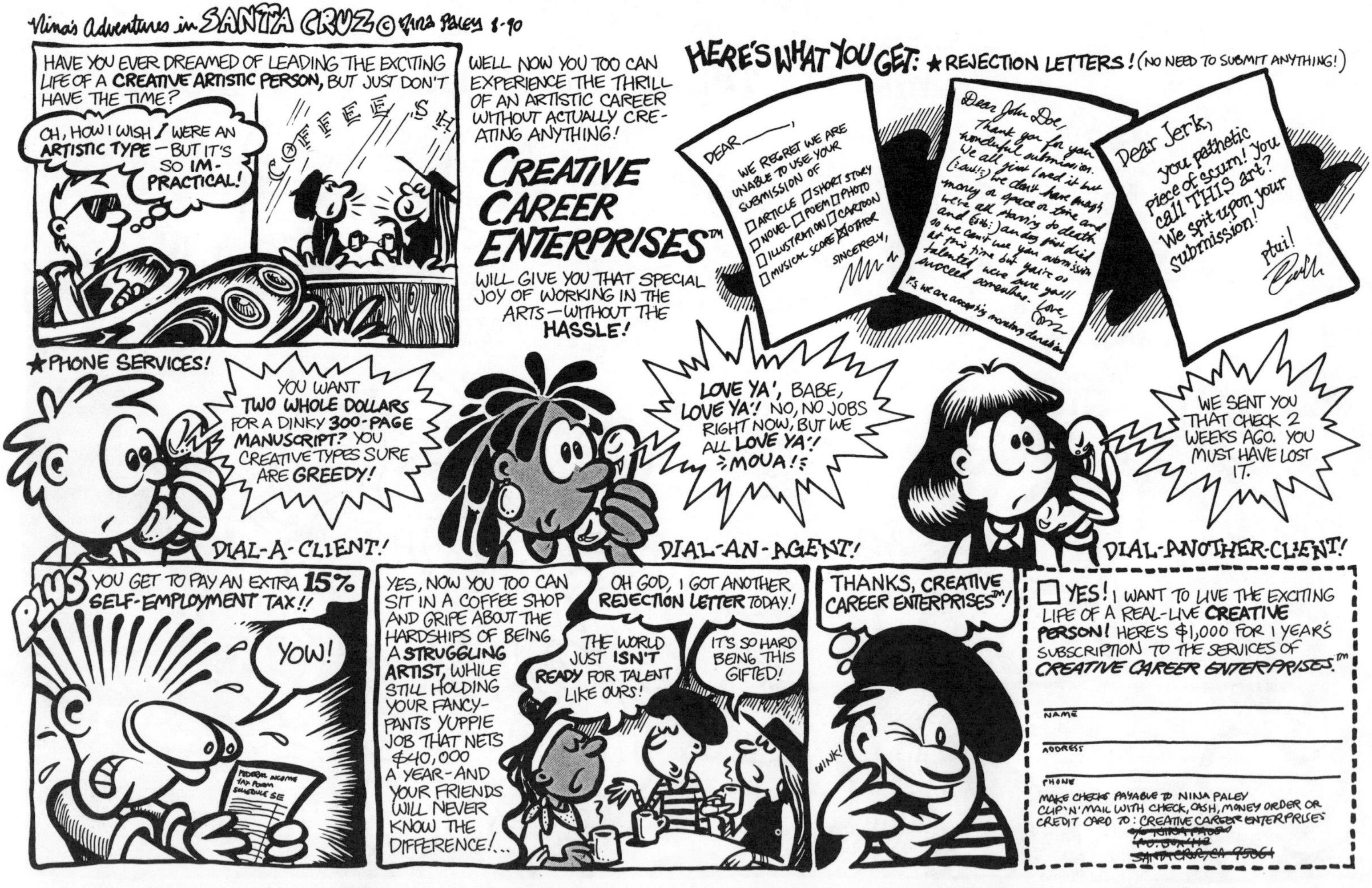
Nina's Adventures in SANTA CRUZ © Nina Paley 8-90
HAVE YOU EVER DREAMED OF LEADING THE EXCITING LIFE OF A CREATIVE ARTISTIC PERSON, BUT JUST DON'T HAVE THE TIME?
OH, HOW I WISH I WERE AN ARTISTIC TYPE — BUT IT'S SO IMPRACTICAL!
COFFEE SH
WELL NOW YOU TOO CAN EXPERIENCE THE THRILL OF AN ARTISTIC CAREER WITHOUT ACTUALLY CREATING ANYTHING!
CREATIVE CAREER ENTERPRISES™
WILL GIVE YOU THAT SPECIAL JOY OF WORKING IN THE ARTS — WITHOUT THE HASSLE!
HERE'S WHAT YOU GET: ★ REJECTION LETTERS! (NO NEED TO SUBMIT ANYTHING!)
DEAR ____, WE REGRET WE ARE UNABLE TO USE YOUR SUBMISSION OF ☐ ARTICLE ☐ SHORT STORY ☐ NOVEL ☐ POEM ☐ PHOTO ☐ ILLUSTRATION ☐ CARTOON ☐ MUSICAL SCORE ☒ OTHER SINCERELY,
Dear John Doe, Thank you for your wonderful submission. We all just loved it but (sob!) we don't have enough money or space or time and we're all starving to death and (sob:) our dog just died so we can't use your submission at this time but you're so talented we're sure you'll succeed somewhere. Love,
P.S. we are accepting monetary donations
Dear Jerk, you pathetic piece of scum! You call THIS art? We spit upon your submission! ptui!
★ PHONE SERVICES!
YOU WANT TWO WHOLE DOLLARS FOR A DINKY 300-PAGE MANUSCRIPT? YOU CREATIVE TYPES SURE ARE GREEDY!
DIAL-A-CLIENT!
LOVE YA', BABE, LOVE YA'! NO, NO JOBS RIGHT NOW, BUT WE ALL LOVE YA'! MOUA!
DIAL-AN-AGENT!
WE SENT YOU THAT CHECK 2 WEEKS AGO. YOU MUST HAVE LOST IT.
DIAL-ANOTHER-CLIENT!
PLUS YOU GET TO PAY AN EXTRA 15% SELF-EMPLOYMENT TAX!!
YOW!
FEDERAL INCOME TAX FORM SCHEDULE SE
YES, NOW YOU TOO CAN SIT IN A COFFEE SHOP AND GRIPE ABOUT THE HARDSHIPS OF BEING A STRUGGLING ARTIST, WHILE STILL HOLDING YOUR FANCY-PANTS YUPPIE JOB THAT NETS $40,000 A YEAR — AND YOUR FRIENDS WILL NEVER KNOW THE DIFFERENCE!...
OH GOD, I GOT ANOTHER REJECTION LETTER TODAY!
THE WORLD JUST ISN'T READY FOR TALENT LIKE OURS!
IT'S SO HARD BEING THIS GIFTED!
THANKS, CREATIVE CAREER ENTERPRISES™!
WINK!
☐ YES! I WANT TO LIVE THE EXCITING LIFE OF A REAL-LIVE CREATIVE PERSON! HERE'S $1,000 FOR 1 YEAR'S SUBSCRIPTION TO THE SERVICES OF CREATIVE CAREER ENTERPRISES.™
NAME
ADDRESS
PHONE
MAKE CHECKS PAYABLE TO NINA PALEY
CLIP 'N' MAIL WITH CHECK, CASH, MONEY ORDER OR CREDIT CARD TO: CREATIVE CAREER ENTERPRISES

Nina's adventures in Santa Cruz

©Nina Paley 3/90

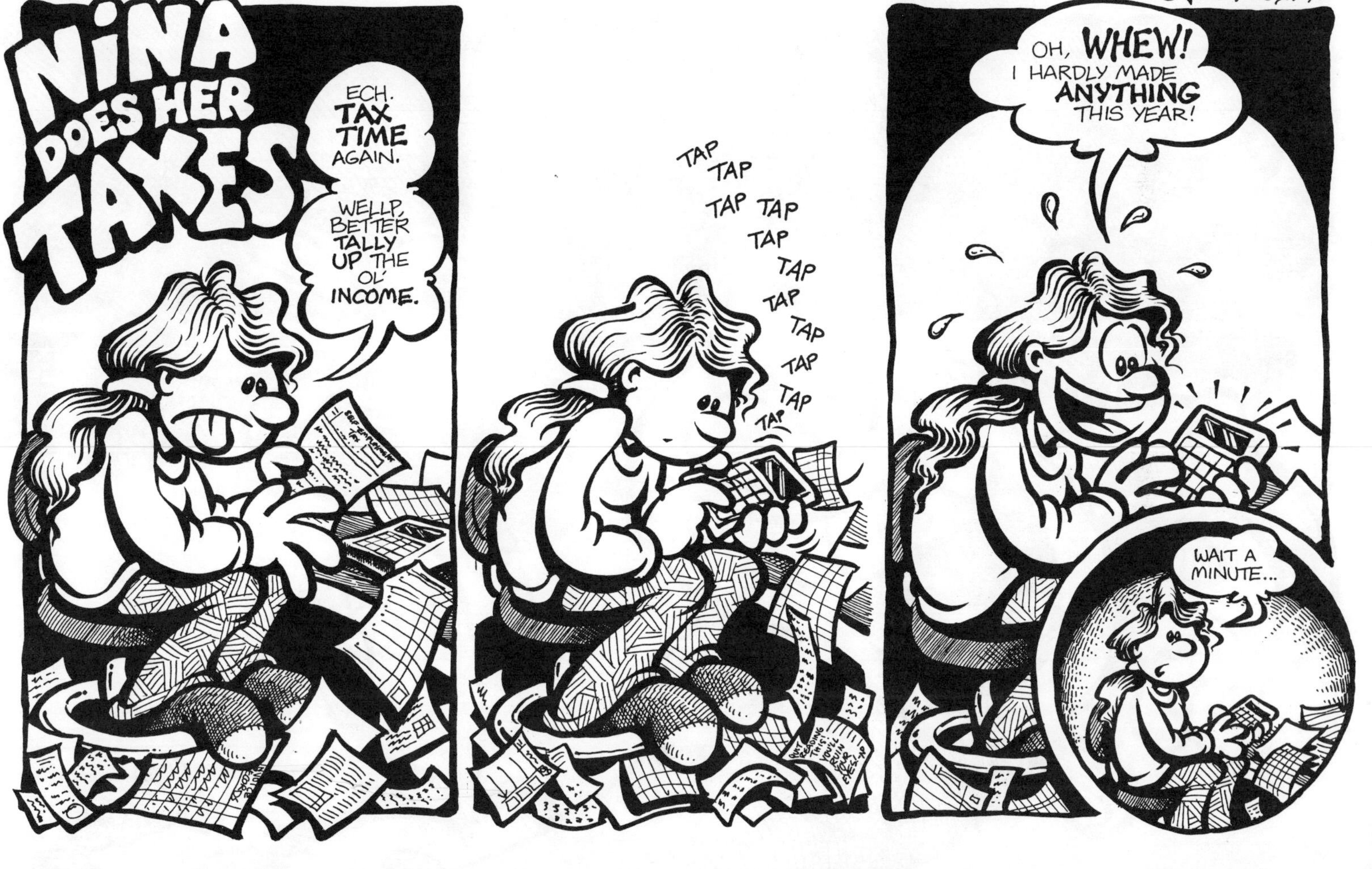
NINA DOES HER TAXES
ECH. TAX TIME AGAIN.
WELLP, BETTER TALLY UP THE OL' INCOME.
TAP TAP TAP TAP TAP TAP TAP TAP TAP TAP TAP
OH, WHEW! I HARDLY MADE ANYTHING THIS YEAR!
WAIT A MINUTE...

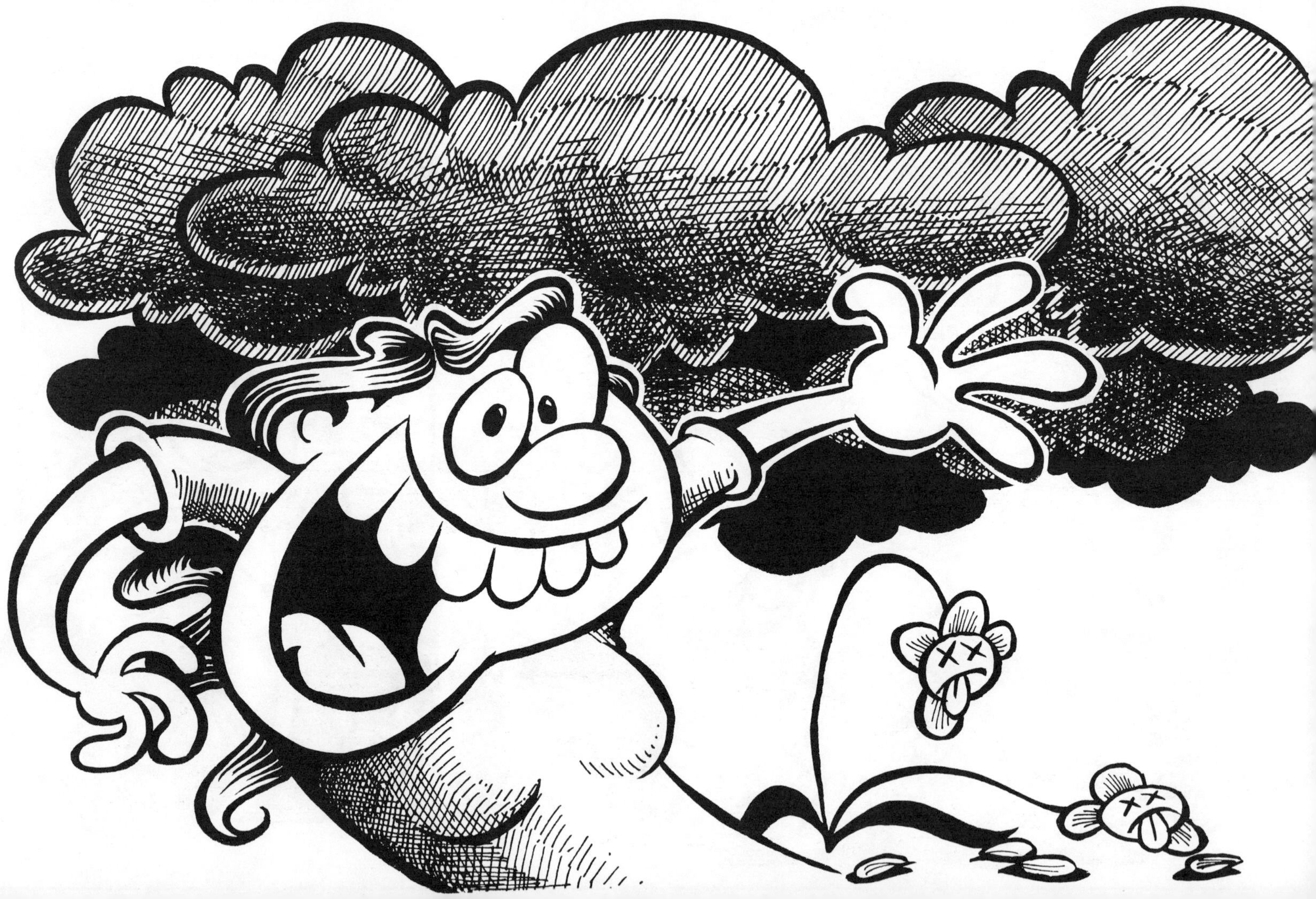

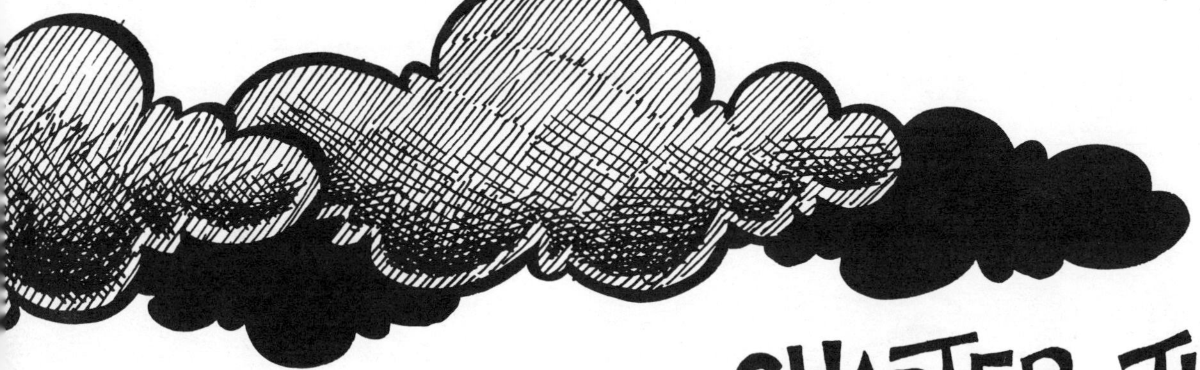

CHAPTER THREE: DEPRESSION IS FUN!

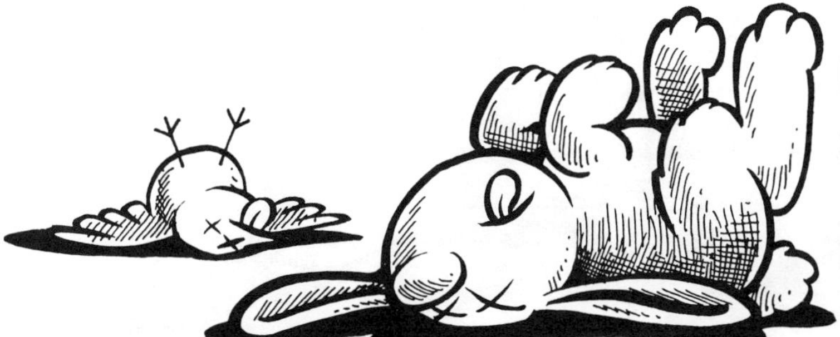

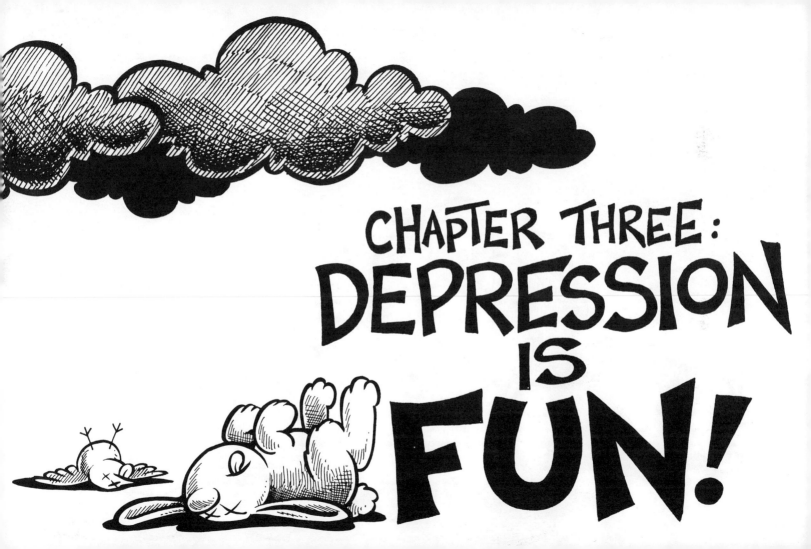

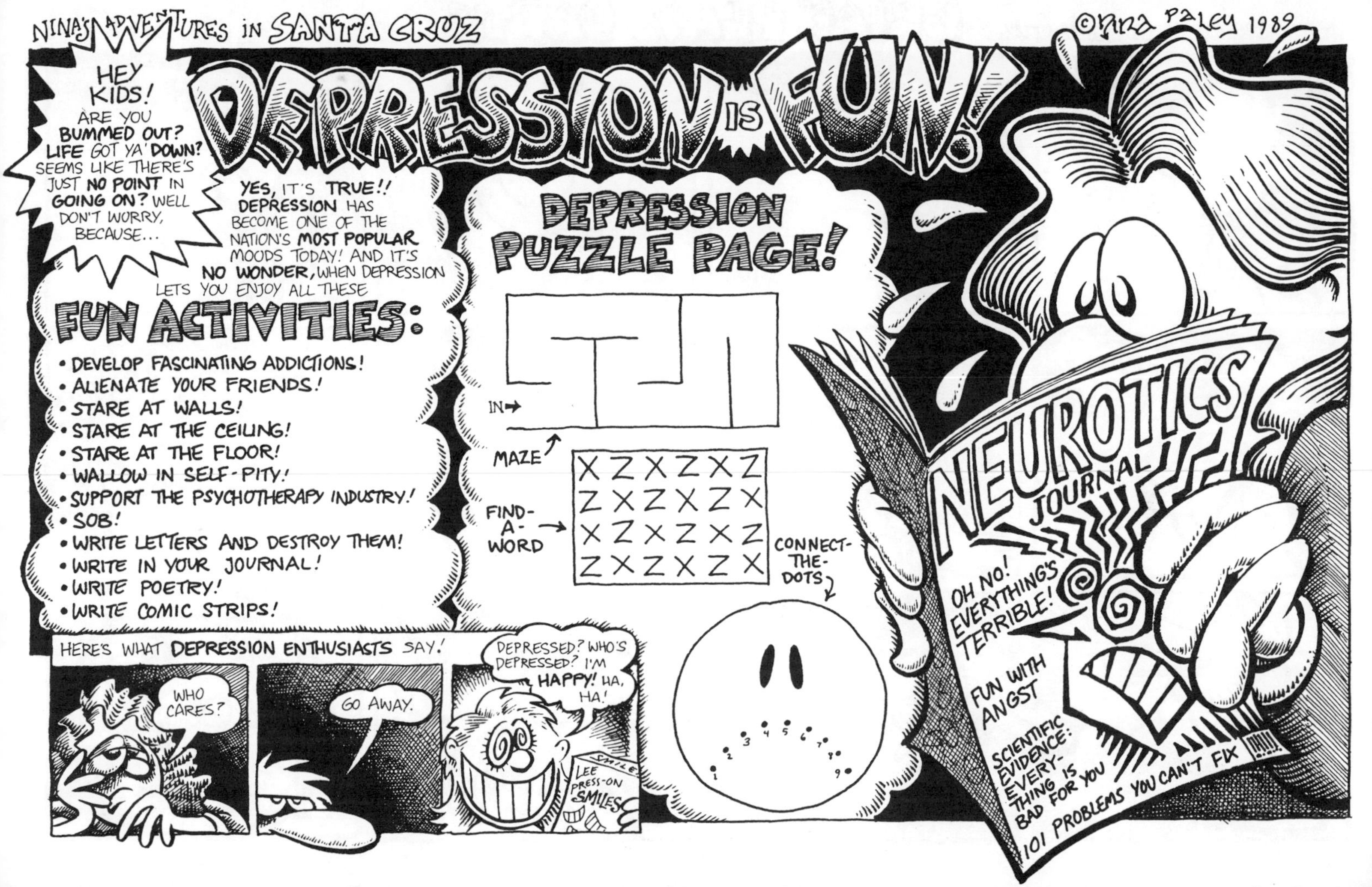
NINA'S ADVENTURES IN SANTA CRUZ
©Nina Paley 1989
DEPRESSION IS FUN!
HEY KIDS! ARE YOU BUMMED OUT? LIFE GOT YA' DOWN? SEEMS LIKE THERE'S JUST NO POINT IN GOING ON? WELL DON'T WORRY, BECAUSE...
YES, IT'S TRUE!! DEPRESSION HAS BECOME ONE OF THE NATION'S MOST POPULAR MOODS TODAY! AND IT'S NO WONDER, WHEN DEPRESSION LETS YOU ENJOY ALL THESE
FUN ACTIVITIES:
• DEVELOP FASCINATING ADDICTIONS!
• ALIENATE YOUR FRIENDS!
• STARE AT WALLS!
• STARE AT THE CEILING!
• STARE AT THE FLOOR!
• WALLOW IN SELF-PITY!
• SUPPORT THE PSYCHOTHERAPY INDUSTRY!
• SOB!
• WRITE LETTERS AND DESTROY THEM!
• WRITE IN YOUR JOURNAL!
• WRITE POETRY!
• WRITE COMIC STRIPS!
DEPRESSION PUZZLE PAGE!
IN→
MAZE
FIND-A-WORD
X Z X Z X Z
Z X Z X Z X
X Z X Z X Z
Z X Z X Z X
CONNECT-THE-DOTS
1 2 3 4 5 6 7 8 9
HERE'S WHAT DEPRESSION ENTHUSIASTS SAY!
WHO CARES?
GO AWAY.
DEPRESSED? WHO'S DEPRESSED? I'M HAPPY! HA, HA!
LEE PRESS-ON SMILES
SMILE
NEUROTICS JOURNAL
OH NO! EVERYTHING'S TERRIBLE!
FUN WITH ANGST
SCIENTIFIC EVIDENCE: EVERYTHING IS BAD FOR YOU
101 PROBLEMS YOU CAN'T FIX

Nina's Adventures in Santa Cruz

BRIAN PLAYS DARTS

©Nina Paley 6/90

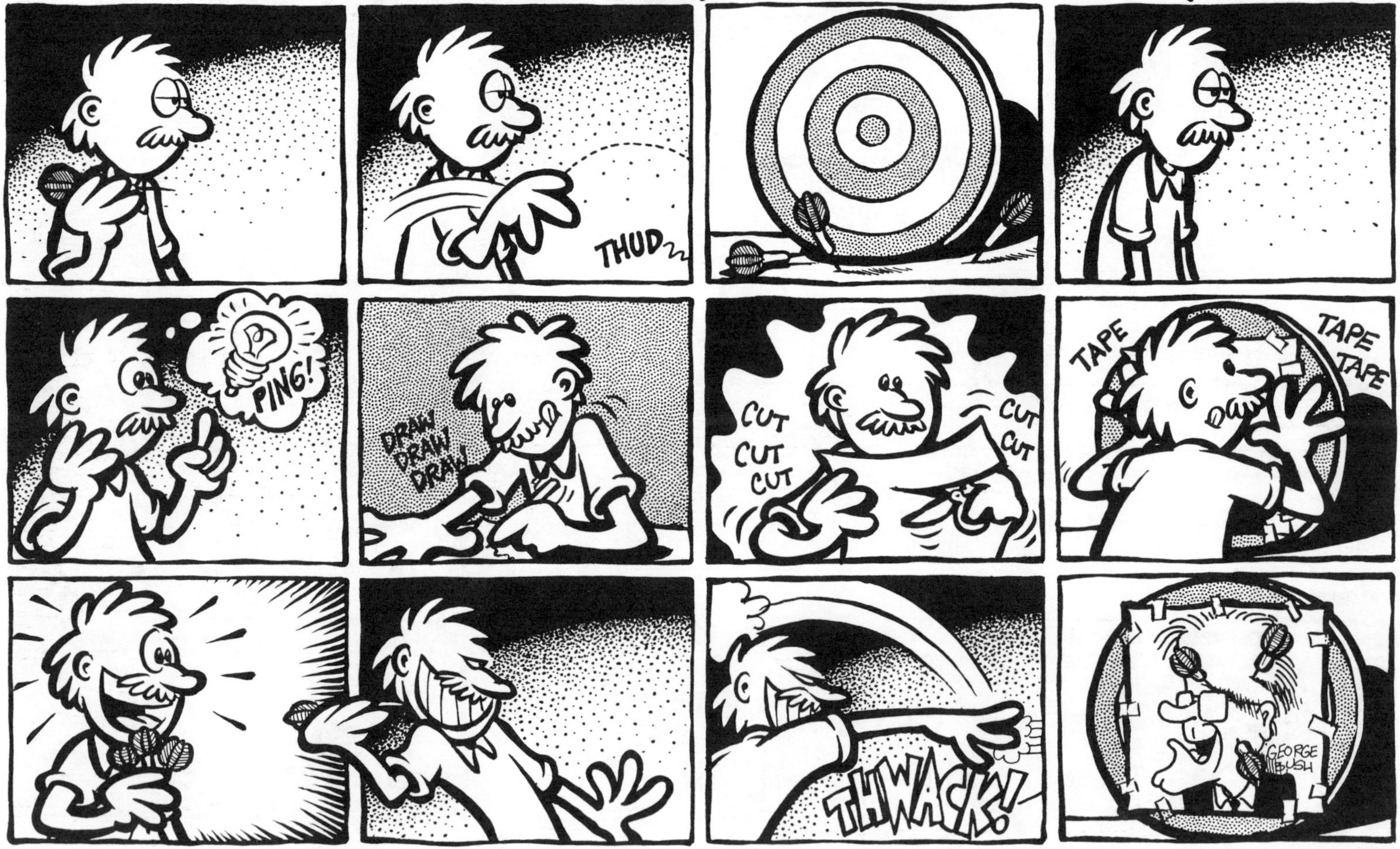
THUD
PING!
DRAW DRAW DRAW
CUT CUT CUT
CUT CUT
TAPE
TAPE TAPE
THWACK!
GEORGE BUSH

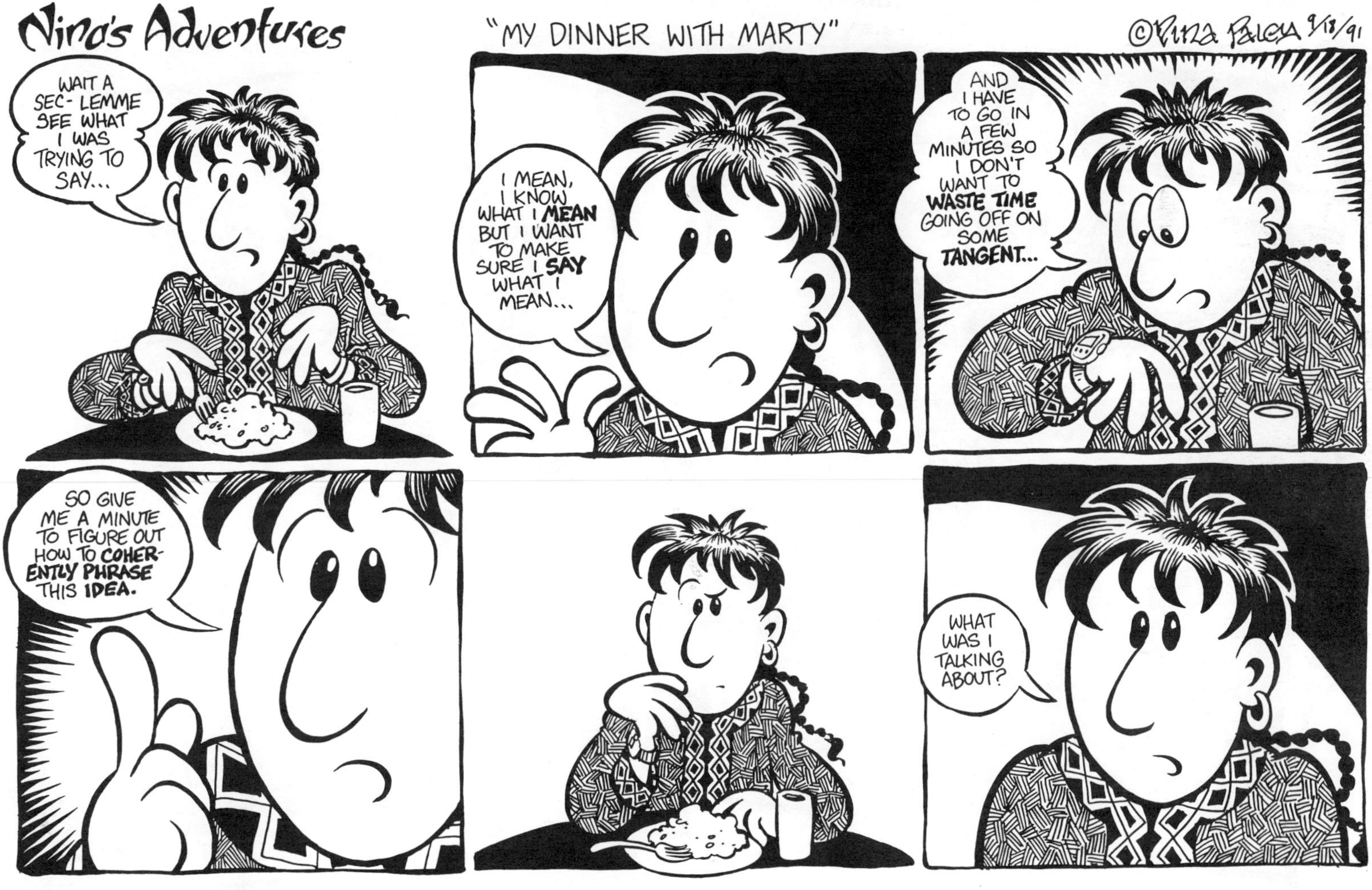

Nina's Adventures
"MY DINNER WITH MARTY"
©Nina Paley 9/18/91
WAIT A SEC- LEMME SEE WHAT I WAS TRYING TO SAY...
I MEAN, I KNOW WHAT I MEAN BUT I WANT TO MAKE SURE I SAY WHAT I MEAN...
AND I HAVE TO GO IN A FEW MINUTES SO I DON'T WANT TO WASTE TIME GOING OFF ON SOME TANGENT...
SO GIVE ME A MINUTE TO FIGURE OUT HOW TO COHER-ENTLY PHRASE THIS IDEA.
WHAT WAS I TALKING ABOUT?

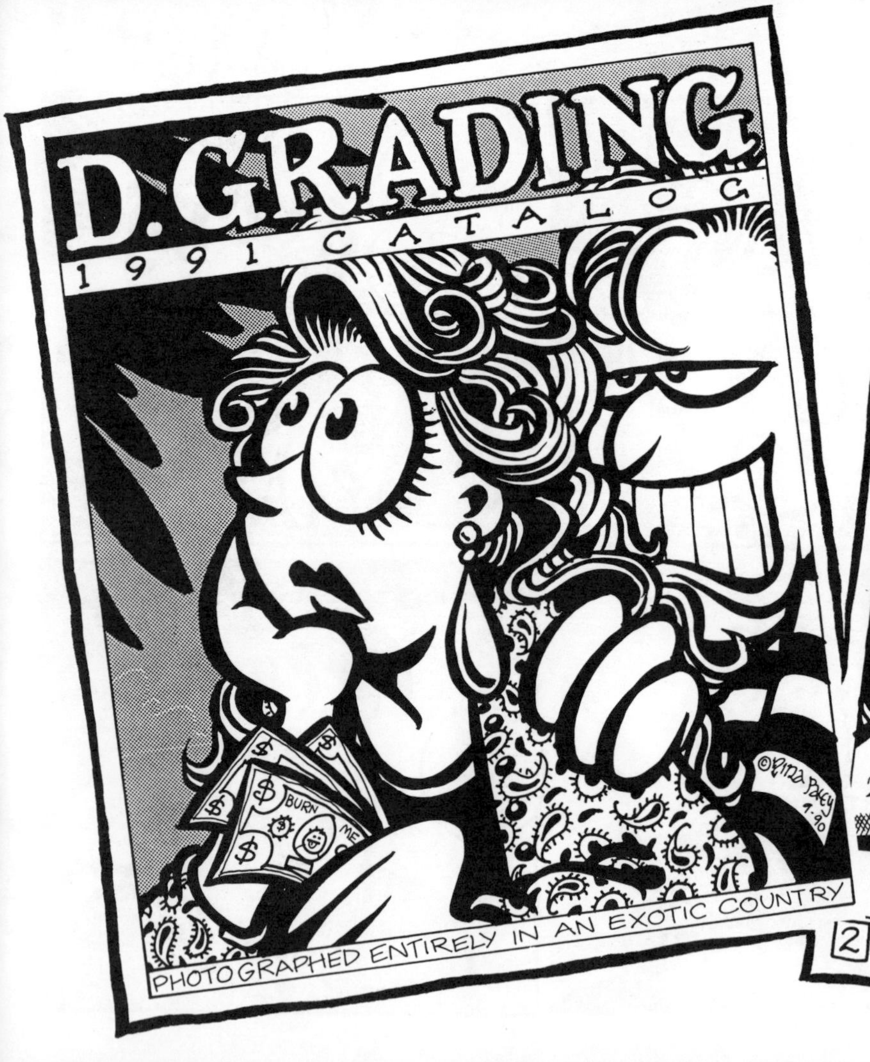
D. GRADING
1991 CATALOG
BURN
ME
©Nina Paley 9.90
PHOTOGRAPHED ENTIRELY IN AN EXOTIC COUNTRY

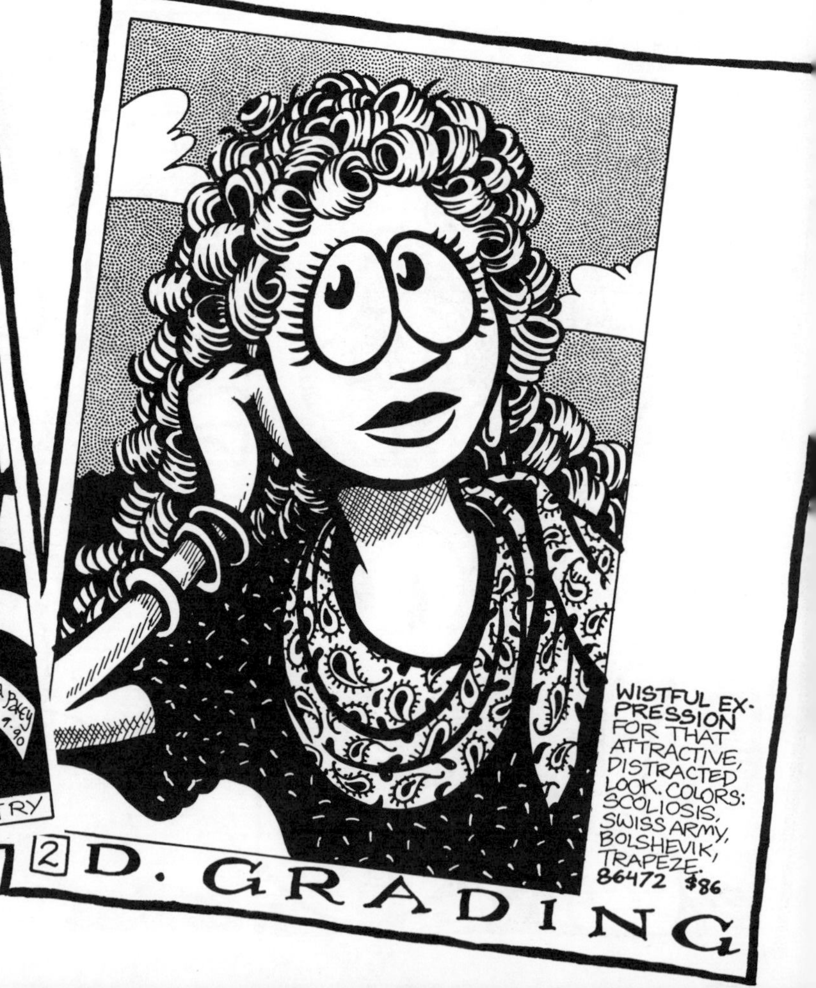
WISTFUL EXPRESSION FOR THAT ATTRACTIVE, DISTRACTED LOOK. COLORS: SCOLIOSIS, SWISS ARMY, BOLSHEVIK, TRAPEZE.
86472 $86
2 D. GRADING

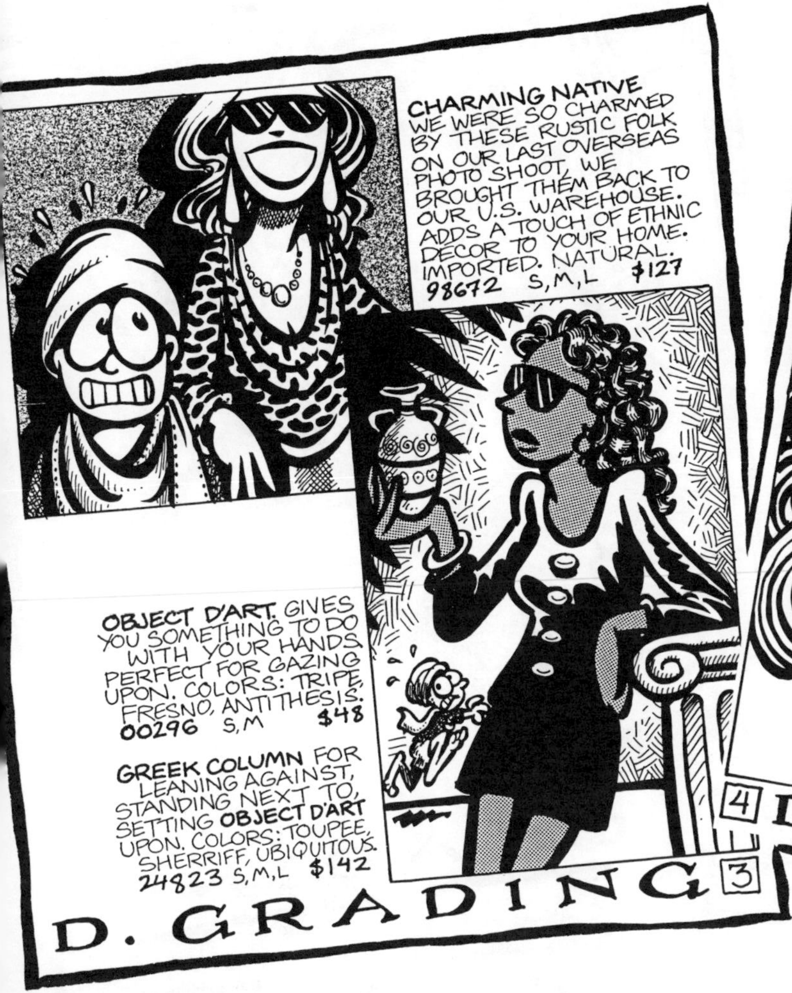
CHARMING NATIVE WE WERE SO CHARMED BY THESE RUSTIC FOLK ON OUR LAST OVERSEAS PHOTO SHOOT, WE BROUGHT THEM BACK TO OUR U.S. WAREHOUSE. ADDS A TOUCH OF ETHNIC DECOR TO YOUR HOME. IMPORTED. NATURAL.
98672 S,M,L $127
OBJECT D'ART. GIVES YOU SOMETHING TO DO WITH YOUR HANDS. PERFECT FOR GAZING UPON. COLORS: TRIPE, FRESNO, ANTITHESIS.
00296 S,M $48
GREEK COLUMN FOR LEANING AGAINST, STANDING NEXT TO, SETTING OBJECT D'ART UPON. COLORS: TOUPEE, SHERRIFF, UBIQUITOUS.
24823 S,M,L $142
D. GRADING
3

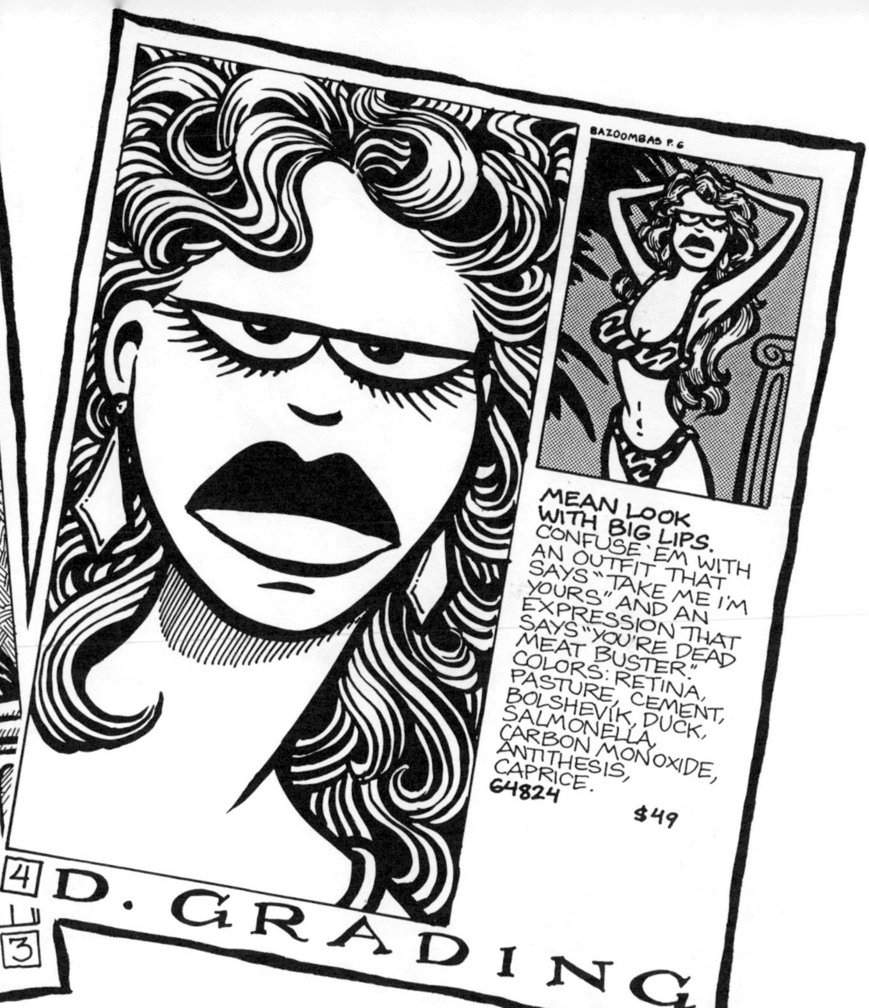
BAZOOMBAS P. 6
MEAN LOOK WITH BIG LIPS. CONFUSE 'EM WITH AN OUTFIT THAT SAYS "TAKE ME I'M YOURS" AND AN EXPRESSION THAT SAYS "YOU'RE DEAD MEAT BUSTER." COLORS: RETINA, PASTURE, CEMENT, BOLSHEVIK, DUCK, SALMONELLA, CARBON MONOXIDE, ANTITHESIS, CAPRICE.
64824
$49
4
D. GRADING

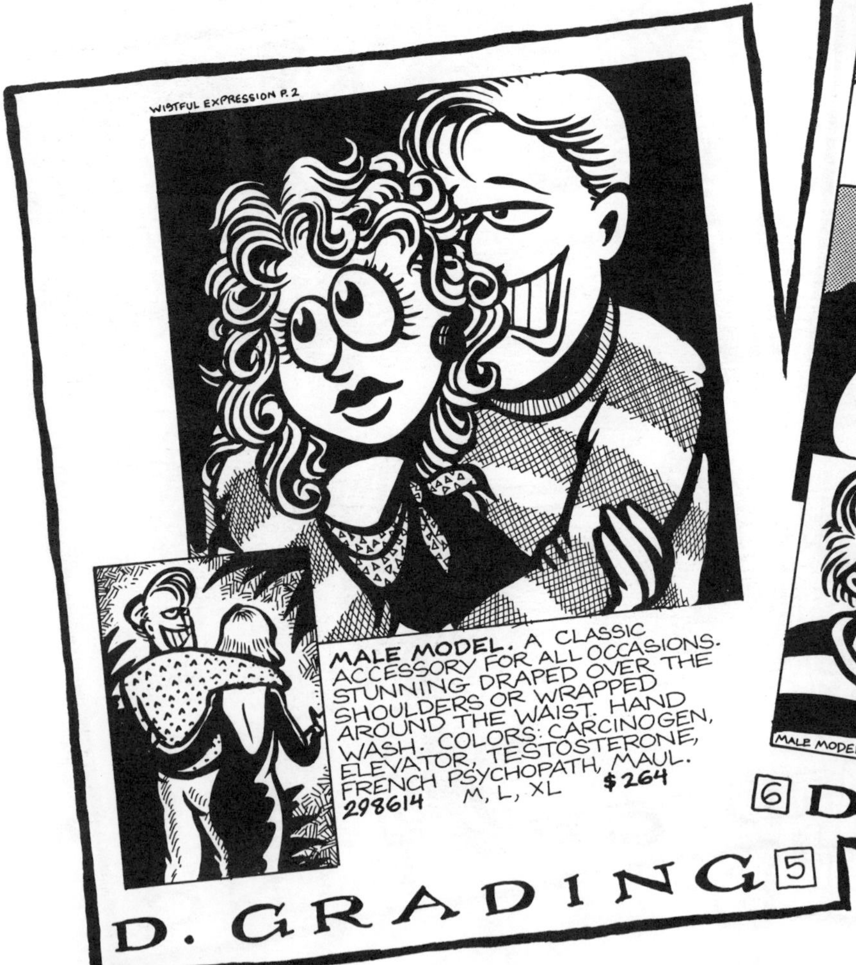
WISTFUL EXPRESSION P. 2
MALE MODEL. A CLASSIC ACCESSORY FOR ALL OCCASIONS. STUNNING DRAPED OVER THE SHOULDERS OR WRAPPED AROUND THE WAIST. HAND WASH. COLORS: CARCINOGEN, ELEVATOR, TESTOSTERONE, FRENCH PSYCHOPATH, MAUL.
298614 M, L, XL $264
D. GRADING
5

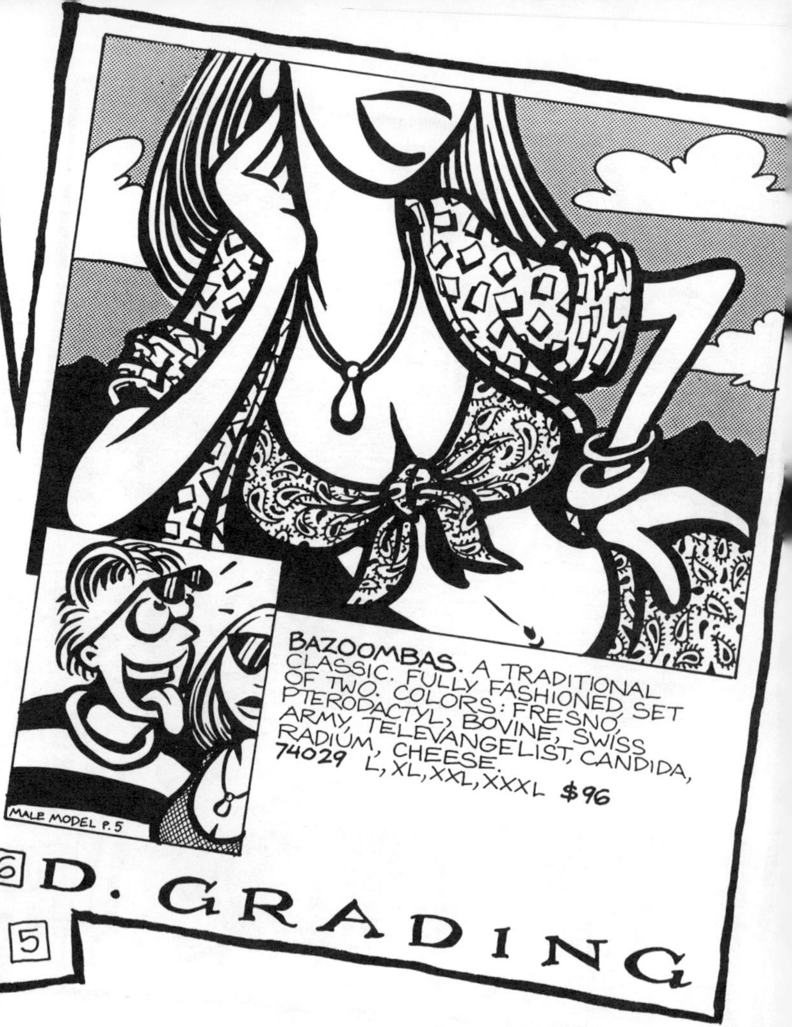
BAZOOMBAS. A TRADITIONAL CLASSIC. FULLY FASHIONED SET OF TWO. COLORS: FRESNO, PTERODACTYL, BOVINE, SWISS ARMY, TELEVANGELIST, CANDIDA, RADIUM, CHEESE.
74029 L, XL, XXL, XXXL $96
MALE MODEL P. 5
6
D. GRADING

THE D. GRADING CATALOG IS © SEPTEMBER 1990 BY NINA PALEY

NAME

ADDRESS

PHONE

#	PAGE NO.	ITEM NO.	I.Q.	WALLET SIZE	DESCRIPTION	PRICE	TOTAL
						SUBTOTAL	
						TAX	
						SHIPPING	
						INSURANCE	
						TIP	
						TOTAL	

FOR PERFECT FIT:

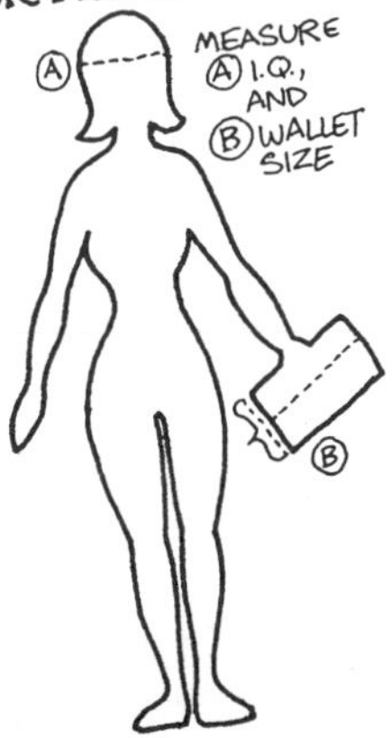

A
B

MEASURE Ⓐ I.Q., AND Ⓑ WALLET SIZE

PAYMENT METHOD:

- ☐ CREDIT CARD
- ☐ CHECK ☐ CASH
- ☐ FIRST BORN

CREDIT CARD NUMBER:

PRINT NAME

SIGNATURE

SEND LOTS OF MONEY TO: NINA PALEY
P.O. BOX 460736
SAN FRANCISCO, CA 94146

D. GRADING
c/o NINA PALEY
P.O. BOX 4112
SANTA CRUZ, CA 95061

JUNK MAIL RATE D. GRADING

(PLEASE REMOVE LABEL AND AFFIX TO FOREHEAD)

TOOTHPICK LEGS. MINIMALIST-STYLED LEGS INSPIRED BY THE CLASSIC TOOTH-PICK. COMPLETELY HAIRLESS. DOMESTIC. COLORS: ARACHNID, FRENCH BANANA, FUME, HYDROCHLORIC ACID, ANOREXIA, HEATHEN, CLOWN.
90872 XXS, XS, S $64

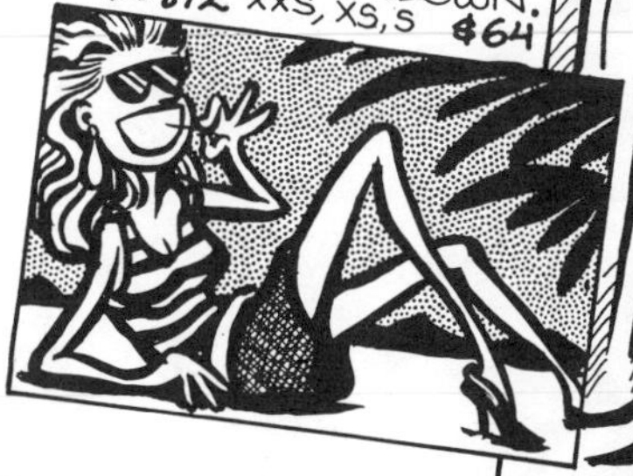

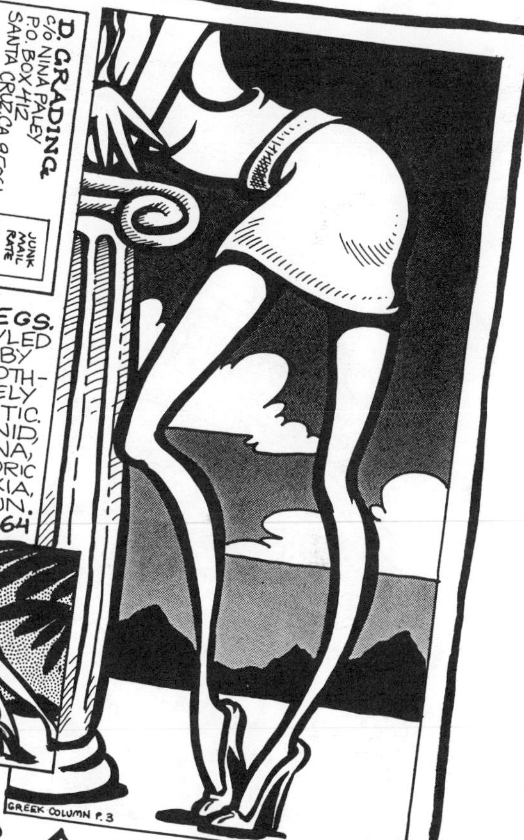

GREEK COLUMN P.3

 D. GRADING

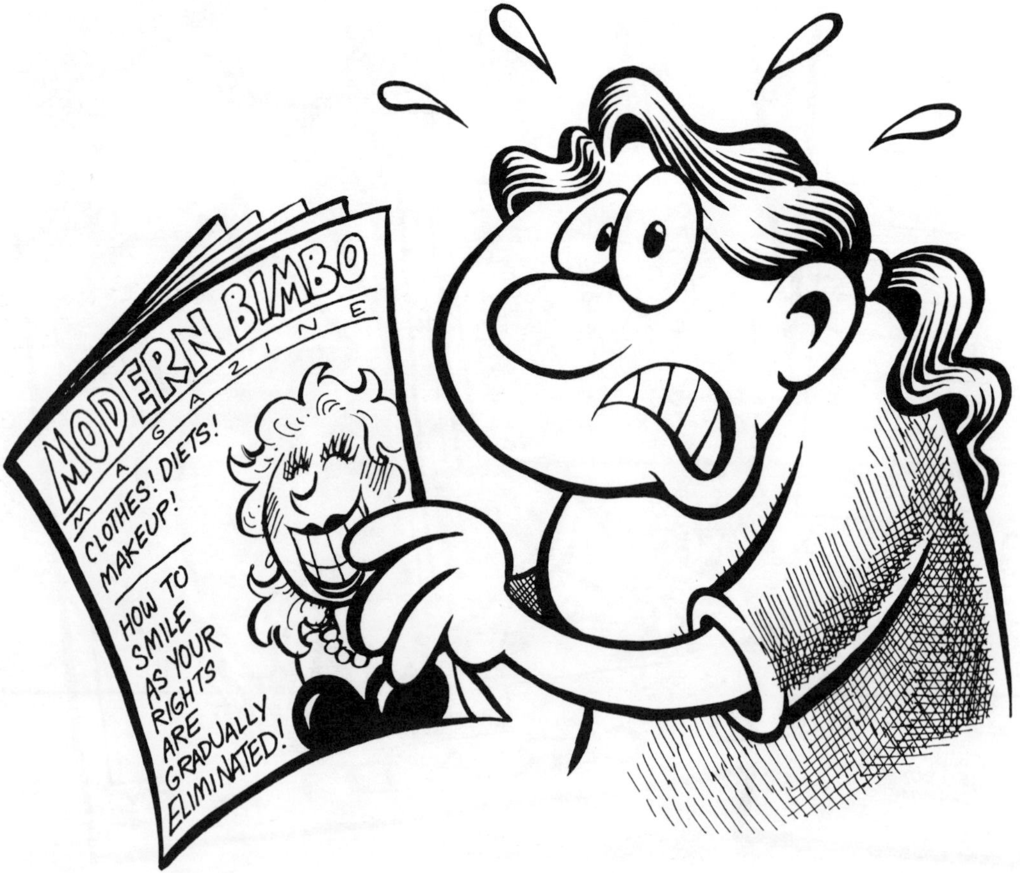
MODERN BIMBO
MAGAZINE
CLOTHES! DIETS! MAKEUP!
HOW TO SMILE AS YOUR RIGHTS ARE GRADUALLY ELIMINATED!

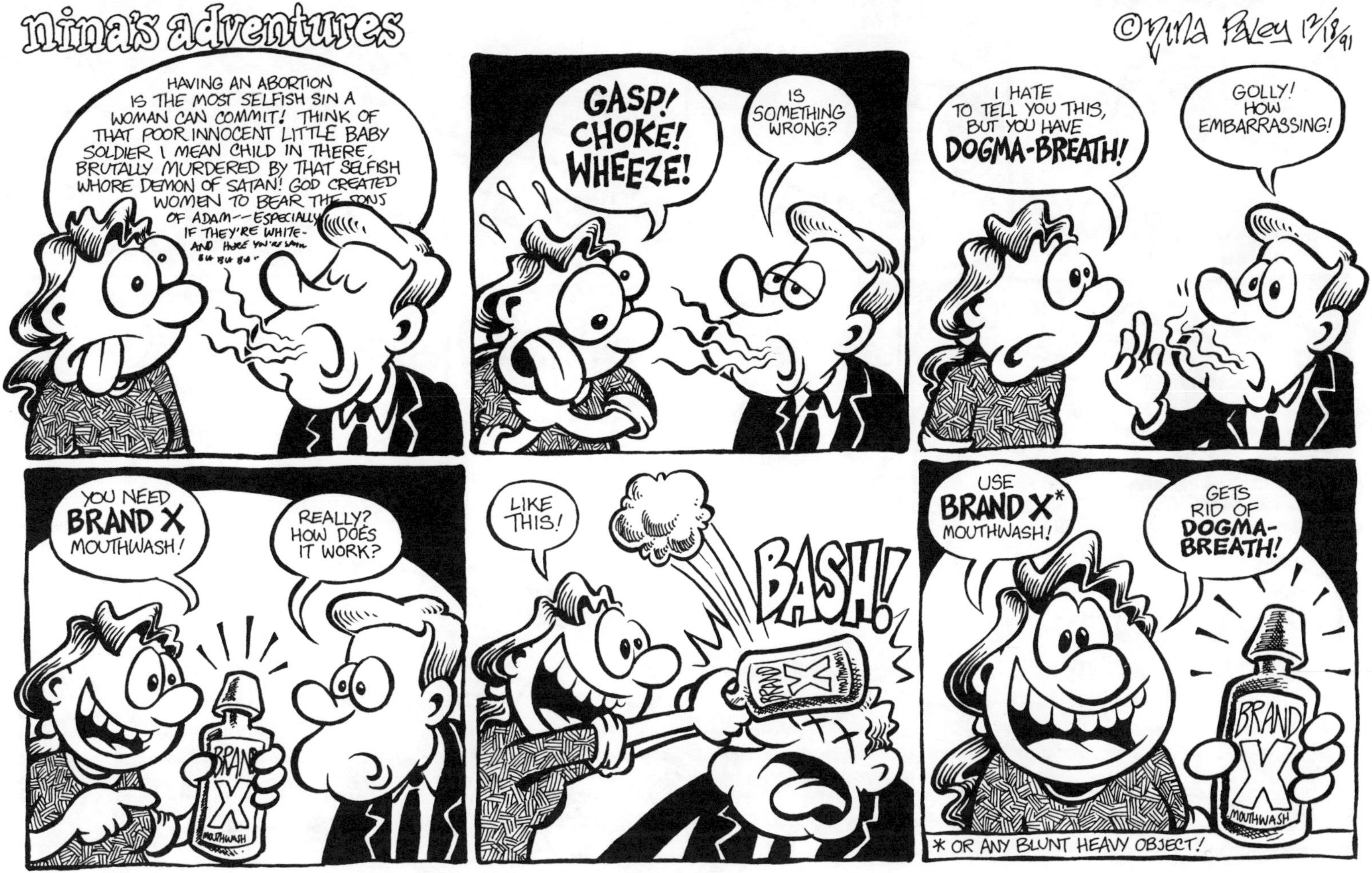
nina's adventures
©Nina Paley 12/18/91
HAVING AN ABORTION IS THE MOST SELFISH SIN A WOMAN CAN COMMIT! THINK OF THAT POOR INNOCENT LITTLE BABY SOLDIER I MEAN CHILD IN THERE, BRUTALLY MURDERED BY THAT SELFISH WHORE DEMON OF SATAN! GOD CREATED WOMEN TO BEAR THE SONS OF ADAM--ESPECIALLY IF THEY'RE WHITE-
GASP! CHOKE! WHEEZE!
IS SOMETHING WRONG?
I HATE TO TELL YOU THIS, BUT YOU HAVE DOGMA-BREATH!
GOLLY! HOW EMBARRASSING!
YOU NEED BRAND X MOUTHWASH!
REALLY? HOW DOES IT WORK?
BRAND X MOUTHWASH
LIKE THIS!
BASH!
BRAND X MOUTHWASH
USE BRAND X* MOUTHWASH!
GETS RID OF DOGMA-BREATH!
BRAND X MOUTHWASH
* OR ANY BLUNT HEAVY OBJECT!

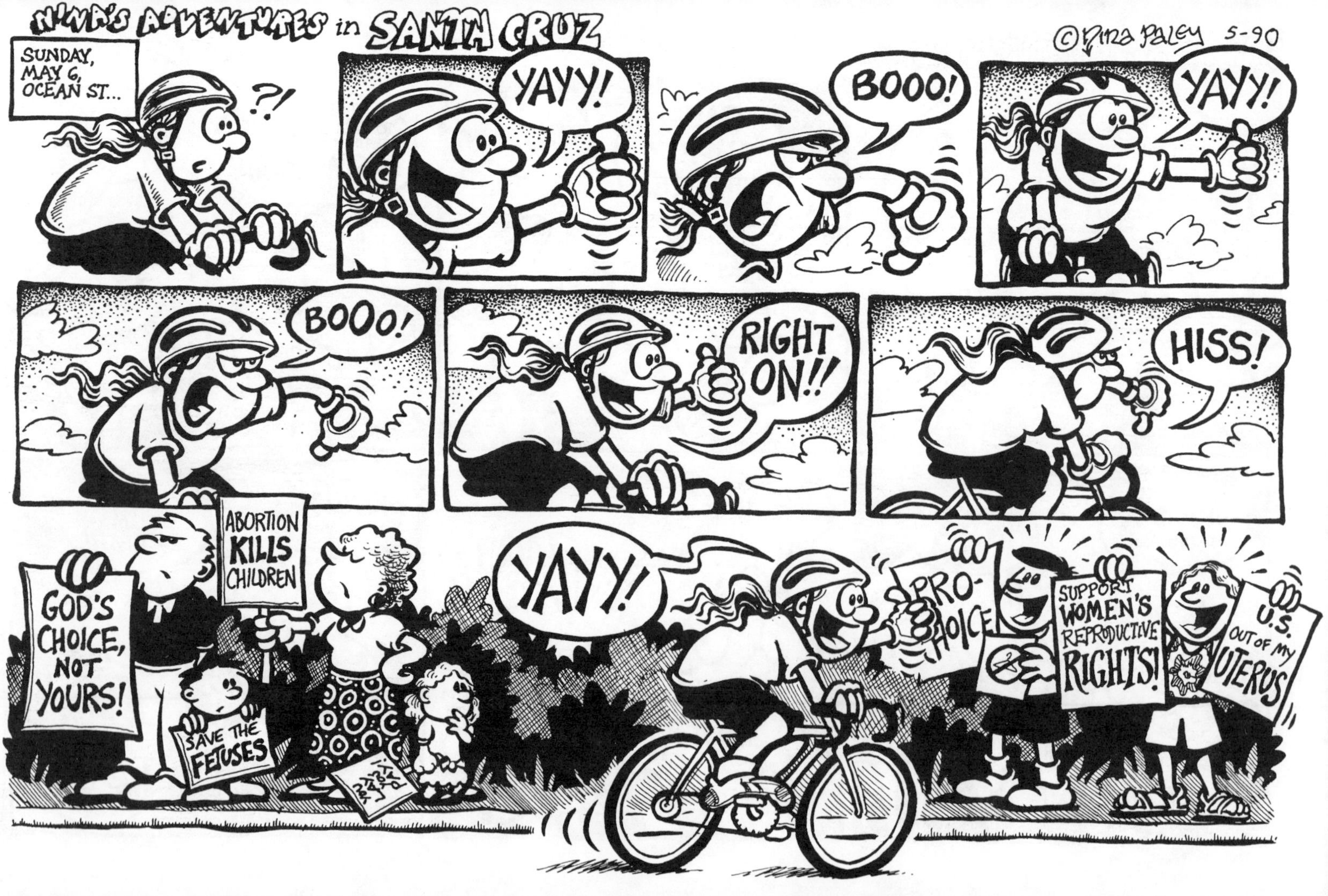

NINA'S ADVENTURES in SANTA CRUZ
©Nina Paley 5-90
SUNDAY, MAY 6, OCEAN ST...
?!
YAYY!
BOOO!
YAYY!
BOOO!
RIGHT ON!!
HISS!
GOD'S CHOICE, NOT YOURS!
ABORTION KILLS CHILDREN
SAVE THE FETUSES
YAYY!
PRO-CHOICE
SUPPORT WOMEN'S REPRODUCTIVE RIGHTS!
U.S. OUT OF MY UTERUS

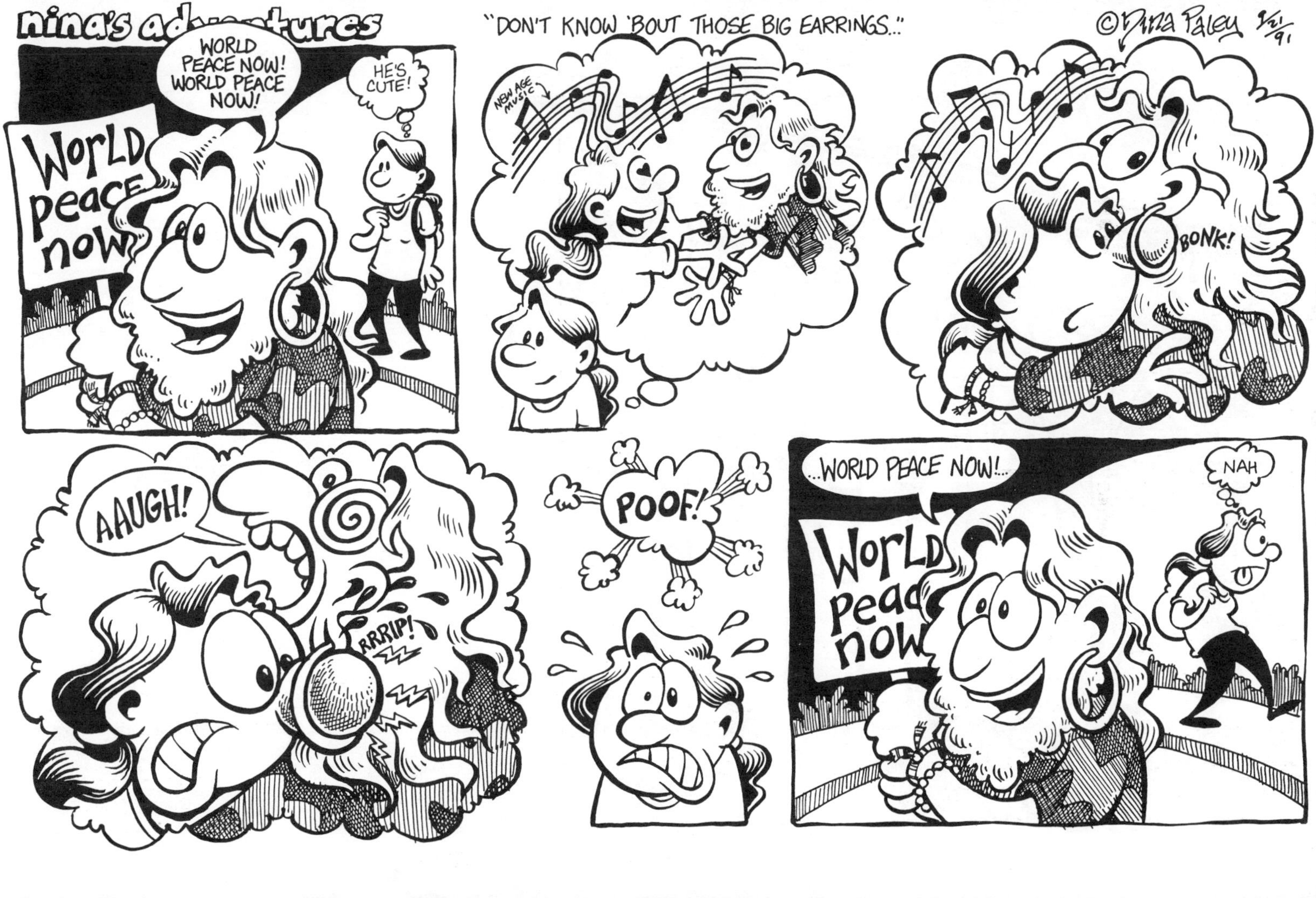
nina's adventures
"DON'T KNOW 'BOUT THOSE BIG EARRINGS..."
©Nina Paley 9/21/91
WORLD PEACE NOW! WORLD PEACE NOW!
HE'S CUTE!
World peace now
NEW AGE MUSIC
BONK!
AAUGH!
RRRIP!
POOF!
...WORLD PEACE NOW!...
NAH

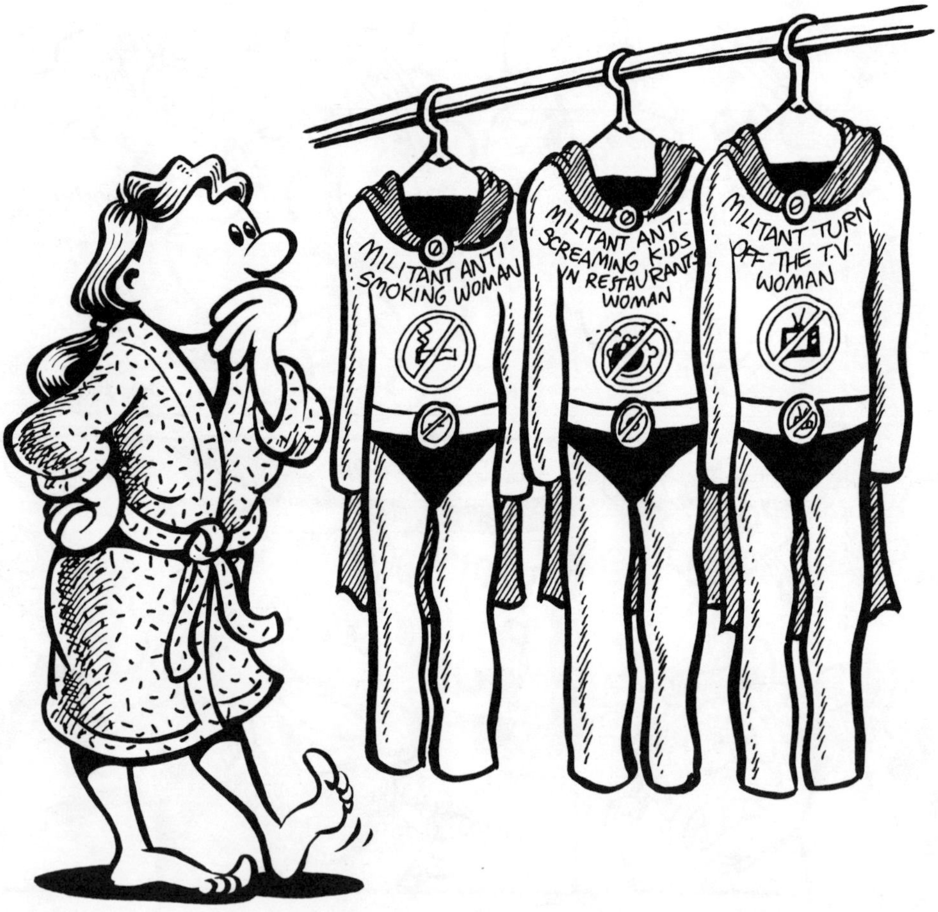
MILITANT ANTI-SMOKING WOMAN
MILITANT ANTI-SCREAMING KIDS IN RESTAURANTS WOMAN
MILITANT TURN OFF THE T.V. WOMAN

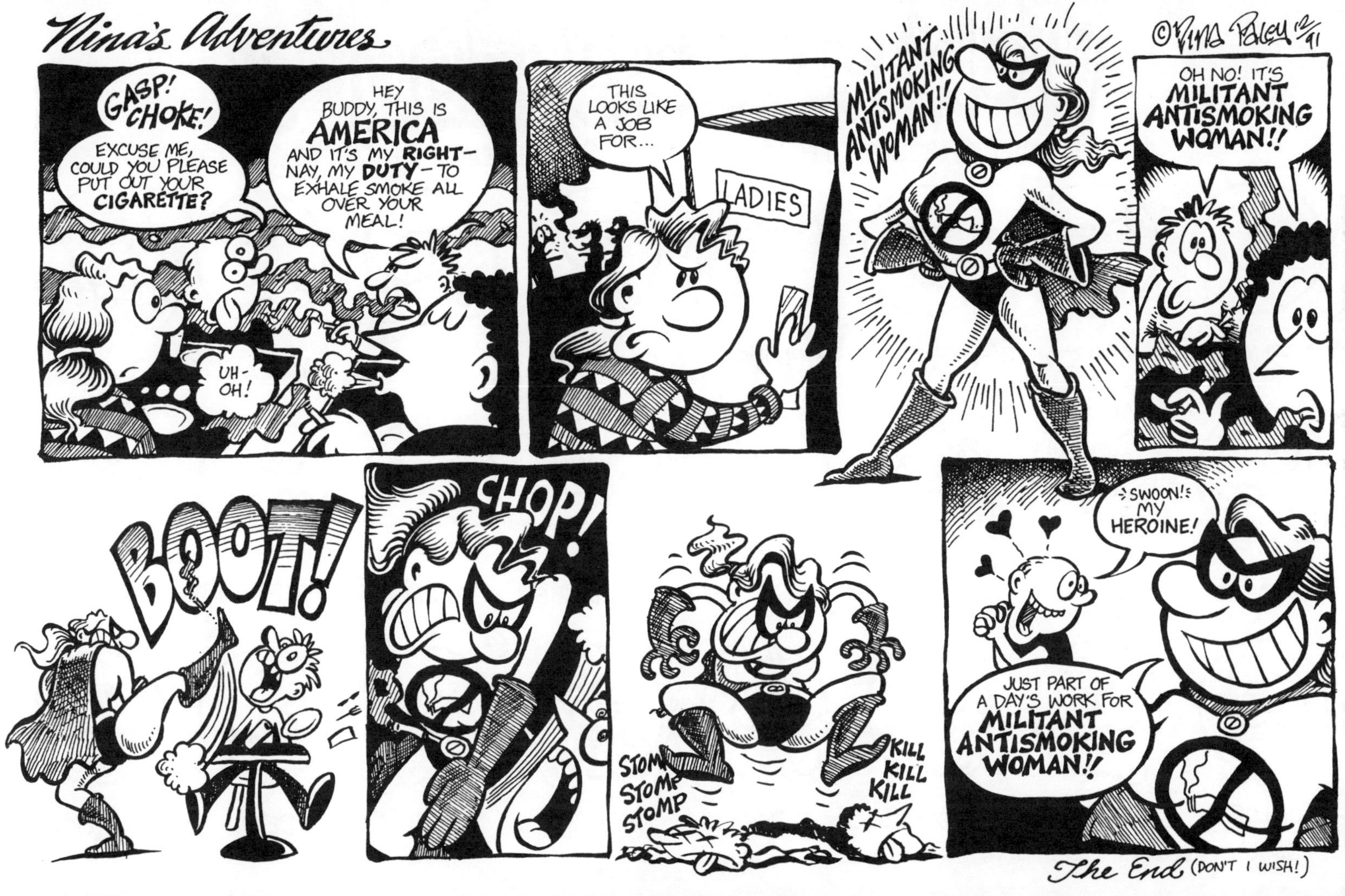
Nina's Adventures
© Nina Paley 12/91
GASP! CHOKE!
EXCUSE ME, COULD YOU PLEASE PUT OUT YOUR CIGARETTE?
HEY BUDDY, THIS IS AMERICA AND IT'S MY RIGHT—NAY, MY DUTY—TO EXHALE SMOKE ALL OVER YOUR MEAL!
UH-OH!
THIS LOOKS LIKE A JOB FOR...
LADIES
MILITANT ANTISMOKING WOMAN!!
OH NO! IT'S MILITANT ANTISMOKING WOMAN!!
BOOT!
CHOP!
STOMP STOMP STOMP
KILL KILL KILL
SWOON! MY HEROINE!
JUST PART OF A DAY'S WORK FOR MILITANT ANTISMOKING WOMAN!!
The End (DON'T I WISH!)

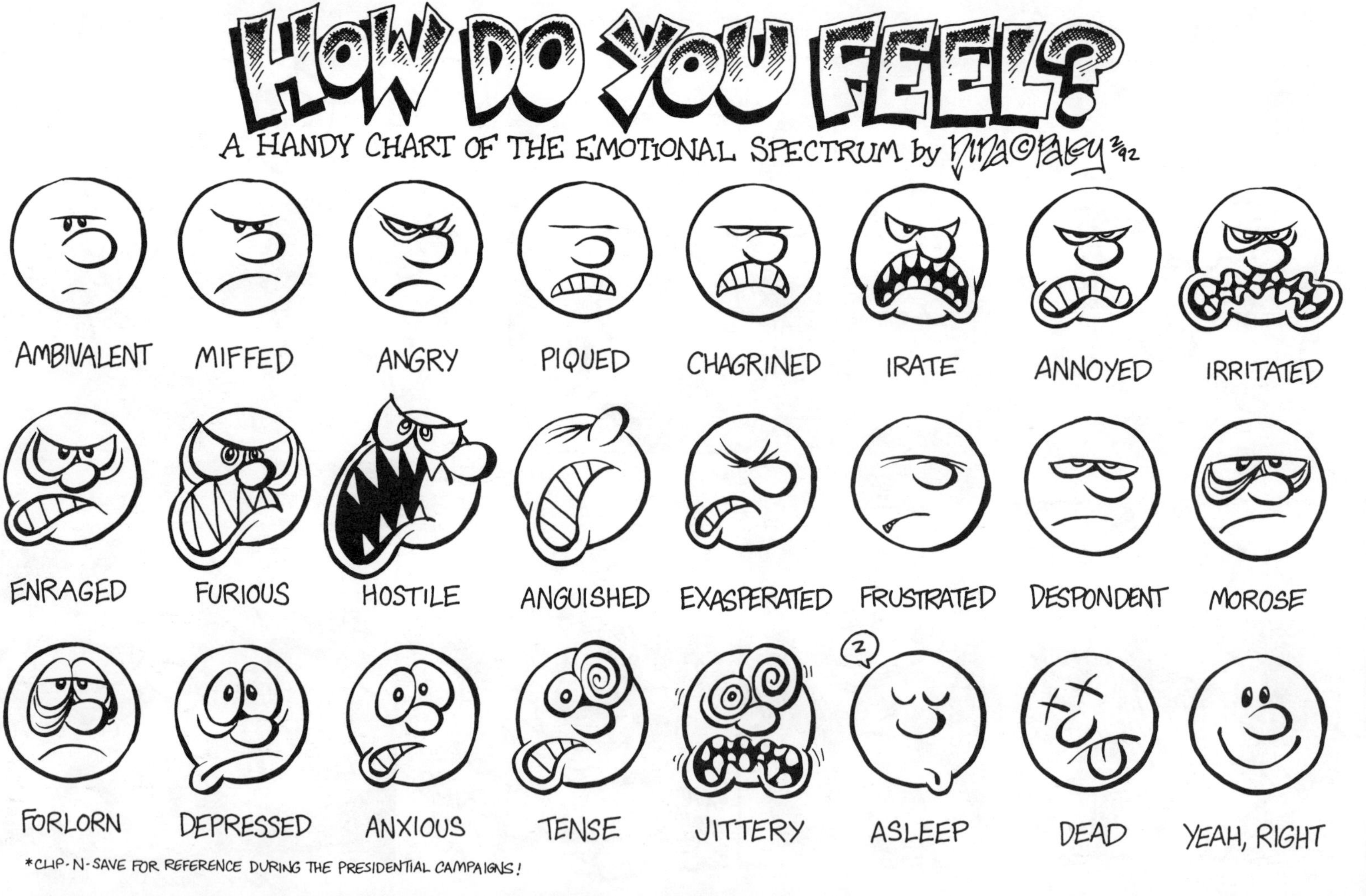
HOW DO YOU FEEL?
A HANDY CHART OF THE EMOTIONAL SPECTRUM by Nina © Paley 2/92
AMBIVALENT
MIFFED
ANGRY
PIQUED
CHAGRINED
IRATE
ANNOYED
IRRITATED
ENRAGED
FURIOUS
HOSTILE
ANGUISHED
EXASPERATED
FRUSTRATED
DESPONDENT
MOROSE
FORLORN
DEPRESSED
ANXIOUS
TENSE
JITTERY
z
ASLEEP
DEAD
YEAH, RIGHT
*CLIP-N-SAVE FOR REFERENCE DURING THE PRESIDENTIAL CAMPAIGNS!

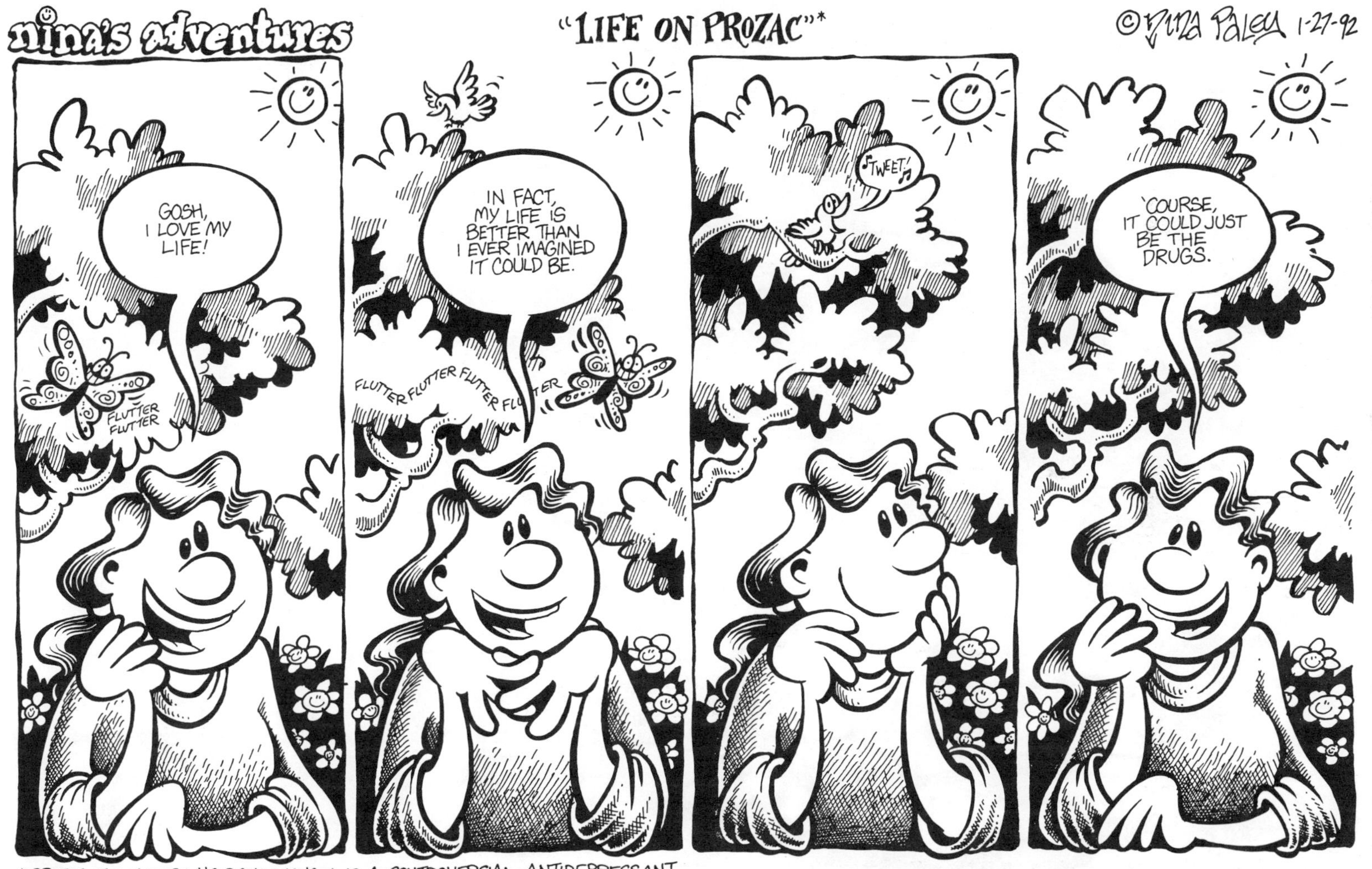

nina's adventures
"LIFE ON PROZAC"*
© Nina Paley 1-27-92
GOSH, I LOVE MY LIFE!
FLUTTER FLUTTER
IN FACT, MY LIFE IS BETTER THAN I EVER IMAGINED IT COULD BE.
FLUTTER FLUTTER FLUTTER FLUTTER FLUTTER
TWEET!
'COURSE, IT COULD JUST BE THE DRUGS.

* PROZAC, FOR THOSE WHO DON'T KNOW, IS A CONTROVERSIAL ANTIDEPRESSANT.

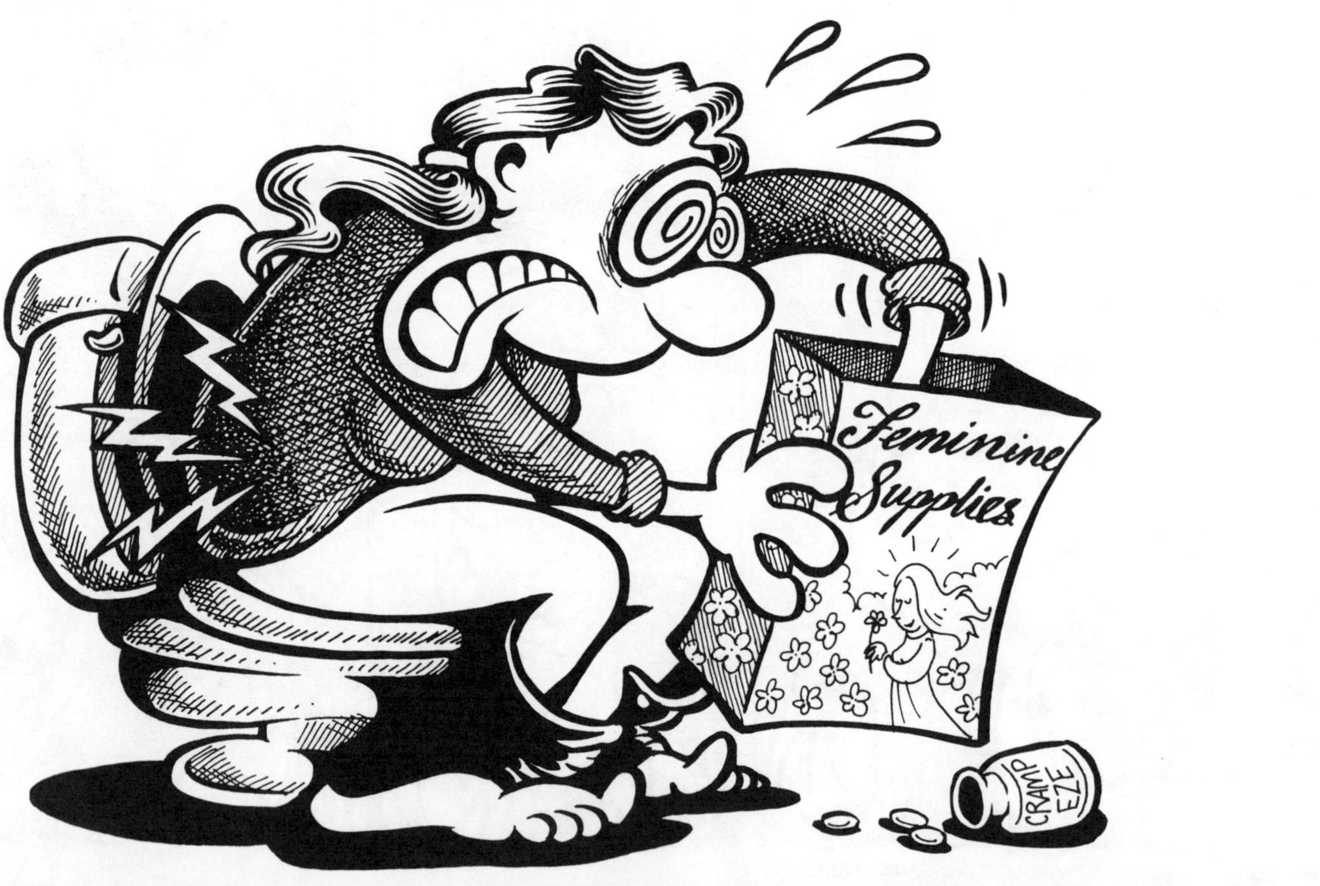
Feminine Supplies
CRAMP EZE

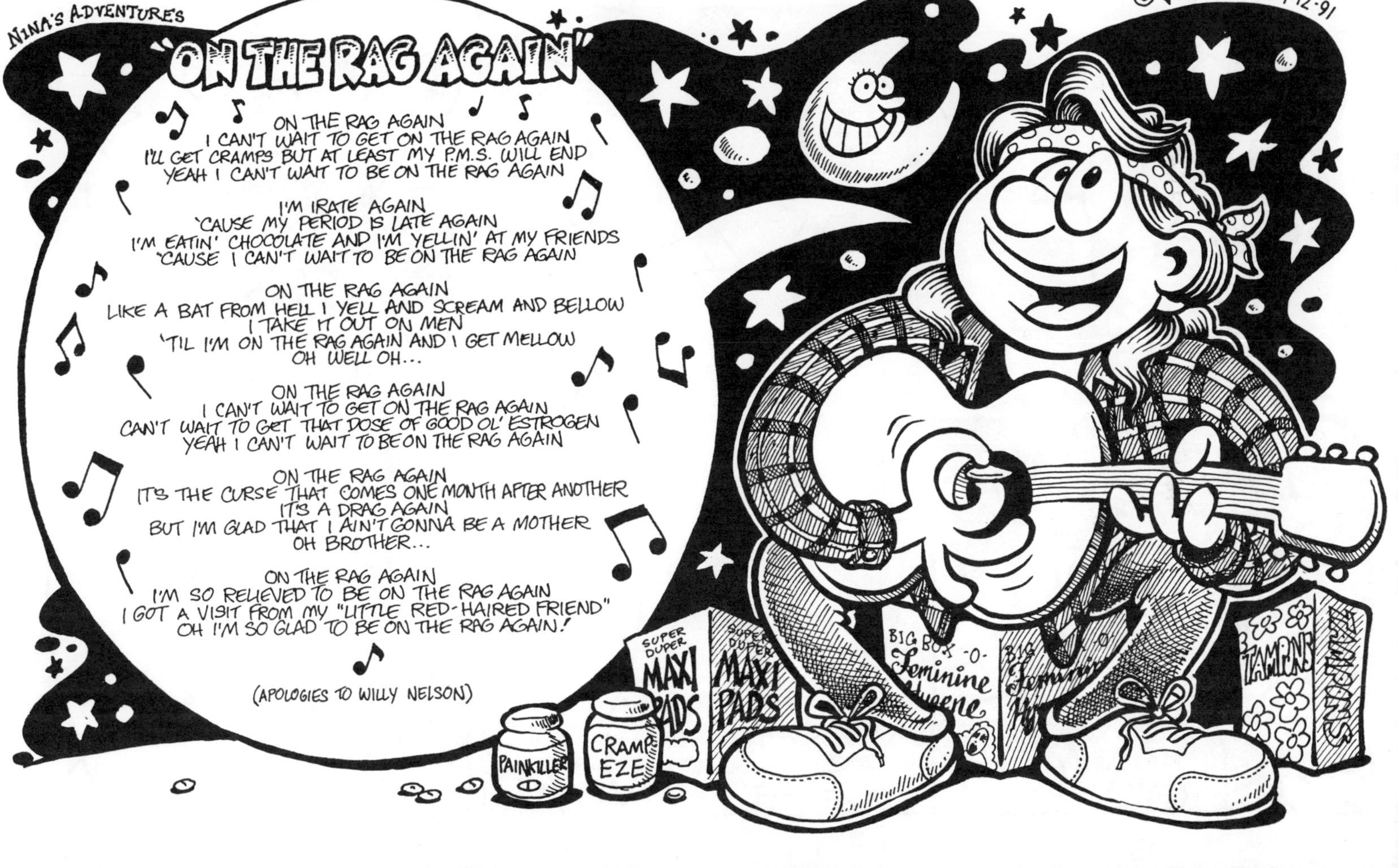
©Nina Paley 9-12-91
Nina's Adventures's
"On the Rag Again"
On the rag again
I can't wait to get on the rag again
I'll get cramps but at least my P.M.S. will end
Yeah I can't wait to be on the rag again
I'm irate again
'Cause my period is late again
I'm eatin' chocolate and I'm yellin' at my friends
'Cause I can't wait to be on the rag again
On the rag again
Like a bat from hell I yell and scream and bellow
I take it out on men
'Til I'm on the rag again and I get mellow
Oh well oh...
On the rag again
I can't wait to get on the rag again
Can't wait to get that dose of good ol' estrogen
Yeah I can't wait to be on the rag again
On the rag again
It's the curse that comes one month after another
It's a drag again
But I'm glad that I ain't gonna be a mother
Oh brother...
On the rag again
I'm so relieved to be on the rag again
I got a visit from my "little red-haired friend"
Oh I'm so glad to be on the rag again!
(Apologies to Willy Nelson)
Super Duper Maxi Pads
Super Duper Maxi Pads
Big Box -O- Feminine Hygiene
Tampons
Painkiller
Cramp Eze

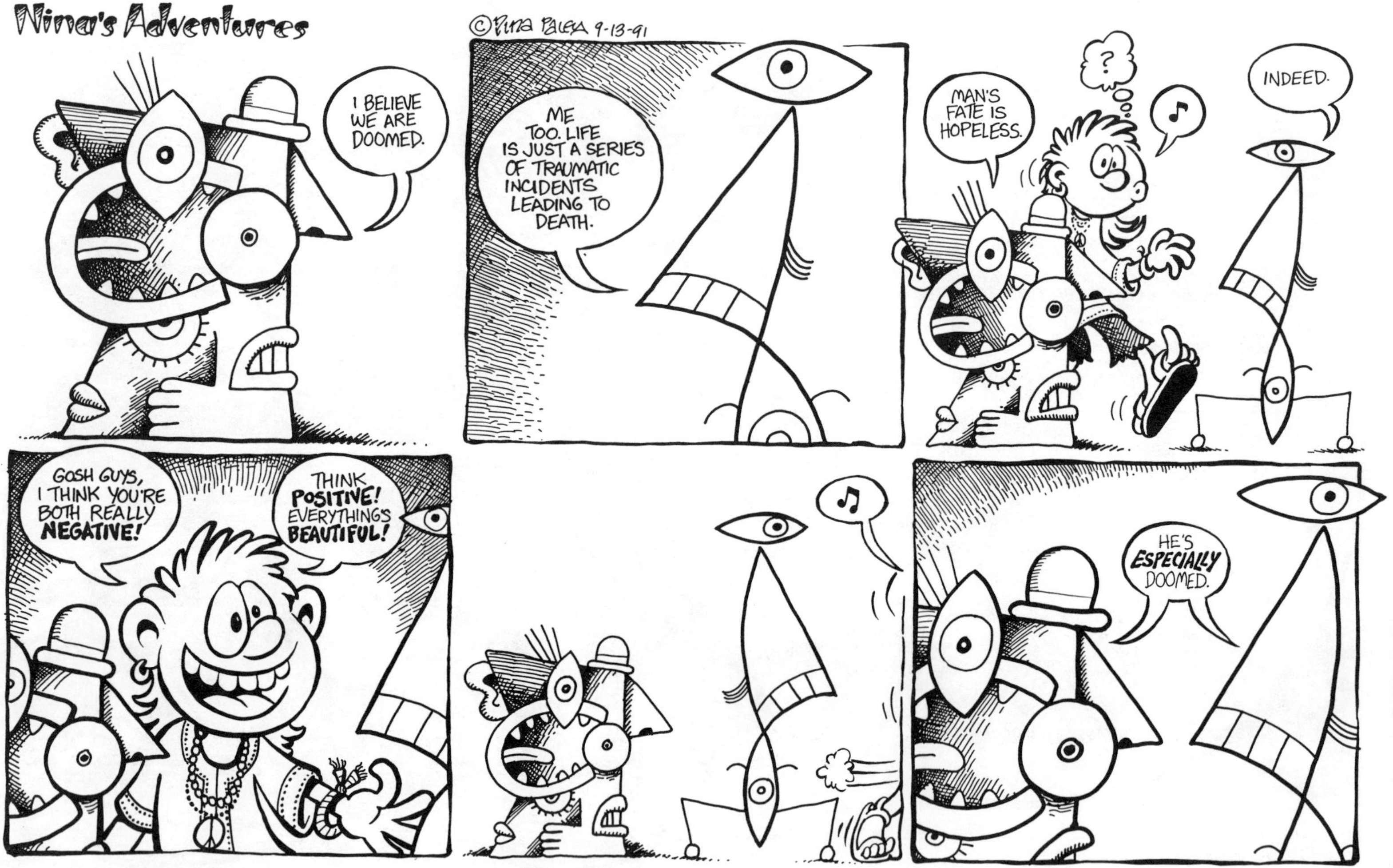

Nina's Adventures
©Nina Paley 9-13-91
I BELIEVE WE ARE DOOMED.
ME TOO. LIFE IS JUST A SERIES OF TRAUMATIC INCIDENTS LEADING TO DEATH.
MAN'S FATE IS HOPELESS.
?
♪
INDEED.
GOSH GUYS, I THINK YOU'RE BOTH REALLY NEGATIVE!
THINK POSITIVE! EVERYTHING'S BEAUTIFUL!
♪
HE'S ESPECIALLY DOOMED.

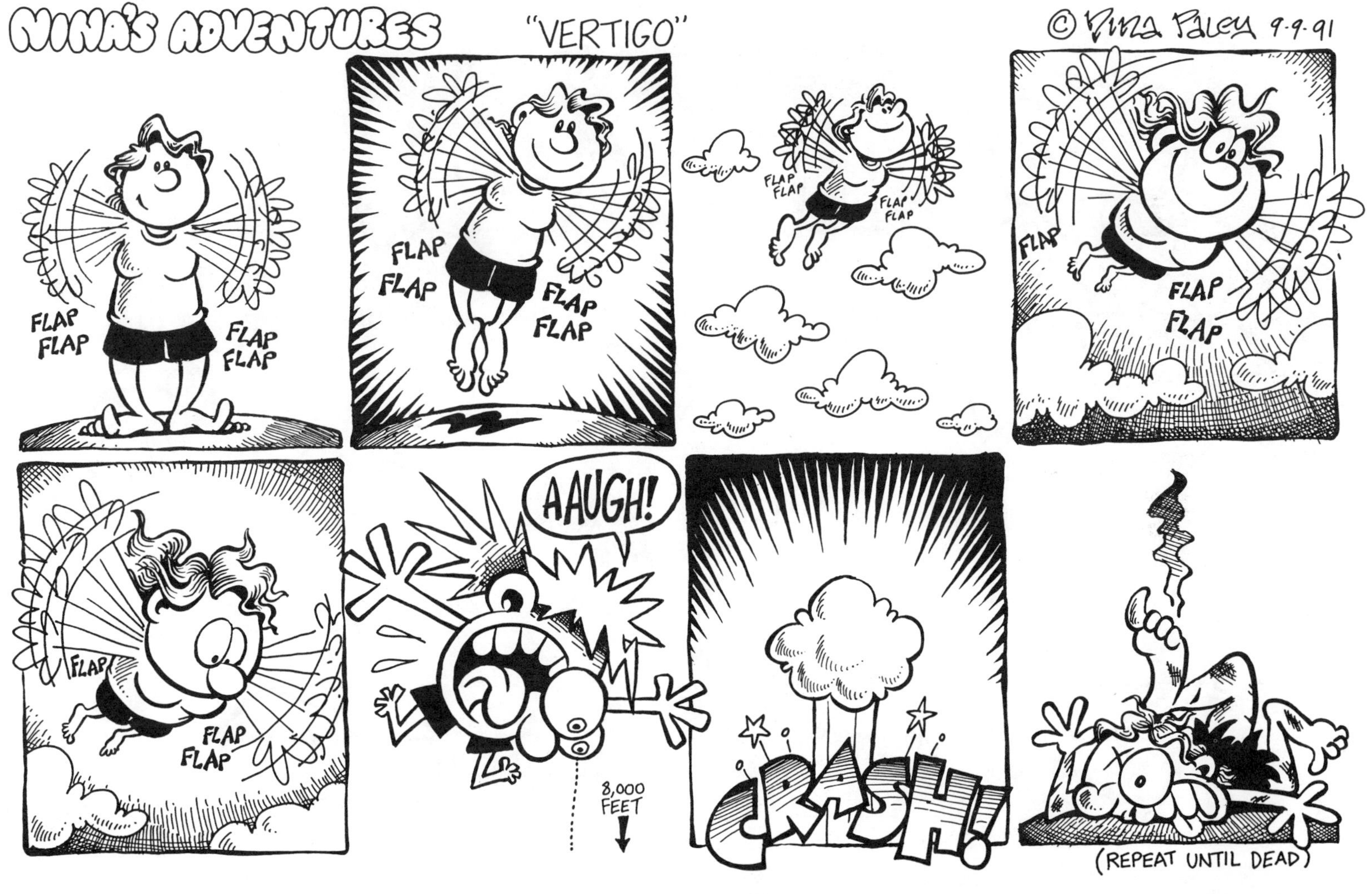
NINA'S ADVENTURES
"VERTIGO"
© Nina Paley 9-9-91
FLAP FLAP
FLAP FLAP
FLAP FLAP
FLAP FLAP
FLAP FLAP
FLAP FLAP
FLAP
FLAP FLAP
FLAP
FLAP FLAP
AAUGH!
8,000 FEET
CRASH!
(REPEAT UNTIL DEAD)

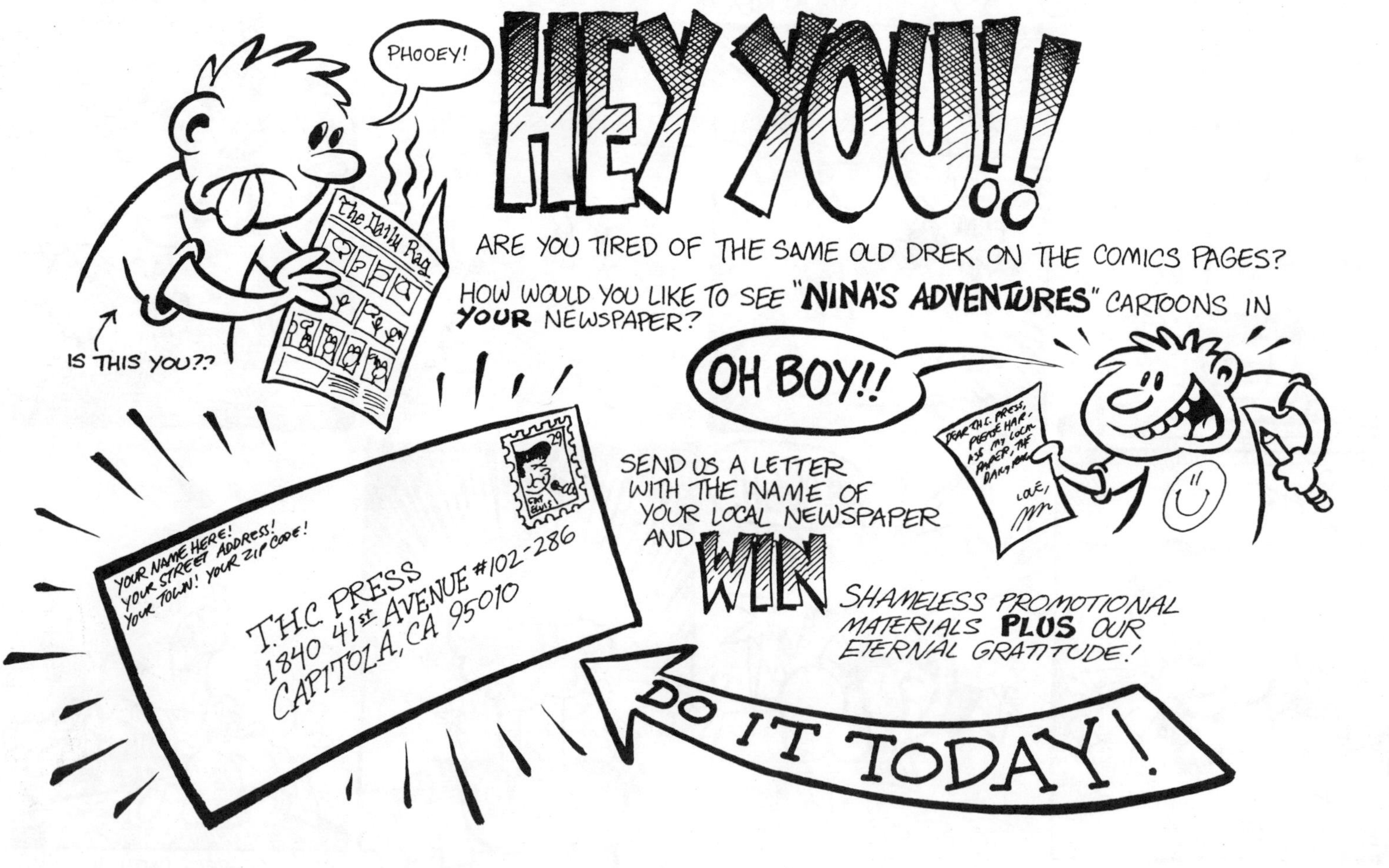
PHOOEY!
The Daily Rag
IS THIS YOU??
HEY YOU!!
ARE YOU TIRED OF THE SAME OLD DREK ON THE COMICS PAGES?
HOW WOULD YOU LIKE TO SEE "NINA'S ADVENTURES" CARTOONS IN YOUR NEWSPAPER?
OH BOY!!
YOUR NAME HERE!
YOUR STREET ADDRESS!
YOUR TOWN! YOUR ZIP CODE!
T.H.C PRESS
1840 41st AVENUE #102-286
CAPITOLA, CA 95010
SEND US A LETTER WITH THE NAME OF YOUR LOCAL NEWSPAPER AND WIN SHAMELESS PROMOTIONAL MATERIALS PLUS OUR ETERNAL GRATITUDE!
DO IT TODAY!

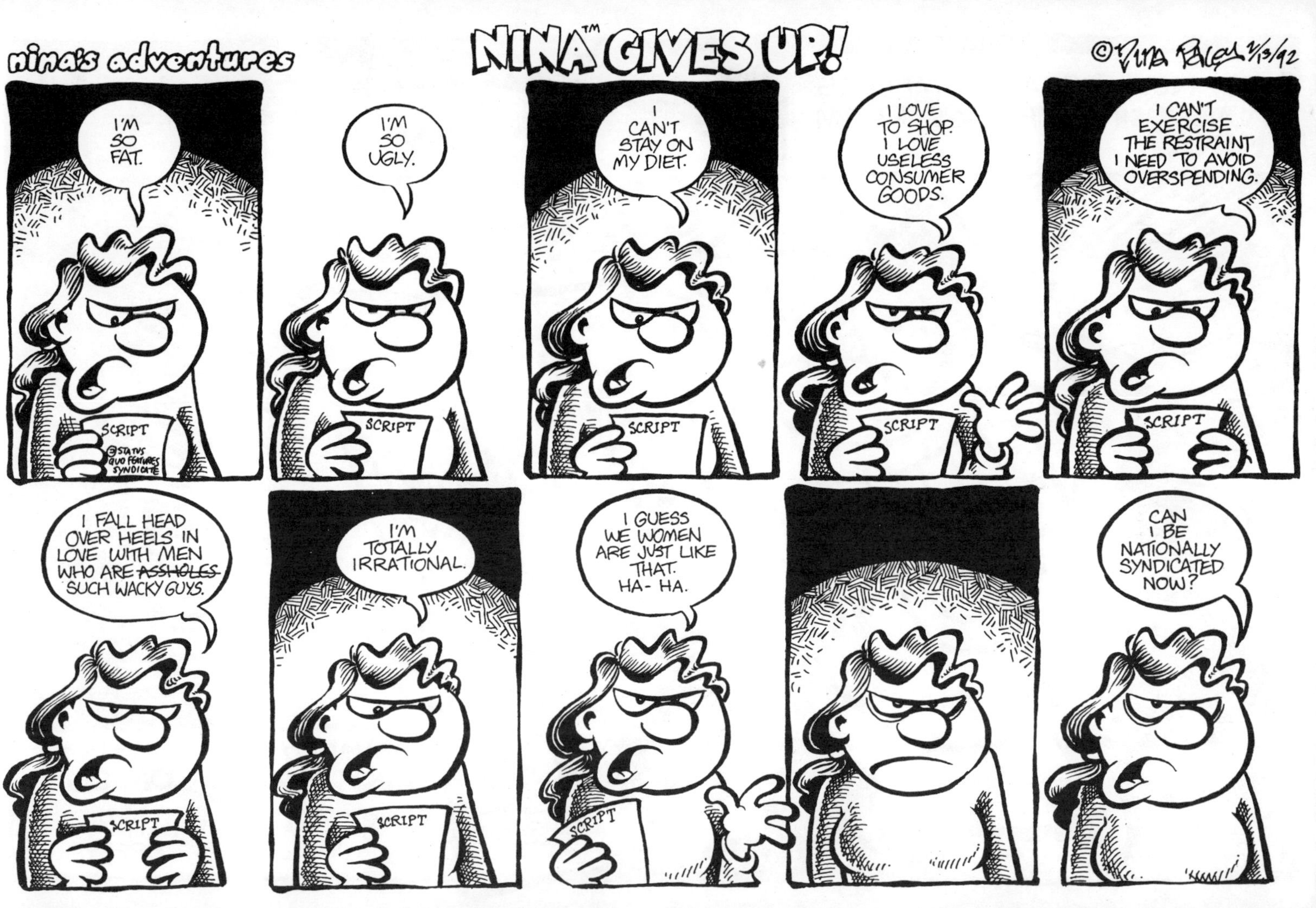
nina's adventures
NINA™ GIVES UP!
© Nina Paley 2/13/92
I'M SO FAT.
SCRIPT
© STATUS QUO FEATURES SYNDICATE
I'M SO UGLY.
SCRIPT
I CAN'T STAY ON MY DIET.
SCRIPT
I LOVE TO SHOP. I LOVE USELESS CONSUMER GOODS.
SCRIPT
I CAN'T EXERCISE THE RESTRAINT I NEED TO AVOID OVERSPENDING.
SCRIPT
I FALL HEAD OVER HEELS IN LOVE WITH MEN WHO ARE ~~ASSHOLES~~ SUCH WACKY GUYS.
SCRIPT
I'M TOTALLY IRRATIONAL.
SCRIPT
I GUESS WE WOMEN ARE JUST LIKE THAT. HA- HA.
SCRIPT
CAN I BE NATIONALLY SYNDICATED NOW?

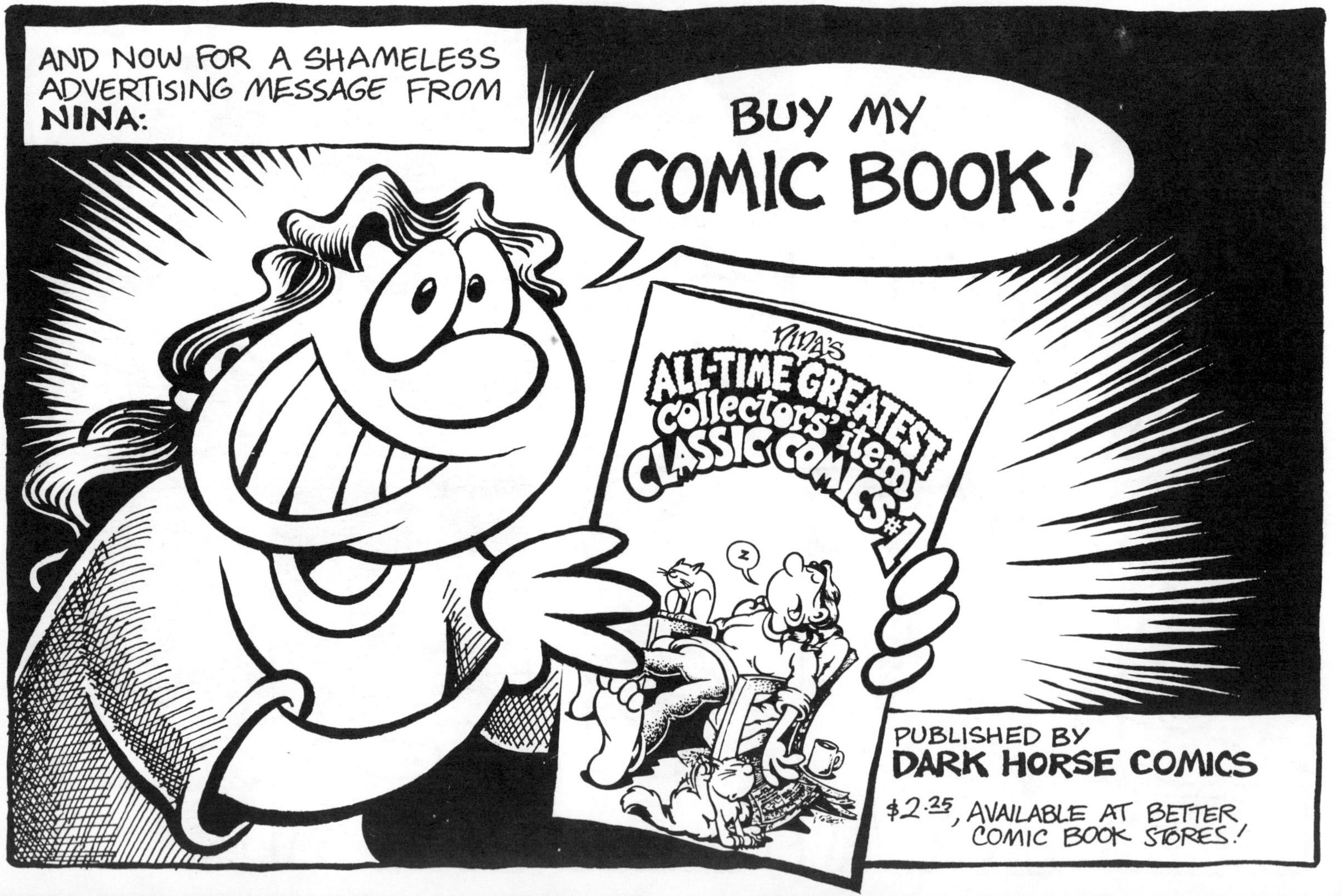
AND NOW FOR A SHAMELESS ADVERTISING MESSAGE FROM NINA:
BUY MY COMIC BOOK!
NINA'S ALL-TIME GREATEST COLLECTORS' ITEM CLASSIC COMICS #1
PUBLISHED BY DARK HORSE COMICS
$2.25, AVAILABLE AT BETTER COMIC BOOK STORES!

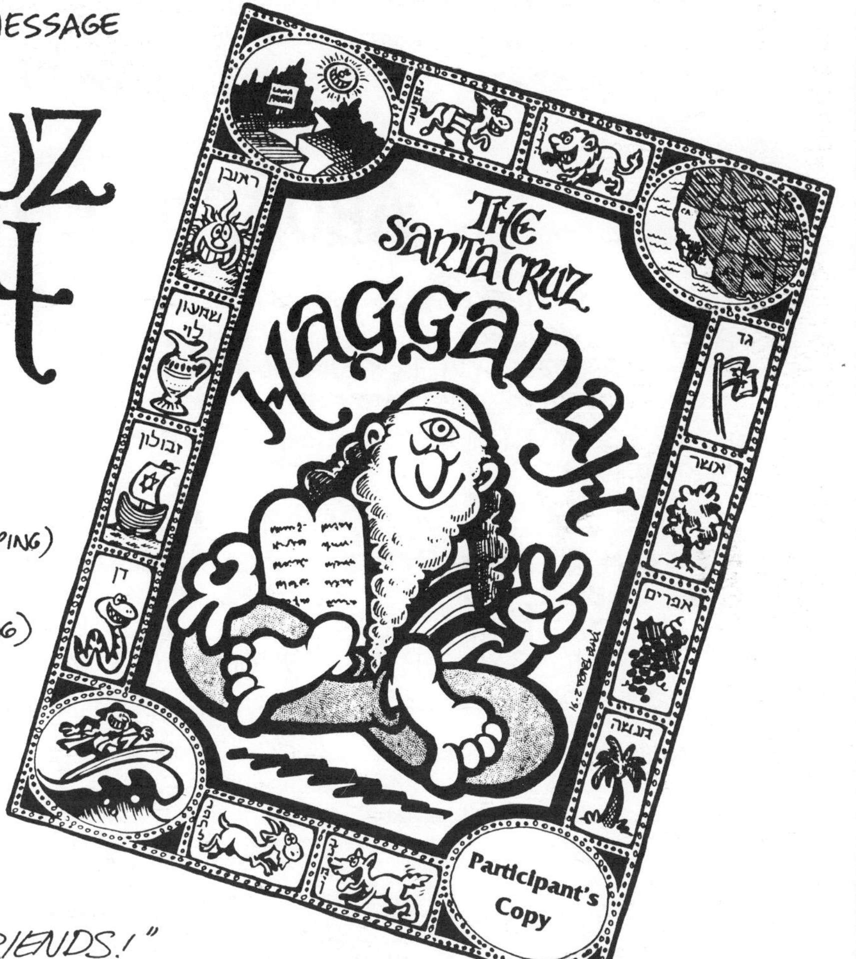
THE SANTA CRUZ
HAGGADAH
ראובן
שמעון
לוי
זבולון
דן
גד
אשר
אפרים
מנשה
Participant's Copy

ABOUT THE AUTHOR

HAILED BY THE *MALAY MAIL* AS A "BUBBLY BLONDE FROM CALIFORNIA," NINA PALEY WAS ACTUALLY BORN (1968) AND RAISED IN URBANA, ILLINOIS. IN 1988 SHE MOVED TO SANTA CRUZ, CALIFORNIA, WITH ASPIRATIONS OF BECOMING A NEW AGE, CRYSTAL-WIELDING HIPPIE. INSTEAD SHE BECAME A CYNICAL CARTOONIST. "THE PAY'S NOT GREAT, BUT AT LEAST I HAVE MY INTEGRITY, SORT OF," SAYS THE BITTER BRUNETTE FROM THE MIDWEST.

HER WORK HAS APPEARED IN NUMEROUS BOOKS AND COMICS INCLUDING **GRATEFUL DEAD COMICS, DARK HORSE PRESENTS, CHOICES, WIMMIN'S COMICS, RIP OFF PRESS, KITTY LIBBER, WOMEN'S GLIBBER,** AND MANY OTHERS. HER WEEKLY COMIC STRIP, "NINA'S ADVENTURES," RUNS IN SEVERAL NEWSPAPERS, AND HER CARTOONS HAVE BEEN EXHIBITED IN CALIFORNIA, EUROPE AND MALAYSIA.

AFTER A BRIEF (THANK GOD) STINT IN AUSTIN, TEXAS, NINA MOVED TO SAN FRANCISCO, WHERE SHE IS CONTENT TO STAY.